Elizabeth G. Martin, Arthur L. I. de Saint-Amand

The Revolution of 1848

Elizabeth G. Martin, Arthur L. I. de Saint-Amand
The Revolution of 1848
ISBN/EAN: 9783337228248

Printed in Europe, USA, Canada, Australia, Japan

Cover: Foto ©ninafisch / pixelio.de

More available books at **www.hansebooks.com**

THE REVOLUTION OF 1848

BY

IMBERT DE SAINT-AMAND

TRANSLATED BY

ELIZABETH GILBERT MARTIN

NEW YORK
CHARLES SCRIBNER'S SONS
1895

CONTENTS

CHAPTER		PAGE
I.	THE FIRST DAYS OF 1848	1
II.	THE OBSEQUIES OF MADAME ADELAIDE	7
III.	COUNT DE MONTALEMBERT	12
IV.	THE CHAMBER OF PEERS	21
V.	M. GUIZOT AND THE COURT	29
VI.	THE CHAMBER OF DEPUTIES	38
VII.	M. DE TOCQUEVILLE	45
VIII.	THE DEPARTURE OF PRINCE DE JOINVILLE	54
IX.	THE DISCUSSION OF THE ADDRESS	65
X.	TWO AMENDMENTS	72
XI.	THE BANQUET SCHEME	80
XII.	THE ARRANGEMENTS FOR FEBRUARY 19	89
XIII.	THE PROGRAMME OF THE MANIFESTATION	97
XIV.	THE TWENTY-FIRST OF FEBRUARY	104
XV.	THE EVENING OF FEBRUARY 21	113
XVI.	THE DAY OF FEBRUARY 22	121
XVII.	THE EVENING OF FEBRUARY 22	129
XVIII.	THE MORNING OF FEBRUARY 23	136
XIX.	THE FALL OF THE MINISTRY	146
XX.	THE FIRING ON THE BOULEVARD	157

CHAPTER		PAGE
XXI.	THE NIGHT OF FEBRUARY 23–24	167
XXII.	THE MORNING OF FEBRUARY 24	177
XXIII.	THE LAST REVIEW	193
XXIV.	THE ABDICATION	200
XXV.	THE DUKE DE NEMOURS	212
XXVI.	THE DUCHESS OF ORLEANS IN THE CHAMBER	221
XXVII.	THE INVASION OF THE CHAMBER	238
XXVIII.	THE PROVISIONAL GOVERNMENT	247
XXIX.	THE SACK OF THE TUILERIES	255
XXX.	THE EVENING OF FEBRUARY 24	265
XXXI.	DREUX	275
XXXII.	FROM DREUX TO HONFLEUR	283
XXXIII.	THE PAVILION DE LA GRÂCE	290
XXXIV.	TROUVILLE	298
XXXV.	THE EMBARKATION AT HAVRE	305
XXXVI.	THE DEPARTURE OF THE DUCHESS OF ORLEANS	313
XXXVII.	THE DUCHESS DE MONTPENSIER	320
XXXVIII.	CONCLUSION	328
INDEX		337

LIST OF PORTRAITS

Louis Philippe.................................*Frontispiece*

	PAGE
Marie Amélie	64
Lamartine	160
Ledru-Rollin	224

THE REVOLUTION OF 1848

CHAPTER I

THE FIRST DAYS OF 1848

THE year 1848 opened sadly. The first article in the *Moniteur* of January 1, announced the death of the "very high and very powerful Princess Eugenie Adelaide Louise, Princess of Orleans, sister of the King, born at Paris, August 23, 1777, daughter of the very high and very powerful Prince Louis Philippe Joseph of Orleans, and of the very high and very powerful Princess Louise Marie Adelaide of Bourbon, died December 31, 1847, at three o'clock in the morning, in the palace of the Tuileries, at Paris." The body of the Princess was lying in a mortuary chapel in the pavilion of Flora. The château, usually so animated on New Year's day, was silent and sombre. No joyous serenades at dawn! No military music! No official congratulations! On the previous day, Louis Philippe and all his court had put on mourning for two months. This mourning was to be for his sister, in the first place, and very soon after for the monarchy. Stricken to the heart by a loss so pre-eminently painful, the old

King could with difficulty restrain his sobs. Marie Amélie, who had always loved her sister-in-law greatly, was not less afflicted than her husband.

New Year's day wore on most gloomily at the Tuileries. At evening-time came a glimmer of light; a messenger of good tidings made his appearance at the château, Colonel de Beaufort, aide-de-camp of the Duke d'Aumale. He brought from Algeria the great news of Abd-el-Kader's surrender. It was Colonel de Beaufort who had been sent by the Governor-general, the Duke d'Aumale, to Sadi-Brahim, to receive the submission of the Emir on behalf of His Royal Highness, and who had also been charged to conduct him from Oran to Toulon, where he had just established him in quarantine under safe keeping. The colonel was received at once by Louis Philippe, and afterwards by the princes. He brought Abd-el-Kader's pistol to the King, and his sword to the wife of General de Lamoricière. Marie Amélie thought the arrival of the conqueror of the Arab camp a happy omen. She hoped that the disasters of 1848 would be succeeded by a prosperous year, and that the vein of ill-luck was at last exhausted.

One might, indeed, have supposed that this event, which completed the conquest of Algeria, would be received with general rejoicings and effect a salutary diversion amidst the parliamentary disputes. But, on the contrary, there was a repetition of what had taken place in 1830.

In his interesting and patriotic work entitled *Vieux-Souvenirs*, Prince de Joinville says: "Shortly after the Palais-Royal fête occurred the taking of Algiers, a deed of national prowess, of courageous and far-sighted policy, a brilliant feat of arms accomplished under the white flag, which ought to have excited enthusiasm, tightened the links between France and its king, and reconciled the nation with its ancient standard. It did nothing at all. The taking of Algiers was received as a piece of ordinary news, and regrets for the tricolored flag were as keen as ever. This was because the tribune and the press — the press above all, that most powerful implement of destruction in modern times — had done their work. The days of the government of the Restoration were numbered. No one had any cause of complaint against it; abroad, as at home, it had assuredly been the best régime that had come into power since 1789. But it had desired to govern paternally, for the welfare of France in the present and its grandeur in the future, and to resist the encroachments of the upstarts who were trying to work it to their own advantage. It had been demolished piecemeal, as everything has been demolished for the last hundred years, in the name of laws and principles which destroy all government and will soon render all society impossible. The hour of 'Take that off that I may put it on' — the one end sincerely aimed at by our revolutions, however one may seek to disguise it — was about to sound."

Admiral Duperré's despatch announcing the taking of Algiers had arrived at Paris, July 9, 1830. The throne of Charles X. was overset before the end of the month. The news of Abd-el-Kader's surrender reached Paris, January 1, 1848. The monarchy of July was at an end by the 24th of February.

People were as ungrateful to the elder branch of the Bourbons as to the younger. Under the Restoration, as under the government of King Louis Philippe, there were Frenchmen unpatriotic enough not to rejoice at the successes of France, because those successes might consolidate a dynasty which they detested.

The reports of the Duke d'Aumale and of General de Lamoricière concerning the surrender of Abd-el-Kader were published in the daily papers of January 3, and should have produced unmingled satisfaction. But ill-natured criticism sought to draw distinctions as to who deserved the greatest praise. The young Prince was begrudged so brilliant a success. The newspapers of the left endeavored to lessen the importance of an event which had been received with enthusiasm in Algeria by both the army and the colonists, and affected to see in it nothing but the result of a lucky stroke npon which the government had no right to pride itself. They blamed the promise made to the Emir of transporting him to Saint John of Acre, where he would be free. They were deferential to General de Lamoricière, because he

was a deputy of the left, but they attacked the
Duke d'Aumale, although his conduct had been irreproachable. The young Prince had foreseen these
unjust accusations from the moment when he ratified the engagements entered into by General de Lamoricière with the Emir. General Cavaignac said
to him at the time: "You may be sure there will be
attacks made, and on you, Prince, especially. The
greater the success is, the more they will try to
belittle it, and even to use it against you." "Oh,
well!" resumed the Duke d'Aumale with a smile,
"General de Lamoricière is a deputy of the left, and
I fancy you are not altogether without friends in the
republican party; you two can parry that." Politics
had so deteriorated the national character that the
tidings of the most fortunate event for France were
received by the opposition not merely with indifference but with hostility.

This was a bad symptom, but the government was
not excessively alarmed by it. The Duke de Broglie
wrote to his son, early in January: —

"The situation here is good without being excellent. The majority are very well united. Nevertheless, there is always some latent trouble. The
events of last year have left their traces, and the
majority, when they feel solidly established, begin
to dream again of reforms and to look for some little
thing or other to destroy. Purses are empty, savings
are used up, and credit and confidence are very slowly
and painfully restored. It will be up-hill work all

through the session. M. Guizot is, as usual, satisfied and confident. Duchâtel is well, but less ardent and enthusiastic. The rest of the ministers seem to be hopeful and in good humor." Uneasiness had not as yet made its way into official circles.

CHAPTER II

THE OBSEQUIES OF MADAME ADELAIDE

THE first ceremony of 1848 was the celebration of Madame Adelaide's obsequies. They took place at Dreux, on January 5. At three o'clock the previous day, the Archbishop of Paris, the clergy of Saint Germain-l'Auxerrois, and the curés of the different parishes of the capital had repaired to the Tuileries and recited prayers in the mortuary chapel in the pavilion of Flora, where the body of the Princess lay. On the 5th, at four o'clock in the morning, the funeral car started for Dreux, accompanied by the Duke de Nemours, the Prince de Joinville, and the Duke de Montpensier.

In her last will, Madame Adelaide had expressed her wish that the care of directing her obsequies and following her mortal remains to the vaults of Dreux should be confided by the King to the princes, without his assisting in person at so painful a ceremony. Louis Philippe did not comply with this desire. He left the Tuileries at one o'clock, January 4, along with the Queen, the Duchesses of Orleans and Nemours, the Princess Clementine and her husband, Duke Augustus of Saxe-Coburg-Gotha. They arrived at Dreux, at eight o'clock in the evening, and were joined the next morning by the King and Queen of the Belgians.

Some time before the end of the old régime, Louis XVI. had purchased from the Duke de Penthièvre, King Louis Philippe's maternal grandfather, the domain of Rambouillet, where rested the remains of the Count and Countess of Toulouse, the father and mother of the Duke, who had them transferred to the vaults of his château of Dreux, where he, also, was soon afterwards interred. As Bossuet said, speaking of the Pharaohs, "He did not long enjoy his sepulchre." The Revolution destroyed the château and broke up the tombs. But when the Duchess-dowager of Orleans, the daughter of the Duke de Penthièvre, returned to France with Louis XVIII., her first care was to restore the vaults to their first destination. She was buried there in 1821, and from that time the chapel of Dreux became the family burying-place of the Orleans family. King Louis Philippe caused what remained of the old château to be repaired and arranged, so as to have a temporary residence, a sort of pious way-station, near the chapel he built amidst these ruins to replace the one destroyed by the Revolution. It was there he spent the night of January 4–5, 1848.

The funeral car, drawn by eight horses draped in mourning, and led by domestics in full black livery, arrived at Dreux at noonday. The three princes who accompanied it alighted from their carriages at the entrance of the town, and followed it on foot. Never since the mournful day which saw the remains of the prince-royal carried within the walls of Dreux, had the town presented a more doleful aspect.

A numerous crowd, coming from all quarters of the surrounding country, thronged the streets while awaiting the arrival of Madame Adelaide's remains. The car was followed by two hundred priests in surplices, belonging to the dioceses of Chartres and of Évreux, and also by two long files of poor people, clad at the King's expense, and carrying candles. The convoy, after having slowly climbed the long ascent which leads to the esplanade of the château, halted at the principal entrance, where it was received by the King with his head uncovered, and dressed in mourning. His sobs drew tears from every eye. For the first time, his green old age seemed to bend under the weight of sorrow. However, without giving his arm to any one, he put himself at the head of the procession. His three sons followed him, as deeply affected as himself. The office for the dead, celebrated by the Archbishop of Chalcedoine, lasted two hours. The King wished to follow the body of his sister into the vault where, between two rows of lighted candles, the tomb, opened for a moment in order to be closed forever, now awaited her. A small number of persons were permitted to attend the sovereign in this final trial. After the *De Profundis*, which, chanted in this subterranean city of the dead, seemed like the voices of the dead themselves, he approached the tomb, sprinkled the coffin with holy water, and then, collecting himself for a last adieu, knelt down on the stone and watered it with his tears.

This was the third time within eight years that Louis Philippe had led a train of mourners to Dreux. He had paid the last respects to his daughter, the Princess Marie, January 4, 1839; to his son, the Duke of Orleans, August 4, 1842. January 5, 1848, came to reopen the scarcely healed wounds of his heart.

Marie Amélie trembled on finding herself again in this chapel, which had been the tomb of so many hopes. Besides the Princess Marie and the Duke of Orleans, two of her children, a boy and a girl who died very young, rested in these vaults, where her own place and that of her husband were already designated. She was to pray there only once more before her death, — on the morning of February 25, 1848, — and then under what terrible conditions! But we will not anticipate.

An hour after Madame Adelaide's funeral the King and his family quitted Dreux. On returning to the Tuileries, the unhappy sovereign found himself more afflicted than before. He could not accustom himself to the thought of never again seeing his sister, and kept staring fixedly at the door through which he had been in the habit of passing every morning from his own apartment into that of this faithful companion of his whole existence. She was his Egeria. and he had lost her just at the moment when he needed her counsels most. However, great as was his sorrow, he continued to fulfil his duties as sovereign with his customary zeal. Nothing could discourage this old man of seventy-four, who knew neither moral nor physical fatigue. Though the private man was afflicted, the public man, the sovereign, had not yet had a moment of weakness. In spite of his grief, he did not view the political situation under a gloomy aspect. He thought that the campaign of banquets, ended in the provinces, would not recommence in Paris. He was aware of the wrath excited in the ranks of the opposition by that phrase in his speech from the throne in which he spoke of "the agitation fomented by inimical or blind passions"; but he was convinced that all this noisy anger was merely a fire of straw which would soon die out. Seeing both his domestic and his foreign policy supported in Parliament by a strong and compact majority, he showed himself irrevocably resolved on not abandoning this majority, which he thought he could draw on as an unfailing source of strength. The Commission on the Address had just been appointed by the Chamber of Deputies, and the nine members elected were all partisans of the ministry. In this first manifestation, the King saw the hope, the certitude, of a great parliamentary victory. He awaited the coming debates with absolute confidence. The old pilot told himself that he had already weathered many a storm, and that so long as he kept his hand on the helm the ship had nothing to fear.

CHAPTER III

COUNT DE MONTALEMBERT

THE discussion of the Address began in the Chamber of Peers on the 10th of January. It furnished to Count de Montalembert the occasion for one of the finest oratorical triumphs of Louis Philippe's reign.

Born in London on March 10, 1810, M. de Montalembert would soon be thirty-eight years old. His mother was an Englishwoman; his father, an *émigré* who had served in Condé's army, was a member of the Chamber of Peers, and Minister of France at Stockholm under the reign of Charles X. He was himself a member of the Upper Chamber, although he had not yet reached the prescribed age for casting a deliberative vote, at the time when, in 1831, he opened a free school with the Abbé Lacordaire, the future Dominican. When prosecuted on this account, he appealed to the jurisdiction of the Chamber to which he belonged, and after having made an eloquent defense he was fined one hundred francs. Already he had sworn eternal enmity to university monopoly. Liberty of instruction was the programme

of his entire public life. He became the chief of
the party called the Catholic party, which, placing
the Church above all forms of government, subordi-
nated all other interests, whatever they might be, to
the interests of religion. "The Catholics of France,"
said he, "are numerous, wealthy, and esteemed; the
only thing they lack is courage. . . . They are accustomed to rely on everything but themselves. . . .
Liberty is not accepted, it is conquered." Half
nobleman, half tribune, an intrepid defender of religious liberty and of down-trodden nationalities, he
maintained his ideas with the zeal and conviction
of an apostle.

There were perceptible analogies between the
sentiments of the leader of the Catholic party and
those of Marie Amélie. Like him, she had the
habit of judging all questions from the religious
point of view. Like him, she was persuaded that
outside of the Church there was no chance of salva-
tion for society. But, more prudent, calmer, and
more circumspect than the impetuous orator, she
displayed her sentiments with less energy and vehe-
mence.

M. de Montalembert was in a state of exasperation
when the year 1848 began. The Swiss Catholics
had just been cruelly defeated by the Swiss radicals.
The matter in dispute was the Sonderbund, the
league formed in 1846 by the seven Catholic cantons,
— Fribourg, Lucerne, Schwitz, Unterwald, Uri, Zug,
and Valais, — for the purpose of resisting the Federal

Diet, which had prescribed the expulsion of the Jesuits, Redemptorists, and other religious congregations. The Sonderbund, supported in vain by the four great continental powers, had been crushed out. Secretly encouraged by England, the Diet had obtained an easy victory. In any case, the forces were wholly disproportionate. The cantons forming the Sonderbund had only 394,000 inhabitants, nearly all of whom were poor, while the population of the much more wealthy cantons under the domination of the radicals was 1,867,000 souls. The forces of the federal army, under command of General Dufour, amounted to 50,000 troops of the first line, 30,000 reserves, and 172 cannons, while the Sonderbund had in all but 25,000 fighting men. After several skirmishes, its principal centre, Lucerne, surrendered, November 24, 1847. Victorious radicalism was inexorable. "It is the will of God," said the Duke de Broglie in the Chamber of Peers, January 13, 1848, "that, after sixty years, we should once more behold conquest with its pitiless demands, military occupation with its greedy exactions, the profanation of holy places, the devastation of holy things, general conscriptions, wholesale confiscations made by revolutionary governments, improvised at the point of the bayonet, and in their turn improvising, in the name of law, inquisition and persecution to the plaudits of the populace."

Paragraph seven of the Address debated in the Chamber of Peers was thus expressed: "The peace

of the Swiss cantons, those ancient and faithful
allies of France, has been disturbed by domestic discords.
It is regrettable that a friendly mediation
could not prevent civil war. We desire that it shall
leave no fatal traces behind it, and that the rights
of all shall be respected. The Helvetian Confederation
will recognize that the situation guaranteed to
it by the treaties, in conformity with all its historic
traditions, is the basis of its repose and the pledge
of security given to neighboring states." It was
apropos of this paragraph that M. de Montalembert,
in the session of January 14, delivered a speech which
was one long cry of anger, grief, and indignation.
"The thing at stake on the other side of the Jura,"
he exclaimed, "is neither the Jesuits nor the national
sovereignty; it is order, the peace of Europe, the
security of the world and of France; that is what
has been vanquished, stifled, crushed at our doors,
at our frontiers, by men who ask nothing better than
to launch the brands of discord, war, and anarchy
from the other side of the Alps and the Jura. Hence
I do not come to speak for the vanquished, but, vanquished
myself, I address the vanquished; that is,
the representatives of social order, of regular order,
of liberal order, which has just been overthown in
Switzerland, and which is menaced throughout
Europe, by a new invasion of barbarians."

The audience shuddered while listening to this
description of the radical triumph: "Do you know
what these haughty conquerors whom they have been

praising to you did on the morrow of the victory? They dared to write with their bloody pen the name of Saint Vincent de Paul in a decree expelling those Sisters of Charity who are an object of veneration, admiration, and respect to all the world. And how have they expelled them? Like wild beasts, shamelessly giving them but three times twenty-four hours to evacuate the canton, without pension and without indemnity, — they, those saintly women, those daughters, not of Ignatius Loyola, but of Saint Vincent de Paul. Nor did they stop there." Then, turning toward those of his colleagues who had served under the standards of the Republic and the Empire, "Do you see," cried the orator, "those armed men ascending that defile of the Alps which many of you have followed? See them climbing that precipitous way which, for so many centuries, millions of Christians, strangers, travellers, have trodden with respect and gratitude; they are going where the French Republic halted with respect, where the body of Desaix, your comrade Desaix, found a tomb worthy of him, where Bonaparte, the First Consul, left the souvenir of his intelligent toleration. . . . And what are they going to do there, these conquerors without a battle? It must be said, they are going to steal; yes, to steal the patrimony of the poor, of the travellers, of those monks of Saint Bernard whom ten centuries have surrounded with their love and veneration. . . . The shameful thing is the victory, a victory won without a struggle, by ten against one, a victory which will present itself to posterity flanked on one side by an expelled Sister of Charity, and on the other by a monk of Saint Bernard, robbed, evicted, and insulted by these cowardly victors."

The Catholic orator had communicated to his auditors the sentiments of indignation which flooded his own soul. As was said by the *National*, a republican journal: "Nobody had ever so moved the desks, the wooden knives, and the lungs of the peerage. This was not agitation, but transport; not spasms, but a sort of high fever. Shouts, bravos, stampings, served as an accompaniment to the effusions of his eloquence. Impassioned himself, almost to frenzy, he spurted over all the benches currents of electricity which made them jump." The Upper Chamber shared M. de Montalembert's emotion all the more easily because it agreed with him in thinking that the triumph of the Swiss radicals foreboded radical victories in other countries, perhaps even in France itself. The orator insisted on the solidarity established between the victors of the Sonderbund and their French admirers, who in their banquets had just been making noisy apologies for the excesses committed on the other side of the Alps. "What was said at the banquets," he exclaimed, "must not be forgotten, and the echo of it should be prolonged as a profound and salutary warning. They did not limit themselves to confounding liberty with the Revolution, and the Revolution with the Convention. They did not merely proclaim that the guillotine was the tribune from which France had spoken to kings and to Europe. They did not simply protest against the aristocracy of capital. No; they went on to hail with enthusiasm the victories and the heroes of Swiss radicalism, as if there were to be found the actual practice of the glorious theories they were proclaiming. . . . They have sought out whatever was most sanguinary, most ignoble, in our Revolution, in order to make of it a sort of programme and justification of the new doctrines they are preaching to the French people. . . . The wolves have discovered that there is no need of disguising themselves as shepherds. Hence they talk like wolves, and men applaud them and drink with them to fraternity and humanity." After defining his position as that of a Catholic, but a liberal Catholic, the orator went on to say: "I defy any one to find a word issuing from my pen or dropped from my lips which was not destined to serve liberty. Liberty! Ah! I can say without a boast that it has been the idol of my soul. If I have any reproach to address myself, it is that I have loved it too well, loved it as one loves in youth, beyond measure, beyond restrictions. But I do not reproach myself; I will continue to serve it, to love it always, to believe in it forever. And I think I have never loved it more, never served it better than on this day when I have striven to tear off the mask of its enemies, who adopt its colors and usurp its flag only to dishonor and to soil it."

The enthusiasm of the peers continued to increase.

As was said by the *Presse:* "The eaglet became an eagle; it soared to a height which the most complaisant friendship had not supposed it capable of attaining. Few orators have ever counted so complete a success in all their lifetime." Here is the burning peroration of this discourse, which called forth frenzied bursts of applause: "For my part, it is my conviction that the greatest of all evils in a political society is fear. Do you know what has been the source of all our catastrophes in this infamous and bloody society which men are striving with all their might to rehabilitate? It is fear. Yes; the fear that honest men have of scoundrels, and even the fear which petty scoundrels have of great ones. Do not be afraid, gentlemen; do not allow the wicked to have the monopoly of energy, of audacity! Let honest men be energetic in well-doing; when needs must, let good citizens be audacious! Let them unite to defend energetically our glorious institutions conquered in 1789 and in 1830. Let us defend them at home and abroad by showing our horror of all that resembles 1793 and 1799. Let this be our policy, this the principle of union between all who at bottom desire the same thing: liberty, order, and peace. Guard liberty above all; learn from what has happened beyond the Jura how dangerous it is not to know how to tolerate, to comprehend, to support even those whose ideas, beliefs, and affections we do not share. Do not forget that this liberty has just been immolated in Switzerland and betrayed by

England, but that the destiny of France is to be forever its standard and protector." When the orator ceased speaking, acclamations resounded from all sides. The peers left their seats and hastened to congratulate him. Among the most enthusiastic was the Duke de Nemours. Never had an alarum produced a greater impression. It was the tocsin which announced not merely the Revolution of February, but all future struggles between Catholicism and radicalism.

CHAPTER IV

THE CHAMBER OF PEERS

A LARGE majority of the Upper Chamber which had so enthusiastically applauded Count de Montalembert's speech was devoted to the King and M. Guizot, and faithfully interpreted the domestic and the foreign policy of the sovereign. It contained few adherents of reform, and the Luxembourg palace appeared to be an essentially conservative centre. The ministry had nothing to fear from that quarter. But if the Chamber of Peers was not a danger to it, neither was it a force. The noble assembly was to play no part whatever in the forthcoming drama. And yet the debates on the Address, which took place there between the 10th and 18th of January, 1848, were more than usually spirited, and even among its members the symptoms of revolutionary effervescence might be detected.

Two members of the aristocracy, the Marquis de Boissy, who had married Byron's mistress, the Countess Guiccioli, and Count d'Alton-Shée, talked like advanced democrats. The latter greatly scandalized his colleagues by making an apology for the Convention, in the session of January 13. The Duke de Pasquier, who presided, thought fit to address him the following severe admonition: "Sir, you should have waited a few years longer before eulogizing the Convention, as you seem to desire; you should have waited until members yet sitting here, who lost their fathers, sisters, and most cherished relatives by the sanguinary decrees of that Convention, had disappeared and left the field clear for the praises you are anxious to bestow."

The discussion over Italian affairs likewise created great excitement. Pius IX., who was elected Pope June 16, 1846, had inspired not only the liberals but even the revolutionary party with the most ardent hopes. Mazzini had written him, September 8, 1847: "Holy Father, be confident, rely on us. We shall found for you a government unique in Europe. We shall know how to convert into impressive action the instinct which is convulsing Italy, from one end to the other. I address myself to you because I deem you worthy to be the initiator of this vast enterprise." At the same period, the King of Piedmont, Charles Albert, wrote to one of his ministers: "We have a pope who is both firm and holy, and who will be able to sustain with dignity the national independence. I have informed him that, whatever may happen, I will never separate my cause from his. A war of national independence which should unite in defence of the Pope would be the greatest good-fortune that could happen to me." These misconceptions were soon to end. Pius IX. was not to be the ally of either Charles Albert or Mazzini. Already the first symptoms of disenchantment were becoming evident. But in France, M. Guizot's adversaries were unwilling to recognize them. In their view, Pius IX. always represented the cause of Italian independence, and the French government was to be Austria's ally against the Pope. Curious spectacle to see the Voltairians of the left reproaching the ministry with not upholding the Sovereign Pontiff, and associating Pius IX. and M. Ochsenbein, the chief of the Swiss radicals, the persecutor of Catholicism, the victorious enemy of the Sonderbund, in the toasts given at their banquets.

In the Chamber of Peers the Pope had enthusiastic admirers. The Vicomte Victor Hugo, as the poet was then styled in official circles, eulogized the Holy Father on January 13, in what was almost a hymn of praise. "This man," said he, "who holds in his hands the keys to the thoughts of so many men, might have sealed up the intelligence of men, and he has opened it. He has set the idea of emancipation and liberty on the highest summit where man can place a light. The eternal principles, which nothing can sully and nothing can destroy, which caused our Revolution and survived it, those principles of right, equality, and reciprocal duty which fifty years ago made their appearance in the world for a moment, always grand doubtless, but ferocious, formidable, and terrible under the *bonnet rouge,* have been transfigured by Pius IX., who has just displayed them to the universe glowing with mildness, sweet and venerable under the tiara. It is, in truth, because their veritable crown is there! Pius IX. is showing the good and secure path to kings and peoples, to statesmen and philosophers, to all mankind. Thanks be to him! He has made himself the evangelical auxiliary, the supreme and sovereign auxiliary of those lofty social verities which the continent, to our great and serious honor, denominates French ideas. He, the master of consciences, has made himself the servitor of reason. . . . He has come to show the nations that it is unnecessary to shed blood in order to fertilize the furrow where germinates the future of free peoples, but that it is enough to spread abroad ideas; that the Gospel contains all charters; that the liberty of all peoples, like the deliverance of all slaves, was in the heart of Christ and should be in the heart of the bishop; that when he wills it, the man of peace is a greater conqueror than the man of war, and a better conqueror; that he who has true divine charity, true human fraternity, in his soul, has at the same time the true genius of politics, and that, in a word, for those who govern men, to be holy and to be great is one and the same thing."

The illustrious poet touched the summit of enthusiasm. "Yes," said he, "I insist upon it, a pope who adopts the French Revolution, who makes of it the Christian revolution, and includes it in that benediction which from the balcony of the Quirinal at Rome he sheds over Rome and the universe, *urbi et orbi*, a pope who does this extraordinary and sublime thing is not merely a man, he is an event." Already presaging Italian unity, the lyrical orator continued: "Yes, gentlemen, I am one of those who tremble in thinking that Rome, ancient and fecund Rome, that metropolis of unity, after having brought forth unity of faith, unity of dogma, Christian unity, is again in travail, and will perhaps bring forth, amid the acclamations of the world, the unity of Italy."

The problems of the future asserted themselves. "Independence! Independence!" exclaimed M. Cousin, during the same session; "what a sacred and dolorous word it is that I pronounce! I myself feel like uttering it in affright, so laden with tempests is it! . . . The Holy See and Piedmont are the two powers whose own character and situation call on them to be the great instruments of Italian regeneration. The Pope is its soul, Piedmont its arm. The Pope has given the signal; it is his part to direct it. It is he who, by virtue of his double title, as temporal prince of the centre of Italy, and above all as pastor of souls, should inspire, sustain, conduct this great enterprise." And, as if he had foreseen the future annexations, M. Cousin added: "The Piedmontese are, in a way, the Macedonians of Italy."

M. Guizot was far from sharing the idea of a crusade of Pius IX. and Charles Albert against Austria.

He desired reforms in Italy, not disturbances, and belonged to that school of politicians who thought that, as France was unable to rectify its own frontiers, it was not called upon to rectify those of other countries. A most distinguished diplomat, Count de Sainte-Aulaire, who had been French ambassador at Rome in the beginning of Louis Philippe's reign, was the interpreter of M. Guizot's policy when, throwing cold water on the inflammatory speeches we have just cited, he said, in the session of January 12: "M. de Montalembert has spoken of the happy and glorious exaltation of Pius IX.; for my part, I shall speak of the anguish of Gregory XVI. at his entry into the pontificate. M. de Montalembert has spoken to you of the legitimate liberalism of 1847; I shall speak to you of the culpable liberalism of 1831. M. de Montalembert has spoken to you of Austria, which, according to him, ought to be mistrusted in 1847; I shall speak to you of the sincere and liberal concurrence lent us by Austria in 1831 in order to obtain liberal reforms. As to Italian liberalism, be on your guard against whatever would tend to excite, exalt, or encourage it beyond due measure. It has no need of anything but sedatives and to be incessantly recalled to prudence and moderation. . . . In fact, gentlemen, I do not believe that anything stable can be realized in Italy at present without the concurrence of Austria. And I am convinced that it can easily be obtained on reasonable conditions." Such was, at bottom, the position of the ministry. Its adversaries judged the Italian question from an entirely different point of view.

In discussing internal affairs the Chamber of Peers showed evidence of tact and prudence. Notwithstanding the steps taken by certain partisans of the ministry, it did not insist upon the words "blind or inimical passions," which had so greatly irritated some minds in the speech from the throne, and appealed in it to legal action and public reason to preserve the repose of the country. On January 18, it voted the whole Address, by a majority of 144 against 23. The next day this Address was presented to the King by the grand deputation of the Upper Chamber. The Duke de Nemours, Prince de Joinville, and the Duke de Montpensier stood at the right and left of the throne. The most important paragraph had been drawn up by Baron de Barante. It ran as follows: "Noisy manifestations in which vague ideas of reform and progress, passions inimical to our monarchical constitution, opinions subversive of social order, and detestable souvenirs were blindly mingled, have disquieted men rather than cast them into perturbation. The Government was obliged to take them into consideration. We are persuaded that such agitations, tolerated by a régime of liberty, are powerless against public order. Yes, Sire, the union of the great powers of the state, the action of the laws, public reason, will suffice to preserve the repose of the country, to bring back wandering minds, and to dispel senseless hopes. The seventeen years during which our dear country has at last simultaneously enjoyed order and liberty, are far from being another phase of our revolutions. This period begins a durable era, and will bequeath to future generations the maintenance of the Charter, the benefits of your reign, and the glory of your name. Sire, may the thought of what you are to France sustain your strength and courage and soften the griefs which have just wounded you in your dearest affections!" The King replied in words full of confidence and serenity. The drawing up and the voting of the Address by the Chamber of Peers had been an incontestable triumph for the ministry. But this was merely a first station on the perilous road which had yet to be travelled. The discussion of the Address by the Chamber of Deputies was about to reunite in a formidable attack all the forces of the opposition.

CHAPTER V

M. GUIZOT AND THE COURT

M. GUIZOT, who was about to begin the desperate struggle which heralded the Revolution, in the Chamber of Deputies, was full of energy and confidence, in spite of the opposition against him which existed in the immediate surroundings of the sovereign. Many persons, even at Court, thought the ministry had lasted too long, and that to maintain it in power might lead to catastrophes. In the royal family the prime minister could count on no supporters except the King and the Duke de Nemours, who was accustomed to share his father's opinions on all questions. The Duchess of Orleans, who was liberal like her husband, believed that a reactionary policy involved grave dangers for the future of the dynasty, and she received deputies who had the same conviction at the Marsan pavilion. Prince de Joinville, not daring to express his mind to his father, who would not allow his sons to offer not merely any criticism but even an observation, however respectful, imparted his uneasiness to his mother, and the Queen was troubled by it.

There was an atmosphere of hostility at Court against M. Guizot, a silent opposition, existing as yet in a latent state, but which already caused the powerful minister serious anxiety, and which he has characterized as follows in his Memoirs: " The people of the Court, I will not call them courtiers, for they are not all such,— there also there is often more sincerity and disinterestedness than one thinks,— the people of the Court, I say, are in politics spectators greatly occupied with what is done or happens, and yet very idle; they behold all events, both great and small, at too close quarters, and they exert no public influence for which they are responsible; they are actors, who live only in the green room. . . . At the Court of Louis Philippe I did not lack partisans and friends sincerely attached to our policy; but I also found fault-finders, malcontents, and more or less outspoken adversaries; and, as the situation became more serious in the country and the Chambers, the anxieties of some and the hopes of others at Court grew more keen, and sought to prove themselves not altogether vain." At the château of the Tuileries, as well as at the Palais-Bourbon, there was a right and a left side, excited and irritated against each other.

So impressed was M. Guizot with such tendencies, that in the early days of 1847 he had spontaneously offered Louis Philippe to withdraw from public affairs in case the sovereign were not resolved to support him energetically. He had said then: "Sire, the Cabinet is greatly attacked, but not merely in the Chamber and by the turbulent public; it is so occasionally near the King himself, in his Court, and perhaps higher still."—"True," replied Louis Philippe, "and I am distressed about it; they even disturbed and troubled my excellent Queen for a moment; but be tranquil, I have reassured her; she clings to you as much as I do." In the same conversation, M. Guizot had said: "At present the King might change his Cabinet from prudential motives, but when the struggle is once begun he could do so only from necessity."—"You know very well," returned the sovereign, "that I am thoroughly resolved not to outstep the constitutional régime, and that I mean to accept all its obligations, even those that are unpleasant; but just now there is no constitutional necessity; you have always had a majority. What should I be yielding to if I changed my ministers now? Not to the Chambers, nor to the clear and recognized will of the country, but to manifestations devoid of all authority but the pleasure of those who make them, and to a commotion which is the evident cloak of evil designs. No, my dear minister, if the constitutional régime wills me to part with you, I shall comply with my constitutional obligations, but I will not make this sacrifice in advance and out of complaisance for ideas I do not approve."

Every day confirmed the King in his resolution not to change a ministry which had a majority in the

Chambers, and whose ideas were in perfect conformity with his. It must be recognized, moreover, that from the standpoint of parliamentary institutions the sovereign's attitude was absolutely correct, and even that he could not modify it without departing from the rules of the constitutional régime. What would the right, which supported the King's policy with such zeal and fidelity, have thought had it been sacrificed to the left? M. Guizot's partisans would probably not have rallied to the support of M. Thiers, and then dissolution would have become an indispensable measure. Now, in the disturbed condition of the public mind, and after the agitation caused by the banquets, would not that have been a dangerous venture? Could the King abandon a Chamber absolutely devoted to him in order to bring about the election of a new Chamber, whose sentiments would at least be doubtful? Would not that have been ungrateful and imprudent on his part?

Moreover, Louis Philippe was convinced that nothing is more dangerous for a government which is opposed than to surrender to the summons of its adversaries. "Who knows," said he to M. Guizot, "how far the declivity they want me to go to would lead me? When one begins to descend he is very near falling." The minister had written to the Duke de Broglie, December 13, 1847: "I need everything I can possibly have in the way of physical and moral force. If I could have it, I would willingly use it in the existing situation, for it suits me. It is lively, but it is clearly defined. At home and abroad we are everywhere face to face with the radicals, and the more I see of them, the more I recognize the enemy in them." The King was entirely of the same mind as his minister. He also would have adopted for his programme: "Radicalism is the enemy." Considering himself the defender of society, menaced in France and elsewhere, he thought it his mission to preserve Europe from revolutionary enterprises, and regarded the policy of resistance as a social necessity. In his view, to call the opposition to the ministry would have been to shut up a wolf in the sheepfold. All that he saw in electoral reform was an approach to universal suffrage, and it was his conviction that universal suffrage would inevitably lead to the Republic or to Cæsarism. As to the parliamentary reform, which, although admitting certain functionaries to the Chamber of Deputies, was to exclude the members of his civil and military families, he considered it an attack made on the dignity of his Crown. He said to M. Dupin: "You want me to dismiss my ministry and summon Molé; but Molé would go to pieces, and after him what is there? M. Thiers escorted by MM. Barrot and Duvergier, who would deprive me of all power and ruin my policy; no, no, a thousand times no. I have a great mission to fulfil, not in France only, but in Europe,— that of restoring order. That is my destiny, that is my glory, and no one shall make me renounce it."

It is certain that the return of M. Thiers to power would have been the condemnation of all the King's ideas, not solely as concerned his domestic policy, but also, and more especially, his foreign policy. Louis Philippe considered the Spanish marriages as the greatest success of his reign, and M. Thiers had been opposed to them. Louis Philippe regarded Lord Palmerston as his principal enemy, and M. Thiers was Lord Palmerston's ally. Louis Philippe, a partisan of the Sonderbund, combated the Swiss radicals; M. Thiers supported them. Louis Philippe sought the alliance of the continental powers, and M. Thiers that of England. The disagreement could not be more complete.

The Duke de Broglie wrote from London, December 16, 1847: "It is clear that the new Cabinet, whatever it may be, will pass under the yoke of Lord Palmerston and M. Thiers, and that France will take rank, behind England, at the head of the radicals of Europe; that is nearly as certain as that two and two make four. Hence I conclude that nothing is of more pressing importance, either for France or for Europe, than the maintenance of the present Cabinet, and that it is essential that the Cabinet itself shall not succumb until after having done all that is honorably in its power to save itself, and that the conservative powers of Europe ought likewise to make every sacrifice for the maintenance of the Cabinet which comports with their honor and dignity." If the Duke de Broglie, who was not a reactionary, was of this opinion, can one be astonished that it was also that of a sovereign who had become absolutely conservative?

Louis Philippe thought he had reached the apogee of his career. He found in the Chamber of Deputies the strongest majority which had ever supported his policy. At last he was playing the part he had so long aspired to in the European concert. He was marching in line with the King of Prussia and the Emperor of Austria, and was beginning to win over the Emperor of Russia. It was no longer France, but England, that was isolated. The revenge of 1840 seemed imminent. Lord Minto's revolutionary mission in Italy irritated the continental Courts, and Louis Philippe thought he was ready to unite with them in checking those tendencies to unity, which, in his view, constituted a danger not simply to his relatives, the Bourbons of Naples, but likewise to the Papacy and France. Not for any consideration would he have changed at such a moment the direction of his diplomacy. "Thiers," said he to M. de Montalivet, "that means war! And I will not annihilate my policy of peace." Moreover, there were negotiations pending which, in the King's view, could not be conducted to a happy termination by any except his existing ministry. The Cabinets of Vienna and Berlin, far from considering the Swiss business at an end, saw in the defeat of the Sonderbund only a new diplomatic phase, in which France was to play the leading part, and the 15th of March,

1848, had been fixed as the date on which the powers would resume their deliberations on this subject. The Duke de Broglie wrote to his son that Lord Palmerston would then be "left entirely alone, fraternizing with the radicals, and with their flag in his hand."

On the other hand, the situation at Rome was becoming complicated. The radicals were beginning to threaten the Pope, and Louis Philippe wanted to protect him. "It was evident," writes M. Guizot in his Memoirs, "that Rome was the centre of Italian events and perils. By taking up our position in Rome we could support the influence, at once reformatory and anti-revolutionary, of Pius IX., by guaranteeing the security and peace of the Catholic Church. On my proposition, the King and his council resolved that, if the Pope were menaced, either from within or without, and should call on us for assistance, we would give it efficaciously. Certain regiments were designated, a commander appointed for this contingent expedition, 2500 men were kept at Toulon and 2500 more at Port Vendres, in readiness to embark for Civita Vecchia at the first signal. I had two long interviews with General Aupick, an officer as intelligent as he was brave, which assured me that he thoroughly comprehended our intention and would conform his conduct to it. By the 27th of January, 1848, all his measures were taken." Louis Philippe was convinced that, by a foreign policy, both liberal and conservative, he could put an end to the hostility of England and appear as the arbiter of Europe, on one condition, — that of retaining his ministry in power. M. Guizot had adversaries at Court, but the King continued to give him all his confidence.

CHAPTER VI

THE CHAMBER OF DEPUTIES

THE Chamber of Deputies should have been a power for the government, but it was only a danger. It should have prevented the Revolution, and it prepared the way for it. To save the throne would have required a disinterestedness which it did not possess. Its duty was to lay aside all questions of self, all competitions for portfolios, and to put the general interests of France above all private ones. Instead of this, the Chamber yielded to mean passions, and did wrong without estimating the consequences. Seldom has an assembly shown less prudence and composure. It marched gaily toward the abyss and plunged into it headlong. Up to the very morning of February 24, 1848, it was under a complete illusion. Not one member of the left, nor of the right, for that matter, suspected what was going to happen. In both camps there was absolute blindness, and if one can reproach Louis Philippe with having deceived himself, one can also say that the whole Chamber was as greatly deceived as he.

The sovereign disdained the agitations in the

Chamber. Its most tumultuous sessions appeared to him extremely soothing in comparison with those of the Convention, which he had witnessed in his youth. The parliamentary storms of the Palais-Bourbon were to his mind nothing more than tempests in a teacup. To M. Sallandrouze, a rich manufacturer who wanted to play the great politician in the Chamber of Deputies, he said, with rather malicious good-nature: "Are your carpets selling well, M. Sallandrouze?" The King thought that all that was necessary to calm down the most exasperated was to offer him a portfolio.

The government of July had, in fact, nothing but the Orleanist element to fear in the Chamber. Neither legitimacy, Bonapartism, nor the Republic, was in question there. M. Berryer conducted himself better toward Louis Philippe than his own most convinced partisans. He had not participated in the banquets, and had loyally shown up their revolutionary character. He had frankly approved the foreign policy of the government, and defended the Spanish marriages. "We received from M. Berryer," writes the Count de Falloux, "the example of patriotism dominating that collective egotism which is called party spirit. . . . It was certainly a temptation to applaud men who turned against the government founded by them the arms they had employed so powerfully against the Restoration. We might have found more than one bitter satisfaction in so doing; we might have sought there for the sanction of principles to which we were reproached for having been faithful. But this satisfaction and this sanction, whether indisputable or not, might become fatal to France, and that was enough to awaken conscientious scruples and make them prevail." Not a single legitimist deputy had appeared at the banquets, and the partisans of the Count de Chambord exercised no influence in the Chamber. They did not lay aside their arms, but they were no longer fighting.

As to Bonapartism, there was not even a question of it in parliamentary circles. There was not a single Bonapartist deputy in the Chamber. MM. Odilon Barrot, Dufaure, de Tocqueville, Lanjuinais, Léon Faucher, de Falloux, would have been extremely astonished had any one told them they would presently be the Ministers of the President of the Republic, Louis Bonaparte! Still more amazed would MM. de Morny, Achille Fould, Abbatucci, Ducos, Billault, Drouyn de Lhuys, Baroche, Magne, Béhic, all of them Orleanist deputies, have been, had it been announced to them that they would be the Ministers of the Emperor Napoleon III.

The republican element was almost null in the Chamber. Not a deputy would have dared pronounce the word Republic or allude to that régime in any way. One alone, M. Ledru-Rollin, was known to have republican opinions. Summoned before the tribunals on this account, he had one day said: "Attorney-general, who gave you the inves-

titure? The minister. I, the elector, I drive out
ministers. In whose name do you speak? In the
name of the King. I, the elector,— and history is
there to bear me out,— I make and unmake kings.
Attorney-general, to your knees! To your knees
before my sovereignty! To discuss my impartiality
is to lay hands upon my electoral crown!" In the
banquets of 1847, at Lille, Châlon-sur-Saône, and
Dijon, M. Ledru-Rollin had used language equally
vehement and declamatory. But if he had attempted
to express himself in the Chamber in such terms he
would have been silenced at once. He had not the
slightest notion of doing so, and when he spoke it
was much more as a lawyer than a demagogue.
His future colleagues in the provisional government,
MM. Dupont (of the department of the Eure), Carnot,
Marie, Garnier-Pagès, never alluded in their speeches
to the possibility of a revolution. Possibly they
would have been content with a change of ministers
and, in case of the death or abdication of the King,
with the regency of the Duchess of Orleans and the
accession of the liberals to power. As to M. de
Lamartine, who in 1847 never made a single speech
in the Chamber, he was living isolated and solitary
in the midst of his colleagues, a general without soldiers, a philosopher without disciples, scornful of
parliamentarism, and awaiting with Oriental fanaticism destinies which no one could foresee.

It was not, we repeat, the deputies hostile to the
dynasty that Louis Philippe dreaded; what he con-

sidered dangerous were the deputies of the dynastic
opposition, of the partisans and founders of the monarchy
of July. The real struggle in the Chamber
was between the contented and discontented Orleanists.
The left, whenever they had been in power,
had employed the very means they now accused the
ministry of using. It was not principles but ambition,
interest, and greed, by which the combatants
were directed. The vassals of a ministry which had
lasted more than seven years, the members of the
right, had become habituated to exploit it to their
own profit. As M. de Tocqueville has observed:
"The event which overthrew it compromised the
entire fortune of this man, his daughter's dowry for
that one, and for still another the career of his son.
It was by such means that nearly all of them had
been retained. The majority had not merely risen
by virtue of their obligingness, but one might say
they had lived on it, were living on it still, and
hoped to continue doing so, since they had accustomed
themselves to the idea that the ministry would
last forever; they were attached to it by that honest
and tranquil affection that one has for his own fields."
Out of the 450 deputies in the Chamber, 200 were
functionaries over whom the government had irresistible
means of action. "If so many conservatives,"
says M. de Tocqueville, "defended the ministry
simply with a view to retaining emoluments
and places, I am bound to say that many of the opposition
seem to me to have attacked it only in the

hope of gaining them. The truth, and a deplorable truth, is that the inclination for public functions and the desire to live off of the taxes is not, among us, a malady confined to a single party; it is the great and permanent weakness of the nation itself; it is the joint product of the democratic constitution of our civil society and the excessive centralization of our government; it is a secret disease which preyed upon all the ancient powers, and which will likewise prey on all the new ones."

M. Guizot, and still more Count Duchâtel, Minister of the Interior since 1840, were past masters in the art of using the functionaries of the Chamber. Born at Paris, February 19, 1803; son of a man who had been Councillor of State under the Empire and peer of France under the reign of Louis Philippe; son-in-law of General Jacqueminot, commander-in-chief of the National Guards of the Seine,— Count Duchâtel's own merit, as well as his great fortune, had obtained for him very considerable personal importance. A member of the Academy of Fine Arts, decorated with the grand-cross of the Legion of Honor, the owner of a magnificent house in the rue de Varenne, he cared less for power than M. Guizot did, and had more than once been credited with the intention of resigning it. However, he had concluded to retain his post so as not to abandon the King at a critical moment. Besides, he thought himself able to settle all difficulties, and looked at matters with his habitual calmness. He knew better than any one else a majority which had been formed and disciplined by him, and he exerted a decisive influence over it. His suave manners, his obliging and benevolent character, and the ease with which he could be approached, had made him many friends. He had not the eloquence of M. Guizot, but his invariably solid language and occasionally good-natured malice probably pleased the majority better than the grave and majestic harangues of the Prime Minister.

However, in spite of M. Guizot's prestige and M. Duchâtel's ability, unmistakable signs of disintegration began to appear in the conservative party. A good many members of the right were wondering whether the ministry had not lasted too long, and thinking it would be well to cultivate the acquaintance of the ministers of the future.

CHAPTER VII

M. DE TOCQUEVILLE

THE debates of the session opened in the Chamber of Deputies on January 20. The discussion of the Address in response to the speech from the throne was the ground selected for a relentless duel between the friends and the enemies of the ministry. For several weeks they had been watching each other with furious animosity, and now feverishly awaited the hour appointed for the struggle. As yet nothing disturbed the optimism of the King, but the Queen's apprehensions were constantly on the increase. Everybody at Court was anxious except the sovereign.

There appeared in the *Journal des Débats* of January 20 an article which described very accurately the general uneasiness. It said: "The discussion will be extremely lively, we may count on that. Every means of preparing opinion for violent action and alarming the public mind has been resorted to. For some days the most absurd rumors have got into circulation and been propagated, nobody knows how or by whom. Sometimes it is the King's health which is said to cause anxiety. The King is sick; no, the King is dead! Sometimes the Communists are about to rise; thirty thousand of them are ready to take arms against the government; even the leader who is to command them, and who will take charge of the redistribution of property, is pointed out. . . . People come and tell you with a mysterious air that the situation is very delicate, that public dissatisfaction is alarmingly evident, that possibly it would be well to prevent an explosion by making some concession to irritated opinion. To look at certain faces and hear certain speeches, one would think that, to use revolutionary language, we were on the eve of a *journée*. . . . These rumors are contradicted or die away by evening, after having been current for several hours; but, all the same, they have produced their effect, and leave vague anxieties behind them. The Bourse is flat, and people end by believing that something has happened, although no one can say what it is." However, the government organ was far from being discouraged. It firmly awaited the approaching struggle. "What it means," it went on, "is that the opposition, having pushed things to such a point, is probably alarmed by the agitation it has caused, and communicates the fear which it seeks to inspire. The banquets were a stroke of despair on the part of the opposition. If this stroke failed, its cause was virtually lost for a long time. It is awaiting that limit beyond which there is nothing but violence and revolution; it has, so to say, pledged itself to the factions to overthrow the ministry. . . . The opposition is afraid and it wants to frighten others." This was the haughty conclusion of the article: "The conservative party will not weaken. You have had recourse to fear, a sorry means! It is a weapon that will break in your hands, as all the others have. We promise you that in advance."

The resistance of the ministry exasperated its enemies. Explosions of anger from all sides were heard from the moment the discussion opened in the Chamber of Deputies. In the *Revue des Deux-Mondes*, the chronicler of the fortnight wrote: "Alas! we are bound to say that for several days we have been present at the saddest of all spectacles, that of the discrediting of great public powers and the decadence of parliamentary debates. If this goes on we shall presently have nothing to envy in the American Congress, where men go with pistols in their pockets." The opposition tactics were to represent things under the most doleful aspect, and to anticipate the most frightful catastrophes for the near future. Of all the deputies, he who sounded the alarm bell most noisily was a doctrinaire of the left, M. Alexis de Tocqueville.

Born at Verneuil, July 29, 1805, M. de Tocqueville was, on his mother's side, the great-grandson of Malesherbes. At the end of the Restoration he had been judge of the tribunal at Versailles. In 1831, along with M. Gustave de Beaumont, his former colleague in that tribunal, he had been commissioned by the government to go and study the penitentiary system of the United States. He brought back from this mission his principal work, *Democracy in America*, which he published in 1835, and which Royer-Collard styled a continuation of Montesquieu. It was this book which gained him admission, in 1839, to the Academy of Moral and Political Sciences, and in 1841 to the French Academy. Becoming a deputy in 1839, he represented the department of Valognes up to the Revolution of 1848.

When special affairs were in question, M. de Tocqueville frequently afforded valuable assistance to the government, but he carried on a continual opposition to M. Guizot. Without being an adversary of the July monarchy, he aided, in spite of himself, to overthrow it. From the beginning of 1847 the situation had looked gloomy to him. "Although," he has written in his *Souvenirs*, "I was far from imagining that the catastrophe was so near and would be so terrible, yet I felt that uneasiness began and gradually increased in my mind and rooted deeply there the idea that we were marching toward another revolution. That marked a great change in my ideas, for the calm and universal depression which had succeeded the Revolution of July had made me believe for a long time that I was destined to pass my life in an enervated and peaceable society. I began to perceive that in 1830 I had mistaken the end of an act for the end of the play."

Such was M. de Tocqueville's disposition when he ascended the tribune, January 27. His language was that of a Cassandra. "People say there is no danger," cried the author of *Democracy in America*, "because there is no riot; they say the Revolution is far away because the surface of society is unruffled. Gentlemen, permit me to say that I think you are mistaken. Doubtless, though disorder does not appear in actions, it has entered profoundly into men's minds. Look at what is going on in the working classes, who are, I admit, tranquil at present. It is true that they are not so greatly tormented by political passions, properly so-called, as they have been in former times; but do you not see that their passions, ceasing to be political, have become social? Do you not see that little by little ideas are spreading among them which point not simply to the changing of such or such laws, ministries, or even governments, but of society itself, to the overthrowing the very strata on which it now reposes? . . . I think we are sleeping at present over a volcano." Describing the general situation in the most alarming colors, the orator proceeded: "Are you not aware, by a sort of instinctive intuition which cannot be analyzed, but which is certain, that the soil is again trembling in Europe? . . . And it is at such a time that you remain calm in presence of the degradation of public morals, for that word is not too strong. I speak without bitterness, I even speak, as I believe, without party spirit; I attack men with whom I am not angry, but at last I am obliged to tell my country what is my profound and settled conviction. Very well! my profound and settled conviction is that the degradation of public morals will lead in a short time, very short perhaps, to new revolutions."

The peroration of this speech resembled a cry of anguish. "Does then," exclaimed the prophet of misfortune, "the life of kings hang by threads firmer and more difficult to break than that of other men? Have you at present the certainty of another morrow? Do you know what may happen in France a year, a month, a day, perhaps, from now? You do not know; but what you do know is that there is a storm on the horizon, and that it is coming toward you; will you allow yourselves to be forestalled by it? Gentlemen, I entreat you not to do so,— I do not ask, I entreat you; I would willingly go down on my knees to you, so real and serious do I think the danger. . . . Avert it while there is yet time; correct it by attacking, not its symptoms, but itself. Changes in legislation have been spoken of. I am extremely inclined to believe that these changes are not merely useful but necessary; hence, I believe in the utility of electoral reform and the urgency of parliamentary reform; but I am not insane enough, gentlemen, not to be aware that it is not the laws themselves which form the destiny of peoples; no, it is not the mechanism of laws which produces great events, gentlemen, but the very spirit of the government itself. Keep the laws, if you choose, although I think you would be very wrong to do so; keep them, keep the men, too, if that pleases you, but, for God's sake, change the spirit of the government, for I repeat to you, that spirit will drag you to the abyss."

The peroration of the speech was received by derisive laughter from the right and hearty applause from the left. When the orator had left the tribune, M. Dufaure took him aside and said: "You have succeeded, but you would have succeeded better yet if you had not outstripped the sentiment of the Assembly, and determined to make us so much afraid." It is curious to remark that M. de Tocqueville has owned that he did not himself put absolute faith in his sinister predictions. He writes in his *Souvenirs:* "The opposition applauded greatly, but through party spirit rather than conviction. . . . And now that I am face to face with myself, and seriously inquire whether I really was so much alarmed as I appeared to be, I find I was not; I willingly admit that the event justified me more promptly and completely than I expected,—a thing which has probably happened to other political prophets better authorized than I to predict the future. No, I did not expect such a revolution as we were about to see, and who could have expected it?" At bottom M. de Tocqueville and his friends were as improvident as M. Guizot, and were laboring to overthrow a monarchy which they supposed themselves to be merely warning.

During the same session, a member of the majority, M. Janvier, made some striking observations to the members of the left: "No matter what you say," exclaimed he, "France has not ceased to be what it has been,—a land of probity and honor. No, no! all conscience, all dignity are not abolished amongst us. Otherwise, you would be in contradiction with yourselves; otherwise, all these reforms which you are offering as an efficacious remedy would be nothing but a vain palliative. Your proposal to restore public morality by such petty means proves that the evil is not as great as you say, even in your own eyes. . . . The constitutional opposition is under a profound delusion. By the very manner in which it accuses us it is doing as much evil as we ourselves; it is trying to create ruins under which we shall all be overthrown in common. And yet it has been severely warned. No one can accuse the radicals of hypocrisy; they have shown a formidable and implacable sincerity; they have reserved it to themselves, when the conservative party is once beaten, to settle their account with the dynastics, as they call them. The radicals are terrible logicians; they will not be slow to avail themselves of the arguments of their allies of a day, in order to demonstrate that it is necessary to cut down to the roots a tree which has produced such bitter fruits for eighteen years." M. Janvier's prediction was more exact, and, above all, more sincere, than that of Count de Tocqueville. Obeying merely their spites and ambitions, the dynastic opposition did not perceive that they were playing into the hand of the radicals. Their thrusts, aimed at nothing but the ministry, were about to reach the throne.

CHAPTER VIII

THE DEPARTURE OF PRINCE DE JOINVILLE

THE hour of catastrophes was approaching. The presence of all of the King's sons would have been none too much to defend the throne against attacks that were imminent. Fate decreed that two of them should be far away from their father when the storm broke. The Duke d'Aumale had been Governor-general in Algeria since October 5, 1847, and was joined there by Prince de Joinville in February, 1848. This Prince beheld things under a very gloomy aspect, yet without believing that a revolution was so near as it actually proved. For several years he had been predicting the gravest sort of complications, and each time he returned from his maritime expeditions he was made uneasy by what he saw at Paris. "When I returned in the winter of 1845," he writes, "the monarchy of July had three years more to live, but it was already sickly. The parliamentary St. Vitus dance satisfied nobody, with the exception of the Jérôme Paturots, to whom it gave a social position. But for one who was contented, how many were envious! Hence Parliament imparted no strength to the government, which the press was almost unanimously attacking. And, by a strange contradiction, the principal reproach addressed to this régime, which every one was striving to discredit and overthrow, was its lack of vigor. How often at this period did I hear those adjurations to 'be strong,' which always ring the death-knell of governments at bay! Although democratic envy, public speculation, and that necessity of destroying which is the essence of the revolutionary spirit were openly pursuing their ant-like task, without other opposition than sterile verbiage and futile hindrances, ordinary social life nevertheless preserved the appearances of health." In Prince de Joinville's view these were deceptive appearances, and he thought the malady would continue to grow worse.

In 1847, the Prince commanded the Mediterranean squadron. He was on board the *Souverain*, in the roadstead of Spezzia, when he wrote to the Duke de Nemours, on November 7, a confidential letter which was found in a drawer when the Tuileries was sacked, and which proves the keenness of his apprehensions. He says in it: "I am troubled by all the events I see accumulating on every side. I begin to be seriously alarmed, and at such times one likes to chat with those in whom he has confidence. . . . The King has reached an age at which one no longer accepts observations; he is accustomed to govern. He likes to show that he does govern; his immense experience, his courage, and all his great qualities make him brave danger audaciously; but there is none the less danger for all that."

Concerning the foreign policy, and notably concerning the affairs of Switzerland and Italy, the ideas of the Prince were diametrically opposed to those of M. Guizot. He writes in the same letter: "What can be done abroad to relieve the situation and follow a line of conduct which would suit the inclinations of our country? It certainly could not be done by an Austro-French intervention in Switzerland, for that would be to us what the campaign of 1823 was to the Restoration. I had hoped that Italy might afford us this counter-irritant, this diversion that we need so badly, but it is too late, the battle is lost here. We can do nothing here without the concurrence of the English, and in letting them gain ground daily we necessarily throw ourselves back into the opposing camp. All we can do here now is to go away, because if we remain we shall be forced to make common cause with the party of retrogression, and that would have a disastrous effect in France. Those unlucky Spanish marriages! We have not yet exhausted the reservoir of bitterness they contain!" We see what Prince de Joinville thought of those marriages which the King and the Prime Minister considered the most brilliant success of the reign.

M. Guizot, who appreciated the lofty intelligence and great qualities of the Prince, tried, but vainly,

to bring him over to his own ideas, especially with
regard to Italian affairs. November 7, 1847, he
wrote him a letter in justification of the French
policy. He has said: "I had it at heart to nullify
in the mind of this capable and resolute Prince the
impression of regret and blame given him by an
imperfect acquaintance with our recent acts in Italy."
In his letter the Prime Minister said: "We are not
united with the absolute sovereigns. We are not
secretly leagued with Austria. Always and everywhere we have openly advised and upheld moderate
reforms, intelligent and regular progress, that truly
liberal and practical policy which applies itself to
the only good that is practicable and to the only
efficacious means of realizing that practicable good.
I am not surprised that this policy is not popular
just now in Italy. The Italians would like something very different. They would like to have
France place at their disposal its armies, its treas-
ures, its government, in order to do what they cannot do themselves; that is, to drive out the Austrians
and establish national unity and representative government in Italy, under some form or another." To
this sentence, a curious prediction of the events of
1859 and 1860, M. Guizot added: "This general
desire on the part of the Italians, is it good or bad
in itself, is it possible to realize it some day, or
forever impossible? I don't examine into that. I
am not making philosophy, history, or prophecy. I
am busy with practical and actual politics. Within

those limits, I say positively that we ought not, that we cannot, undertake on Italy's account what we have not been willing to undertake on account of France; that is, the territorial and political rearrangement of Europe, taking the spirit of war and revolution as our fulcrum." As to England, whose concurrence the Prince would have desired, the Prime Minister thus expressed himself: "I am not disturbed, sir, by the gust of popularity which England just now enjoys in Italy,—an empty and vainglorious popularity. England is giving Italians words and semblances which please them; she will give them nothing else, and they must soon find that out for themselves." This sentence likewise was an exact prediction.

Hardly had Prince de Joinville received M. Guizot's letter when he quitted the fleet and returned to France. He had not quite finished his two years of command at the head of the Mediterranean squadron, and should not have been replaced until spring. But as he was much fatigued and out of health, he asked to be relieved from his duties, and on November 26, 1847, resigned his command to Admiral Tréhouard. "I returned to Paris," he writes in his *Souvenirs;* "in what state did I find it? Politics had invaded everything. Always tiresome, it was about to become fatal to men of order, and glorious for the agents of disorder, as events but too quickly proved." The Prince agreed with M. Guizot no more on domestic policy than on foreign affairs, and his presence at the Tuileries was not at all agreeable to the Prime Minister. Hence he did nothing to retain him when, the doctors having declared that the climate of Algiers would be good for the Princess de Joinville, the Prince announced his intention of taking her there and spending the rest of the winter with her near the Duke and Duchess d'Aumale. The Queen, who felt more keenly than any one the near approach of danger, would have liked to keep beside her a son whose energy inspired her with absolute confidence. She entreated him to remain, and he was himself hesitating whether or not to start, when he finally yielded to the King's advice, and especially to the wishes of his sister, the Queen of the Belgians, who had great influence over him. At the moment when he decided upon going there appeared, for that matter, to be a certain lull in the situation. The chronicler of the fortnight wrote at the time in the *Revue des Deux-Mondes:* "At last we have entered the waters of parliamentary discussion, with all sails standing, and that sort of fog which hovers regularly over every opening of the session is beginning to blow away. . . . During the vacation a thousand exaggerations accumulate and grow in the forced silence of the government. They pile up, they make, so to say, a snowball, and end by forming a sort of obstruction in the public thoroughfare. Clouds roll together and hang above what it is agreed to call the political horizon, and the legislature opens surrounded by this smoky atmosphere; but little by little light breaks through. What is said from the tribune pierces, dispels, and dissipates these vapors; the current of discussion sweeps them away and purifies the air; people find again where they stand, rely on themselves, put themselves in place, and almost always in the same place. There is nothing new under the sun, and what one sees to-day is always, or nearly always, seen. . . . We are convinced, for our own part, that there is, according to the formula, 'Something to do,' and that something will be done before the close of the present legislature; but, even if the ministry should think as we do, it could not condemn in advance a majority with which it cannot but be satisfied; and, in truth, it would be asking far too much of human nature to ask it to disapprove a Chamber which is still supporting it against the most violent attacks." There was the same continuous optimism in official circles.

The Court, after having plunged into profound mourning on account of Madame Adelaide's death, had now resumed its usual aspect. The Queen reopened her salon, January 25, for a small evening party, which broke up very early. The *Moniteur* gave the following report of it: "The royal family were assembled. The King and Queen received S. A. R. the Count of Syracuse, S. A. R. Prince Paul of Würtemberg, the Ambassador and Madame the Countess Apponyi, the English Ambassador and Lady Normanby, the Ambassador of Sardinia and the Marchioness of Brignole-Sale, the Ambassador of

Belgium and the Princess of Ligne, the Minister of Prussia, the Russian chargé d'affaires, the Minister of Sweden and the Countess of Lowenhielm, the Minister of Tuscany and Madame Peruzzi, the Ministers of Holland, Bavaria, and Würtemberg, the Duchess of Dalmatia, the Princess of Wagram, the Princess of Bagration, the Duchess Decazes, the Minister of War and Madame Trézel, the Minister of Justice and Madame Hébert, the Minister grand-master of the University and the Countess of Salvardy, the Minister of the Marine and the Duchess of Montebello, and many peers, deputies, and generals. The reception lasted until ten o'clock." To see these quiet family evenings spent in the Tuileries, no one would have suspected the formidable storm that was gathering above the château. Prince de Joinville has spoken in his *Souvenirs* of these evenings, which slipped away so pleasantly in the family salon, well named so, since princes and princesses, young and old, large and small, assembled there after the repasts, which were always taken in common. "In this salon, situated on the first story, between the pavilions of Flora and the Horloge, my mother," says the Prince, "sat working tapestry near a round table lighted by shaded wax candles, with our young princesses and the ladies-in-waiting near her. Sitting on a bench of the billiard room adjoining the salon, the King received the despatches brought by his chief of the Cabinet and read the *Times*, the only journal he read daily. It was there that visitors who desired to speak with him, principally diplomats, came to look for him, while ladies who came to call sat around the Queen's table, where the conversation was general, although occasionally soporific. It revived when ladies came whose wit or beauty closed up the ranks of the men dispersed about the salon. This was the case whenever Mesdames de Saint-Aulaire and de Castellane were seen to arrive; or those charming diplomatists, the Princess de Ligne, Mesdames Formin Rogier, de Stockhausen; or, again, three sisters, the daughters of M. de Laborde, Mesdames Delessert, Bocher, Odier. Three superb Englishwomen, the Sheridan sisters, had formerly made a sensation there. Now it was the turn of the Princess Mathilde, then in the full splendor of her beauty."

The Queen, who was the finished type of a princess of the old régime, received with perfect kindliness and extreme amiability. Always mistress of herself, she allowed no trace of the anxieties and preoccupations which assailed her to appear upon her noble countenance, and hid her secret anguish in the depths of her heart. Yet, when she bade adieu to the Prince de Joinville she could not restrain her tears. This was on January 30, 1848. In spite of the early morning hour and the severe cold, Marie Amélie was resolved on accompanying her son and her daughter-in-law as far as the Orleans station. She forgot neither the composure the Prince had displayed when he was on horseback, beside his father, at the time of Fieschi's assault, nor the heroism he had given proof of in Mexico and in Morocco. She felt that the menaced throne needed just such a defender, and one might have said that when she pressed him in her arms at the moment of departure, a secret voice announced to the unhappy mother that when she next saw him it would be in exile.

The Prince and Princess de Joinville embarked at Port Vendres, on the steam frigate *Cacique*, and landed at Algiers, February 9.

The Duke and Duchess d'Aumale went into the roadstead to meet them. A few minutes later, their Royal Highnesses were received at the landing by all the city authorities. At ten o'clock in the morning, the two princesses, in an open carriage accompanied by an immense procession, at the head of which rode the two princes, turned toward the government palace, passing slowly through a densely packed crowd, which incessantly applauded them. Splendid weather, a summer in mid-winter, favored this ceremonious entry. And yet, in spite of the enthusiasm of the colonists, the natives, and the army, in spite of his joy at again seeing his brother who was so successfully filling the post of Governor-general of Algeria, Prince de Joinville was sad. "I arrived," he says, "full of sombre presentiments, and convinced that by dint of determining to respect those so-called legal shackles which paralyze governments, and embarrass revolutionists so little at any time, we should end by being swamped, and hear the fatal hour, the *too late* of all revolutions, begin to strike. The only thing was that I did not suppose that moment was so near." In spite of his pessimistic feelings, the Prince did not suspect that at the time when he was installing himself in Algiers, the July monarchy had but a few more hours to live.

MARIE AMÉLIE
QUEEN OF THE FRENCH

CHAPTER IX

THE DISCUSSION OF THE ADDRESS

THE discussion of the Address in the Chamber of Deputies was the prologue of the Revolution. It brought into prominence the absolute divergences existing on all questions between the personal views of the sovereign and the ideas of the opposition. All that was said concerning foreign policy by the orators of the left seemed to the King merely the development of a warlike policy, and Louis Philippe gloried in preserving the pacific character of his reign. M. de Lamartine, who had not made his appearance in the tribune for eighteen months, returned to it with a bitter criticism of all the diplomatic proceedings inspired by the King. "Ever since the Spanish marriages," he exclaimed, "France, in direct contradiction to her nature and to centuries of tradition, has had to become Ghibelline in Rome, sacerdotal in Berne, Austrian in Piedmont, Russian in Cracovia, French nowhere, anti-revolutionary everywhere." Encouraging the Italian movement with all his might, he added: "Underneath the government of France is France itself, France, liberal in its sympathies, persevering in its friendships, and which will ever salute with glory and enthusiasm the resurrection of Italy." As M. Guizot was saying in reply: "It would need a greater lack of foresight than I am able to conceive, not to be aware that if France should take sides with the Italian movement, you would instantly see the four powers forming anew against us," M. Odilon Barrot interrupted him with: "Send your contingent into Lombardy, plant your tricolored standard there."

The same discord existed between the Crown and the members of the left on the Swiss question. "They say," exclaimed M. Thiers, in the session of February 3, "that the men who have just triumphed in Switzerland are radicals, and they think they have said everything in accusing them of radicalism. I am not a radical, gentlemen, as the radicals know right well. But understand my sentiments clearly. I belong to the party of the Revolution, whether in France or in Europe. I hope that the government of the Revolution may remain in the hands of moderate men; I will do all in my power that it may continue to do so; but, although this government should pass into the hands of men less moderate than I and my friends, into the hands of violent men, even were they radicals, I would not abandon my cause for that reason; I shall always belong to the party of the Revolution." That phrase alone was enough to hollow out an abyss between Louis Philippe and M. Thiers.

On questions of foreign policy, the ministry had had a majority of eighty votes. In matters of domestic policy this majority was about to diminish, until it reached forty-three.

The real combat, the hand-to-hand struggle, began February 7, over the banquets and the reform. M. Duvergier de Hauranne's language was especially violent and bitter. "Let it be well understood, well recognized," said he, "that we do not come here to plead against the ministry before the majority; we come to plead before the country against both ministry and majority." He recalled what M. Guizot had written in 1820: "I should say that I do not dispute the peril; only, in my opinion, it is the ministerial system which renders it immense. It is the counter-revolution by which the Revolution is menaced. Let us hear no talk about the Jacobins from those who are themselves using all their power; let no one threaten us with their apparition when they seem to be doing all they can to resuscitate them." Taking the offensive, M. Duvergier de Hauranne exclaimed: "You accuse us of being moved by blind or inimical passions; we accuse you, we, of founding all the hopes of your domination on base and avaricious passions. You accuse us of giving strength by our speeches to the extreme parties, who wish to overthrow social and political order; we accuse you of furnishing, by your acts, to the extreme parties the fulcrum, the lever, which was lacking to them." The orator ended by declaring himself ready to associate himself "to those who, by a striking act of legal resistance, desire to test whether a simple police order suffices to confiscate the rights of citizens," and then he added these haughty and threatening words: "I have said, and I repeat it, we should be unworthy of liberty if, strong in the rights given us by the Constitution, we were about dastardly to recoil before a ministerial ukase."

The members of the left took a malicious pleasure in opposing M. Guizot personally. "I will terminate this part of the discussion," said M. Léon de Maleville, February 8, "by the citation of an inexhaustible author, from whom, I grant, we borrow a great deal, and whose authority we shall weaken in the end by quoting him so often. This is what M. Guizot said in 1830: 'Citizens have the right to assemble for the purpose of talking over public affairs; it is well that they should do so, and I shall never dispute this right; never will I attempt to weaken the generous sentiments which lead citizens to come together and communicate their sympathetic opinions.'"

Count Duchâtel, Minister of the Interior, replied by proving that the members of the opposition were not less inconsistent. What had happened in 1840, under the ministry of M. Thiers, when M. Léon de Maleville was under-secretary of state? When there was question of giving political balls and banquets by subscription, some were authorized and others interdicted, and both had addressed themselves to the authorities in order to obtain the authorization apparently considered necessary. M. Duchâtel appealed to the laws of 1790 and 1791, conferring on the authorities the right to oppose public reunions whenever they seemed likely to disturb order, and ended by declaring that government, performing its duty, would never quail before manifestations, let them be what they might.

Notwithstanding the energetic conclusions of his discourse, M. Duchâtel had spoken without bitterness and even with a certain good-nature. Recalling the epithet "blind," which had excited such wrath in the speech from the throne, he said: "We would all agree perfectly not to submit to such epithets."

The speech delivered the next day, February 9, by the Keeper of the Seals, M. Hébert was, on the contrary, that of a public prosecutor. M. de Tocqueville says in his *Souvenirs:* "M. Hébert was still an attorney-general in the very marrow of his bones; he has the face and the characteristics of that employment. . . . However, he was neither stupid nor unjust, but he had a mind naturally headstrong and stiff, which always went too far and never knew how to turn back or stop in time, and which became violent without being aware of it, through sheer ignorance of slight differences. M. Guizot must have attached slight importance to conciliation when he sent such an orator into the tribune under such circumstances." As the Keeper of the Seals was saying: "I persist in believing that what was done by the banquets was done without law, against the law, and that people should not be able to do it without recognizing and submitting to the law," M. Odilon Barrot, in a rage, rose and cried out: "But Polignac and Peyronnet did not talk like this!" The confusion was at its height. M. Hébert replied: "I protest against your accusations. Far from arresting my courage, far from making me recoil, they but demonstrate to me more and more that I am right, that I am displaying the truth, that I have touched the wound. This wound can be healed only by the just and persevering maintenance of the laws, in spite of those who wish to throw them off." The entire opposition were now on their feet, with their hands stretching out toward the ministerial benches. "Yes," cried M. Barrot, "you, ministers of the popular Revolution of July; you, whose power has been sanctioned by the blood of the martyrs of liberty, you, are disputing a right which the ministers of the Restoration, at the very moment when it was about to be destroyed, recognized and respected! That is what I say; and it is a fact that cannot be wiped away. That which was respected by M. de Polignac has been violated by you!" On both sides, exasperation reached its utmost limits. Never had a more tumultuous session been known. Those deputies who were least irritated invoked the president's authority to restore order. The president had vanished. The session broke up in inexpressible agitation. In the evening M. Duchâtel wrote to M. Guizot: "The effect of the session was not very favorable. Hébert was too dictatorial at the close. That is what is thought by everybody I have seen since the session. The Chamber must be calmed down. We are going straight toward a riot, for which all my measures are taken. Wholly yours." The republican journal, the *National*, hailed in these vehement incidents, "the prologue to another drama, far more interesting and much more real." This drama was the approaching Revolution.

CHAPTER X

TWO AMENDMENTS

ALL means of conciliation were not yet exhausted. Two conservatives, M. Desmousseaux de Gioré and M. Sallandrouze, proposed to the Chamber of Deputies two amendments in the drawing up of the Address, the adoption of which would have tranquilized men's minds and might have averted a revolution.

The first of these amendments was debated February 11. It proposed to suppress the words "blind or inimical passions," and to substitute these in place of the sentence containing them: "Rely on the public reason, enlightened by our free discussions, and the manifestation of all legitimate opinions." One makes sad reflections on the poverty of parliamentarism when one thinks of the importance attached to keeping or abandoning a couple of epithets. The future of a monarchy was to be settled over a question like that.

M. Desmousseaux de Gioré supported his amendment with calmness and moderation. He insisted on what the phrase "culpable manœuvres," inserted in a speech from the throne, had cost Charles X., and on the danger of digging an abyss between the King and a part of the Chamber. "What are you doing?" said he. "You are going to close the doors of the King's palace to the members of the constitutional opposition. You are going to end this monarchical, assuring, consoling spectacle of the concurrence of all sincere and legitimate opinions around the head of the state." He added that the amendment contained nothing hostile to the ministry, which would retain the confidence of the Chamber even if these two epithets in the Address were suppressed. Unfortunately, M. Guizot was determined on keeping them at all hazards. His obstinacy was relentless. One of the most skilful of parliamentary tacticians, M. Dufaure, tried in vain to open his eyes to the danger of "bitter and irreconcilable language." In vain he added: "In such political circumstances as ours, is it prudent for the majority of the Chamber to declare itself against a hundred deputies as attached as it is, as I am, to the institutions of our country, as determined as we are to defend them whenever they are threatened? Gentlemen, this would be an act of the highest imprudence, you would enter upon a path of which you do not know the ending, and you would be preparing events which you cannot foresee." If the ministry refused the amendment, there would be war to the uttermost. If it accepted it, the deadlock would be over at once. M. Guizot was inflexible.

Great emotion was displayed while the vote was being taken. This was done at first by sitting and rising. The vote having been declared doubtful, a *viva voce* vote was resorted to, which lasted three-quarters of an hour, in the midst of the most lively agitation. The adversaries of the monarchy feared nothing so much as the adoption of an amendment which might save it. The *National* avowed this as follows: "When in this assembly of more than four hundred members the president, having put to vote M. Desmousseaux de Giore's amendment, in which the existence of the ministry was at stake, said: 'The vote is doubtful,' we had a sort of vertigo, our blood rushed back to our heart, an involuntary cry escaped from our breast: 'They are escaping us!' Luckily the ballot came to reassure us." In fact, as has been very well observed by M. A. Granier de Cassagnac, the adoption of the amendment would have overthrown the ministry, as to which the demagogues cared very little; but, by putting an end to the existing struggle, it would have deprived them of the alliance of the opposition, which they needed in order to raise a riot. The "inimical passions" lost the support of "blind enthusiasms," the game was up for the time being. That was what agitated the *National* for an instant. But the republican journal was victorious. The conciliatory amendment was rejected by a vote of 228 against 185. The monarchical army was divided into two camps bitterly opposed to each other. Complying with ministerial injunctions, M. Sauzet, president of the Chamber, had voted on a question where parliamentary usages made it his duty to refrain. The opposition let him know that not one of its members would again appear at his house. They also resolved at the same time never to present themselves thereafter at the King's palace.

The ministry rejoiced none the less over its deceptive success. It was about to gain another Pyrrhic victory the next day, in the session of February 12, by rejecting an amendment offered by M. Sallandrouze, which was in these terms: "In the midst of varying manifestations your government will be able to recognize the real and legitimate wishes of the country. It will take, we hope, the initiative in the wise and moderate reforms demanded by public opinion, among which the chief place should be given to parliamentary reform." M. Sallandrouze was a great manufacturer, a carpet-maker, very devoted to the July monarchy, and a notorious conservative. A school-fellow of the Duke of Orleans, he had been received with special marks of favor at the Tuileries, even after that Prince's death. The Court tried in vain to make him withdraw his amendment. He developed it with propriety and in measured terms. "You want to prevent violent reforms," said he; "make wise reforms in time. That there is something to be done I think there is no need of proving. Does not some new voice rise daily from the benches of the majority to warn the ministry? Are not the most loyal men, and even those who are the greatest sticklers for party discipline, forced to ask themselves whether they have not already sacrificed their personal opinions to this discipline? There is, therefore, something to be done, and if I suggest in especial that you should carry the principle of parliamentary reform, it is because it seems to me that this question, above all, has now reached its maturity. . . . Every involuntary concession is a blunder, but in the existing state of things government can comply with dignity with all that is demanded by public opinion, and do so in a suitable degree. The country would thank it for taking the initiative; later on, it would probably be different, and let us know, gentlemen, whether power would not then have to choose between the weakness of a forced concession, and the folly of open resistance to public opinion?" M. Sallandrouze ended thus: "Rest assured that the amendment I have the honor of submitting to the Chamber is not the result of premeditated hostility to the ministry; it is the loyal warning of a sincere and convinced conservative; it is the necessary consequence of that policy, at once moderate and progressive, which we promised the electoral body should triumph in this Chamber."

Count de Morny, the future Minister of Napoleon III., occupied at this time a seat among the most conservative members of the Chamber of Deputies. Especially devoted to M. Guizot, he made a last effort to induce him to say at least a few pacificatory words, to make some promise of future reforms. M. Guizot replied to this speech from one of his most loyal partisans by admitting that the question of parliamentary reform ought to be examined before the present legislative body finally dispersed, but he added that he would give no personal pledges. "The Cabinet," said he, "will make sincere efforts to maintain the unity of the conservative party on this question, so that it may be the entire body of that party which shall give the solution of it to the country. . . . If that is not possible, the Cabinet will leave to others the melancholy task of presiding at the disorganization of the conservative party and the ruin of its policy." In reality, this language was nothing but plea in bar.

When M. Guizot came down from the tribune, a large number of conservatives hastened to the ministerial bench and implored the president of the council to lessen the force of his imprudent declaration. He maintained an imperturbable silence. The Sallandrouze amendment was rejected by 222 votes against 189. The ministerial majority was constantly on the decrease. It was not more than 43 votes. M. de Rémusat had been able to establish two facts: the division in the conservative party and the irresolution of the government. An instant later the Address, in its entirety, was voted, by 213 against 3. The whole left had abstained from voting.

In the evening, M. Guizot wrote to the King: "The defile is passed, and one of the most difficult that we have ever crossed. I have made no promises. If I had not said what I did say, the amendment would have been adopted and the Cabinet overthrown. There will be a great deal to reflect on during the next session; for if unity cannot be restored in the conservative party, the dissensions I have just postponed will break out, and the opposition will infallibly profit by them. In any case, the King is left perfectly free."

Louis Philippe thought himself the victor. February 14, at ten in the evening, he received at the Tuileries the great deputation from the Chamber of Deputies, who had been commissioned to present the Address. On the right and left of the throne stood the Duke de Nemours and the Duke de Montpensier. Nearly all the conservatives had accompanied the deputation. The members of the opposition remained away. The sovereign's countenance evinced the most profound satisfaction during the reading of this Address, in which occurred these words: "Sire, in devoting yourself to the service of our country, with that courage which nothing abates, not even the blows which strike at your most cherished affections; in consecrating your life and that of your children to the care of our interests and our dignity, you strengthen daily the edifice which we have founded, together with you; rely on our support to aid you in defending it. The agitations roused by inimical passions or blind enthusiasms will subside before the public reason, enlightened by free discussion and the manifestation of all legitimate opinions." After having thanked the deputies, the King descended from his throne and came toward them, greeted on all sides with applause. "Gentlemen," said he, "I am much affected by seeing so many of you around me, and very sensible of these acclamations." Who would have suspected, on that evening, that ten days later the throne on which Louis Philippe had just seated himself, for the last time, would be given to the flames?

CHAPTER XI

THE BANQUET SCHEME

THOUGH the ministerial majority had been diminished, it was still considerable. The opposition, vanquished within the Chamber, did not accept its defeat, but swore to take its revenge outside. There were differences at first over the manner of protest to be adopted. The left hesitated between a wholesale resignation of their seats, and a participation in a banquet then in course of preparation in the twelfth arrondissement. M. Marie, a future member of the provisional government, said to the radicals on the morning of February 13: "If we are ready for a revolution, give your banquet; if you are not ready, there will be a riot, and I don't want that." The same day there was a reunion of nearly all the members of the opposition, in the Durand café on the Place de la Madeleine. M. Marie's proposal to resign *en masse* was rejected, and the banquet plan adopted. M. Thiers, who had not uttered a word at the reunion, said to M. Marie as they were coming out: "You were entirely right; a wholesale resignation was the only sensible thing to do. The government has eighty thousand men; all the strategetical measures are decided on." M. Marie answered: "You ought to have upheld that opinion."

Extra-parliamentary agitation had just been resolved upon. The opposition laid down as its principle the absolute maintenance of the right of assembly. February 15 an article appeared in the *Journal des Débats*, which said: "It is not enough for the opposition to have had sixty banquets during the legislative interval; it means to have them in every quarter of Paris, with a tribune which shall respond in the evening to the legislative tribune. And then the students will have theirs! the *Montagnards*, the Communists, theirs! For if the right is absolute, it is so for everybody." The ministerial journal added: "There was no law when, at the opening of the Revolution of July, the National Guard closed the clubs with the simple words: 'Nobody can pass.' Must all reunions, no matter what, be allowed to go on at present? This is a question we put to industry, to commerce, to all who have business in their own houses and who do not think it would be the finest thing in the world to bivouac in the streets and fight the riot." Official optimism was beginning to be a trifle less imperturbable. The *Débats* of February 15 thus pointed out the danger: "When peers of France, when deputies go to erecting another tribune external to the legislative precinct, they are signing their own abdication; they are making ready their own oppression, theirs and ours, that of the minority as well as that of the majority! What! when the pages of history are not yet turned, when the future is written in the past,— almost in the present,— in lessons so bloody, how can those who are not enemies be,— let the word be spoken without gall or bitterness,— how can they be so blind? The clubs, the perpetual banquets, the tribune in the streets, the law in the public square, all this is the absorption, annihilation of all constitutional powers! It is there that oppression is, and tyranny, the brutal and sanguinary hand that would place itself upon the mouth of liberty!"

However, the banquet of the twelfth ward was organized. The members of the dynastic opposition wanted to make of it something soothing and inoffensive, which should tend to the greater glory of the left centre and the detriment of the republicans, — a sort of judicial banquet in which they would content themselves with posing merely a simple question of right, and from which every factious element should be carefully excluded. They meant to select some private house instead of a public one, in which to hold it. There should not be more than a thousand subscribers. Not a cry should be uttered. Even that of *Vive la Réforme!* should be interdicted. They told themselves that a riot would merely strengthen the tottering system, while a legal protest would suffice to overthrow the ministry and assure the triumph of the reform. M. Odilon Barrot estimated the situation, not from the revolutionary standpoint, but as a lawyer. To his mind, the banquet ought to be merely a tribunal in which the case might be argued quietly. To keep the people away as much as possible, the time selected ought not to be a holiday, and the banquet should take place in some little-frequented locality. The original plan had been to give it on a Sunday, in the faubourg Saint-Marceau, and to charge only three francs a ticket. M. Odilon Barrot and his friends thought this plan too democratic. They managed to have it settled that the banquet should occur on Tuesday, February 22, in a lonely quarter, at six francs a head. The place chosen was a vacant house belonging to a M. Nitot, and situated at Chaillot, near the Etoile barrier, in a street then called the rue du Chemin-de-Versailles, but since named rue du Banquet. It was agreed, moreover, that the list of guests should be settled by a committee. As M. Odilon Barrot has said in his Memoirs: "M. Garnier-Pagès himself denied admission to M. Ledru-Rollin and his co-believers." No manifestation from the left centre was desired. Hence it was necessary to exclude republicans.

By an excess of caution it was resolved to submit the whole programme to another reunion of those deputies, of all shades of opinion, who had voted the amendments favorable to reform, and especially to find out whether they would repair in a body to the banquet.

The reunion took place February 19, in the same room of the Durand café where the first one had been held. M. Odilon Barrot already foresaw the difficulty of preserving the private and pacific character of the demonstration, and possibly felt the rising of the popular tide. M. de Falloux says he presided with visible ill-temper and discouragement. In the midst of the tumult he was heard to make this characteristic remark: "It is really incredible that we cannot deliberate calmly when we are taking possibly the most serious resolution we have ever taken in our lives." The language of the leader of the legitimists gave certain Orleanists, more perspicacious than the rest, something to think about. As M. de Falloux has justly observed, M. Berryer would neither speak nor act against the fundamental interests of society. "When those interests were in peril, he defended them as sincerely, as warmly, as if the crown had been on the head of his king and the power in his own hands." Insisting on the perilous character of the projected manifestation, he endeavored to demonstrate that the opposition was placing itself on ground that would crumble beneath its feet.

A certain hesitation was produced. M. de Lamartine began speaking: "The crisis is grave," said he, "the circumstances are critical, the dangers may be great for the responsibility of the resolute men who march in the van in the name of their country. Gentlemen, I am still more convinced of it than the previous speaker; it would be blindness not to see it; it would be weakness to conceal it from you. . . . But what is our situation? We are placed, by the provocation of the government, between shame and danger. Shame! Gentlemen, perhaps we might be great enough, generous enough, to accept it for ourselves. I feel myself capable, you feel yourselves capable, of that sacrifice. Yes! our shame rather than a drop of the blood of the people or of the soldiers on our responsibility. But the shame of our country! but the shame of the constitutional cause! but the shame of the nation's rights and character! No! no! no! we ought not, we cannot do it; we cannot, either in conscience or in honor accept it." The melancholy author of the *Méditations Poetiques* and of *Jocelyn* employed the language of the most vehement demagogue. "We should return to our departments," cried he, "saying to our constituents: This is what we bring back to you from that field of legal battle to which you sent us to fight for you, — the débris of your constitution, the ruins of your liberty of opinion, ministerial despotism in the place of national rights! We have put the neck of France under the feet of a minister! No! no! that is not possible! we should no longer be men! This would no longer be a people! We ought to hand in our resignations that very moment, disappear, and annihilate ourselves in public disrepute."

After a series of still more inflammatory tirades, M. de Lamartine denied that he desired a revolution.

He concluded thus: "Gentlemen, let us speak coolly; the moment demands it. Let us know clearly what we are going to bring about in France on Tuesday. Is it a sedition? No! Is it a revolution? No! May God long defer the necessity for one in our country! What is it, then? An act of national determination and faith in the omnipotence of the legal right of a great country." M. de Lamartine's speech won over nearly all his auditors. It was decided that the banquet should take place on Tuesday, February 22, and that they should assemble at ten o'clock in the morning of that day to go thither in procession.

During the meeting in the Durand café, M. Thiers, who was unwilling to commit himself, and so lessen his chances of becoming minister, had, to use the expressions of M. de Falloux, found the means of being neither absent nor present, and of reviewing his troops without taking the chief command. He remained all the time at the door of the room, seeing and hearing all that went on, sometimes approving by a nod or a gesture the most violent language, but not pronouncing a single word. When it was over, he walked away in company with M. de Rainneville and Count de Falloux. "Are you not alarmed," the latter asked him, "by all we have just seen and heard?" "No, not at all." — "And yet, this looks very much like the eve of a revolution." M. Thiers gaily shrugged his shoulders, and replied in a tone of the most ingenuous security: "A revolution! a revolution! One can easily see you do not know the government and are unacquainted with its forces. I know them, for my part; they are ten times stronger than any possible riot. With a few thousand men under command of my friend, Marshal Bugeaud, I would answer for everything. See here, my dear M. de Falloux, excuse me for telling you, with a frankness that cannot wound you, the Restoration died of nothing but stupidity, and I warrant you that we shall not die as it did. The National Guard is going to give Guizot a good lesson. The King has good ears, he will hear reason and surrender in time." Thereupon M. Thiers quitted MM. de Falloux and de Rainneville, who walked on, repeating: "After all, M. Thiers may be in the right. The King and his ministers are so well prepared to defend themselves that no one will dare attack them."

The hero of the day had been M. de Lamartine. The next day he wrote to one of his friends: "Yesterday there was a last reunion of the opposition. The camp was in a state of demoralization. Berryer had just got done with the legitimists, making a good speech, and concluding to withdraw. I was implored to answer him. I did so in a twenty minutes' improvisation of such a sort that everything was renewed as by fire. Never yet had my feeble words produced such an effect. Everything you ever read of mine is sugar and honey compared with this speech." The political poet was not slow to write of the speech he now gloried in. It was apropos of his speech of February 19, in the Durand café, that he wrote in his *History of the Revolution of 1848:* "Lamartine trusted somewhat to luck. Virtue trusts in nothing but prudence when the peace of states and the lives of men are in question. He tempted God and the people. Lamartine reproached himself severely for this fault. It is the only one that lay heavy on his conscience throughout the course of his political life. He did not seek to lessen it in his own eyes or those of others. It is a grave error to throw back on God what God has left to the statesman: responsibility. To do that is to defy Providence. The wise man never defies fortune, but foresees and deprecates it." Strange and truly unexpected reflections on the part of the man who, by his writings, speeches, and actions, contributed more than any one else to the February Revolution!

CHAPTER XII

THE ARRANGEMENTS FOR FEBRUARY 19

THE government did not even seem alarmed by the decisions arrived at in the Durand café. The revolutionary elements still hung behind the scenes, and nobody imagined that they were about to come out on the stage. In the eyes of M. Odilon Barrot and his friends, the banquet was to be an extra-parliamentary manifestation, but one that would preserve parliamentary appearances, a manifestation of the country as constituted by law, of the just medium, the middle class, and the National Guard, in which the proletariat would not be represented. Neither the opposition nor the ministry desired a real battle. All they dreamt of was simple skirmishes, or, rather, a sort of duel which the seconds were expected to prevent at any cost. "A singular circumstance," writes M. Barrot, "and one which proves how great was the confidence felt by all of us, was that the ministers themselves delegated two of their friends, MM. de Morny and Vitet, to come to an understanding with us about the programme of the banquet."

Count de Morny, who was to play such an important part under the Second Empire, was at this time one of Louis Philippe's most loyal adherents. Born at Paris, October 23, 1811, he had been a brilliant officer of cavalry before becoming a political man. He served with distinction in Africa, under the eyes of the Duke of Orleans, who took a very special interest in him. Mentioned several times in the order of the day, he was decorated for having saved the life of General Trézel. Having sent in his resignation in 1838, he was deputy from Puy-de-Dome from 1842 to the end of the July monarchy. Much attached to M. Guizot, he always sat in the ranks of the conservative majority, but he wished that the ministry should consent to prudent reforms, and had expressed that wish in an essay published by the *Revue des Deux-Mondes*, January 1, 1848. Conciliatory, courteous, and very self-possessed, M. de Morny seemed the most suitable person to bring about an agreement between the opposition and the Cabinet. M. Vitet was made his coadjutor, and on the same day in which the reunion had taken place in the Durand café, these two, representing the majority, had an interview with MM. Léon de Maleville, Duvergier de Hauranne, and Berger, representing the opposition. The five negotiators signed that day an official report which, in their opinion, should avert all conflict. This document stated that the question in litigation was a legal one. The government should consent to allow the offence to reach a point

where it could be legally verified, in order that as
result of a condemnation pronounced, in default, by
a justice of the peace, the legal question could be
submitted to the enlightened jurisdiction of the Court
of Cassation. The five negotiators, as legal and honest men, animated by a wise and patriotic intention,
agreed on the following conditions: —

"The deputies of the opposition shall do everything humanly possible to prevent the disturbance of
order. They shall peaceably enter the banquet hall,
in spite of the warning of the police commissioner
who will be stationed at the door, and who will inform them, immediately on their arrival, that they
are violating an ordinance of the prefect of police
(the point being as important to the dignity of the
reunion as that of the agent of authority). They
shall take their places. As soon as they are seated,
the police commissioner shall prove the offence and
state the facts against M. Boissel, or any other person, by declaring to the assembly that it must break
up, or he, the commissioner, will be obliged to employ force to make it do so.

"To this injunction M. Barrot shall respond by
a brief address, in which he will maintain the right
of assembly; he will protest against this abuse of
authority on the part of the government; he will
declare that all he desired was to have the question
legally decided, and he will induce the assembly to
separate peaceably, declaring, however, that it yields
only to force. He will make the assembly compre-

hend that any rebellion or insult to a public officer would change the case completely, and miss the end aimed at by the opposition. It is loyally agreed that he shall make no speech against the government and the majority, and that, in fine, he will not give the reunion the appearance of a banquet accomplished in spite of the government.

"As soon as he is through speaking, the deputies will set the example by retiring themselves, and on going out they will declare, in order that the people outside may not make a mistake and become irritated, that they have accomplished what they came for, and have taken the only way of reaching a decision."

The five negotiators were especially anxious to spare the dignity of both the conservatives and the opposition. They promised to use their influence over the official organs of their parties, — *Débats, Conservateur, Constitutionnel, Siècle, National,* — in order that no provocative or sarcastic articles should envenom their readers' minds. . . . The attitude of the opposition was to be treated as a dignified and moderate one, the government not accused of weakness nor of having taken a step backward, and the degree in which it was to use its authority considered as the sincere desire to keep the promise made in the discussion, that of arriving at a judicial solution. "Lastly, the deputies of the opposition promise not to patronize, preside at, or encourage by their speeches or their presence any banquet in Paris or elsewhere which is forbidden by the municipality, until the decision of the Court of Cassation, and not to attack the government concerning the means it may think itself obliged to employ for preventing others from being organized."

M. Odilon Barrot, so optimistic at that time, has since made the following reflections in his Memoirs: "It may be admitted that it was rather puerile on both sides to hope that in the existing state of excitement everything would happen according to the programme. It proves, at all events, how far the ministers themselves were from dreading the result of this loyal agitation. It never came into the mind of any one of us that this manifestation, thus left to itself, might degenerate into a revolution." It is certain that in the evening there was a real relief from the strain. The conciliatory official report had not yet been made public, but the sense of it was known, and there was rejoicing in both camps. The Turkish ambassador gave a grand ball that evening at his residence, which was the house now occupied by the Artists' Union Club. There M. de Tocqueville met M. Duvergier de Hauranne, one of the five negotiators. "Courage, my dear fellow," he said to him, "you are playing a dangerous game." To which M. Duvergier de Hauranne replied without any sign of fear: "Rely on it, all this will turn out well; besides, we must risk something, in any case. There is no free government which has not passed through similar trials."

The next day, February 20, the arrangement concluded between the five negotiators was submitted to the council of minsters and fully ratified by them. After the council, Count Duchâtel went to call on the Duchess of Orleans. The Princess seemed well satisfied with the result, and agreeably surprised that the King had interposed no obstacle.

M. Sauzet, president of the Chamber of Deputies, found the arrangement magnificent. "It was not," he writes, "a spectacle without grandeur nor an ordinary homage to that respect for laws which is the dominant character of the epoch, to see on one side the government, with its powerful organization and its influence over military discipline, and on the other, the opposition, with its moral ascendency over the enthusiasm of the disturbed masses, inclining together before the pacific toga of a justice of the peace, and submitting the dispute between these two great forces of the country to the most humble delegate of the inviolable hierarchy of the magistracy." After citing this passage from M. Sauzet's book, *La Chambre des députés et la Révolution de Fevrier*, M. Dupin adds: "*Verba et voces! Idle words!* I think, on the contrary, that this transaction was in reality a desertion of principles on the part of both the opposition and the ministry; neither was fully persuaded of being strictly in the right. Hence, what might have been expected, happened. This first capitulation precipitated the complications they wanted to prevent." However, the same M. Dupin who, in his Memoirs, judges so severely the agreement arrived at, had at first applauded it. "Not only," writes M. Guizot, "did the King approve the arrangement, but satisfaction was evinced in the privacy of the royal family and the midst of the conservative party. On learning the result some hours after the council, M. Dupin cordially congratulated the Keeper of the Seals, and told him of his own accord that he would go himself, as attorney-general, to be the spokesman of the government and defend its rights before the Court of Cassation, if it were called upon for a decision."

The government imagined that the litigation was merely a judicial question, and thought it could rely on the magistracy. "The magistrates," says M. Guizot again, "maintained a fitting reserve, but everything indicated that their opinion on the score of legality was in line with the conduct of the government; there was room to hope that the crisis would have a tranquil issue; the most moderate men of the republican opposition appeared to have resigned themselves to it." M. Garnier-Pagès, who, four days later, was to be a member of the provisional government, thus expressed himself concerning the arrangement of February 19: "We were about to show the world the magnificent spectacle of a whole people risen in defence of a right, vindicating respect for law, calmly deploying the imposing but pacific masses of its force, accomplishing in fine, without tumult and with sovereign majesty, a great act of political faith. Certainly this result was enough, and the opposition could not dream of a greater triumph." M. Garnier-Pagès thought thus, and so did all those who, like him, would have been contented with reform. But the men of action in the republican party thought very differently. What they desired was the overthrow of the monarchy. A peaceful legal solution would have been their despair.

Meanwhile the ministry remained convinced that the banquet of the 22d would be only an empty sham. Count Duchâtel considered the affair terminated, but, on that same Sunday, February 20, some one came at ten in the evening to warn him that the opposition journals declined the arrangement. At first he would not believe it, but he was obliged to submit to the evidence when the proofs of the programme to be published the next morning were brought to him an hour later. Then the minister perceived that the opposition chiefs had stipulated for a party of which they were not masters. The revolutionists were entering on the scene. Things were about to change their face.

CHAPTER XIII

THE PROGRAMME OF THE MANIFESTATION

ALL day long, February 20, the success of conciliatory ideas had been believed in by both camps. The ministry was determined to carry out loyally the agreement arrived at by the five negotiators, and the deputies of the constitutional opposition ardently desired that there should be no trouble in any quarter. The organizers of the banquet had appointed a sub-committee specially charged with taking the measures necessary for the preservation of public tranquillity. M. Odilon Barrot wanted to be a minister, not a rioter. He was in absolute good faith when he supposed himself able to guarantee the pacific character of the coming manifestation. "These," he says in his Memoirs, "are the precautions we had deemed necessary in order to avoid all disturbance; instead of leaving the crowd to itself, and by way of introducing some sort of order, we had agreed that all members of the National Guard who were present should wear their uniforms, but carry no weapons except a sabre; that they should assemble by the number of their legions, in order that, knowing each other, it would be easier to exercise a due surveillance; the same plan was agreed on for the schools, each of which was to assemble under its own banner, and likewise for the deputations from the departments. Each corps was thus summoned to exercise over itself a discipline which would not, according to us, be less efficacious for being voluntary." The sub-committee raised the question: —

"Are the National Guards who join the procession to wear or not to wear their sabres?" As there was a difference of opinion, a member said jocosely that the sabre was not prescribed, but it was not forbidden, and everybody began to laugh.

M. Maxime du Camp says in his *Souvenirs de l'année 1848:* " M. Odilon Barrot, in opening the cave of Eolus to find the zephyr which might gently waft his bark into the ministerial haven, had unchained the tempest." But on the 20th of February he did not yet suspect it. And yet the people were beginning to make this chief of the middle classes, this friend of the National Guard, somewhat uneasy. "Up to that time," he says, "we had to deal with the middle classes or the educated youths of Paris; but now came M. Guivard, demanding that we should admit the working classes, who likewise desired to take part in the manifestation; he assumed responsibility, moreover, for perfect tranquillity. The question was referred to me, and I did not decide without considerable hesitation on admitting the working classes on the same condition we had established for the other classes of citizens; namely, that they should assemble by occupations and under distinct banners, in order that all those who should compose these different groups should answer to each other and exercise a reciprocal restraint." The deputies of the constitutional opposition were trying to convince themselves that such measures would suffice to prevent all collision. They had caused it to be adopted as the order of the day that any one who made a disturbance should be considered a provocator and immediately driven from the ranks.

A programme was to announce all the precautions taken and insist on the peaceable character of the manifestation. "It was our mistake," adds M. Barrot, "to leave this programme to be drawn up by the journalists who were members of the committee, thinking that it was sufficient to have thoroughly explained its meaning and principal dispositions for them to conform to these in the publicity they would give it." The parliamentarians took the second place, and the hour of the men of action was about to strike.

The man who drew up the programme which was about to touch a match to the powder was M. Armand Marrast, the chief-editor of the *National*. M. de Lamartine, in his *Histoire de la Révolution de 1848*, has thus expressed himself on the subject of this sheet: "The *National* was the journal of republican opinion, the toothing-stone (*pierre d'attente*) of the future revolution. Nevertheless, as the Revolution was as yet nothing more than a distant presentiment to the masses, this journal did not have an immense circulation in the country. People read it through a certain curiosity, which desired to know what even the least probable contingencies of the future might be holding in reserve. . . . This journal seemed to waver between the acceptance of monarchical government and a profession of republican faith. At times it appeared to come to too intimate terms with the purely dynastic opposition. It lost few occasions of favoring the opinions, tactics, and political views of M. Thiers." M. Armand Marrast was a republican of the Athenian sort, a man of wit and a fine scholar. As M. de Lamartine says again: "The genius of his style was mischievousness, not hatred. Never a sanguinary image, never a fatal souvenir, never a provocation. The sensuousness of the political artist instead of the sombre fanaticism of the sectary, the horror of vulgarity, the disgust for Jacobinism, the dread of proscriptions, the relish for letters, eloquence, toleration, for glory in liberty, was the republican ideal of M. Armand Marrast."

Born in 1801, at Saint-Gaudens, he had made himself a name by his opposition to the government of King Louis Philippe. He had no fortune, and his beginnings had been very modest. After having taught philosophy at the college of Saint-Sever, in the Landes, he came to Paris under the auspices of General Lamarque. While editor of the *Tribune*, he was condemned to prison for the violence of his polemics, but had escaped the penalty by taking refuge in England. Returning to France when an amnesty was proclaimed, he became, after 1841, the principal editor of the *National*.

M. Armand Marrast had thoroughly comprehended that any republican attempt would fail unless supported by the constitutional opposition. Nothing except its adhesion could put the public on the wrong scent, make the government wary in its attempts at repression, and thus increase the chances of the riot. The bold and skilful journalist had neglected no means of maintaining apparent concord with the deputies of the dynastic opposition; he lavished fine speeches and courtesies on them, and adorned the chain he had hung about their necks with silk and flowers.

The sub-committee, to which had been referred the necessary measures for the maintenance of order, had been summoned to meet on February 20. MM. Armand Marrast, Perrée, Merruau, Pagnerre, Biesta, Havin, and d'Alton-Shée were the only members present. M. Armand Marrast took up a pen and wrote out the programme of the *Manifestation réformiste*. It began thus: "The general committee charged with organizing the banquet of the twelfth ward thinks it ought to recall the fact that the object of the manifestation to take place next Tuesday is to claim the legal and pacific exercise of a constitutional right, the right of political reunion, without which representative government would be only a mockery." The order of the procession was regulated thus: —

"The deputies, peers of France, and other invited guests shall assemble at eleven o'clock next Tuesday morning at the usual headquarters of the parliamentary opposition, No. 2 Place de la Madeleine;

"Subscribers to the banquet who belong to the National Guard are requested to assemble in front of Église de la Madeleine, and to form in two parallel lines, between which the guests shall place themselves;

"The procession will be headed by those superior officers of the National Guard who shall be present to join in the manifestation;

"Immediately after the invited guests and the banqueters a file of officers of the National Guard will take their places;

"Behind these, the National Guards will form in columns, according to the number of their legions;

"Between the third and fourth columns the students from the schools, led by commissioners chosen by themselves;

"Then the National Guards of Paris and the environs, in the order designated above;

"The procession will start at 11.30, and march by way of the Place de la Concorde and the Champs-Elysées toward the banqueting-place."

The document concluded in terms of prudence and pacification, intended to keep up to the last the tenacious illusions of the constitutional opposition.

The National Guards were requested to come unarmed, and the citizens to refrain from shouting and carrying flags or other exterior signs. "The committee hopes," it said, "that every man present will conduct himself as a functionary whose duty it is to see that order is respected; it confides itself to the presence of the National Guards, to the sentiments of the population of Paris, which desires public peace with liberty, and which knows that in order to secure the maintenance of its rights it has no need of any but a peaceable demonstration, such as befits an intelligent and enlightened nation, conscious of the irresistible authority of its moral force, and which feels assured that it can attain its legitimate desires by the legal and calm expression of its opinion."

When M. Marrast had finished reading aloud the document he had just drawn up, M. Merruau, editor of the *Constitutionnel*, asked that it should be submitted to the approbation of M. Odilon Barrot. M. Marrast did not meet the latter until evening, in a house where he was dining. Being pressed for time, M. Marrast did not even read him the programme, but contented himself with explaining its principal provisions: "Yes, that is well," said M. Barrot, "but take care not to add anything calculated to compromise the opposition." The programme was then taken as speedily as possible to the three republican journals, the *National*, the *Réforme*, and the *Democratie pacifique*, which published it in their next morning's edition.

CHAPTER XIV

THE TWENTY-FIRST OF FEBRUARY

SUNDAY, February 20, had been a lull in the storm. Monday, the 21st, was a day of disturbance and excitement. The programme of the reformist manifestation changed things from top to bottom. As M. de Tocqueville has remarked, "One might have called it a decree emanating from the provisional government, to be founded three days later." This programme was about to change the banquet into an insurrection. Like the public, the major part of the members of the constitutional opposition only learned this when they read the morning papers. They began to reap what they had sown.

For the rest, there was a slight difference between what M. Marrast had written and what M. Barrot would have desired. The latter has himself acknowledged this in his Memoirs. "M. Armand Marrast," he says, "though without altering the fundamental provisions that had been agreed on, thought proper to invest the preparatives with a sort of semi-official character, and talk very much as a prefect of police on duty might have done. This defect of form, which, moreover, was merely one of journalistic editing, was not of such a nature as to occasion a dissolution of the agreement between the government and us!" Such was not the opinion of the ministry. M. Guizot and his colleagues all thought that nothing was left of the pacific arrangement of February 19.

There was, in fact, no further question of a soporific, parliamentary, and, so to say, judicial banquet, but of an immense popular manifestation, a rendezvous of all the enemies of the dynasty. As M. Guizot had predicted several weeks before, in a conversation with M. de Morny, the affair of the reform was no longer in the Chamber; it was passing into "that illimitable, obscure, seething world on the outside which mischief-makers and boobies call the people." In this programme the ministers beheld a usurpation of powers, an organization of disturbance, a scandal, a provocation which no regular government could permit. Respecting this, we point to the curious avowal of a member of the provisional government, M. Garnier-Pagès. "If the opposition," he says, "were allowed to strike such authoritative blows in Paris, to convoke the National Guard, to enlist the population, the artisans, the schools; if its orders were listened to and executed, the government was no longer in the hands of the ministers, it belonged to the opposition; even M. Guizot's resignation became useless. If, on the contrary, the usurpation were not tolerated, if the Cabinet should resist, there would be war, war with that redoublement of fury which results from the violent rupture of a peace that had begun."

There is room to remark, moreover, that the arrangement of February 19 had been far from gaining universal approbation. Many political men had seen in it an act of weakness, a dangerous concession, a first capitulation. Such was notably the opinion of a peer of France very devoted to King Louis Philippe, Count de Pontécoulant. In his *Souvenirs historiques* he says: "That the opposition should allow itself to be led astray by its blind confidence in its strength and its usual lack of foresight of the evils it was about to cause, was a simple thing to which, for the last eighteen years, we had unfortunately become accustomed; but that grave and serious men could consent to follow it through the obscure windings of a political comedy whose ending it was so easy to foresee, is something which posterity will find it hard to understand, no matter how or by what eloquent tongue soever it may be excused. The ministry, in accepting a false position, exposed itself to all the inconveniences which, in politics, are its inevitable result. Its tolerance seemed a lack of confidence in its own good right and its means of making it prevail; it wanted to prevent a collision, and it proceeded to hasten its explosion by itself summoning its adversaries to the public square; in a word, it ought to have known by experience that disorders in the streets, like all abuses of liberty, are always easier to be prevented in France than they are to be repressed." The ministers themselves doubted the efficacity of the compact, and learned without regret that it had been denounced.

At ten o'clock in the morning the Cabinet assembled at the Ministry of the Interior. "What do you think of the banquet at present?" said M. de Salvandy to M. Hébert, who was entering the room. "I think, and think more than ever, just what I have always thought about it," responded the Keeper of the Seals; "that it ought not to take place, and that there is ground for interdicting it." "In that case," returned M. de Salvandy, "we are all of the same mind." The unanimous decision of the ministers was immediately communicated to the King, who approved of it entirely.

The government had decided to enter the path of repression, and so warned the public. It had a placard posted up, written, it is said, by M. de Morny, and signed by the prefect of police, M. Gabriel Delessert: "Inhabitants of Paris! An inquietude injurious to labor and to business is prevalent among us. It proceeds from the manifestations that are preparing. . . . The manifesto published this morning by the journals of the opposition raises another government at the side of the real government of the country, that which is instituted by the Charter and which rests upon the majority in the Chambers; it calls for a public manifestation dangerous to the repose of the city; in violation of the law of March 22, 1831, it convokes the National Guards and stations them in advance in double lines, by the number of their legions, with officers at their head. There is no room here for doubt; the clearest and best-established laws are violated. The government will know how to make them respected; they are the foundation and the guarantee of public order." It was decided to publish, at the same time, an order of the day from General Jacqueminot, reminding the National Guards that they could not assemble in that capacity without the command of their chief, an order from the prefect of police formally interdicting the banquet and, finally, the ordinance concerning disorderly gatherings in the streets. The most energetic military measures were prepared, in virtue of a plan of resistance decided on since 1840 by Marshal Gérard. On the morning of February 22 Paris was to be occupied by an army of troops amounting to thirty-one thousand men.

MM. Odilon Barrot and Duvergier de Hauranne tried in vain several palliatives intended to heal this breach, — changes of wording, insufficient explanations, etc. It was too late. On arriving at the Chamber of Deputies, they learned that the government would maintain the policy of resistance, greatly to the joy of the whole conservative party. The session was comparatively quiet. They were already conscious that the question was being discussed beyond the precincts of the Palais-Bourbon.

M. Barrot expressed himself more like a doctrinaire than a tribune. "I fear," said he, "lest what authority is doing at this moment in the interest of order may be, on the contrary, only a cause of profound trouble in society. . . . I will say that even in the situation they are making for us, the first need, the first duty of every man, whatever opinions he may hold, is to employ every possible means of influence or authority in his power to avert the misfortunes which I foreese. . . . I declare that if it rested with me to banish them from the country, to appease this excitement which your inopportune measures will surely increase, I would do it with all the strength of my convictions. Gentlemen, my rights end there; I cannot go further. It is the government which is charged with the maintenance of order and tranquillity in the country; it is for it to weigh the gravity of the circumstances, and it is it, above all, which bears the responsibility."

Count Duchâtel's reply was energetic and calm. Never had the minister spoken with more moderation or authority. "The law against street disturbances is violated," said he; "the law concerning the National Guards is violated. . . . We are unwilling that on the occasion of a banquet, a manifestation contrary to all the laws, and the proclamation of a government improvised at the side of the legal government, should be tolerated in the city of Paris." As M. Barrot was replying, some one shouted to him: "You must avow or disavow the programme."

"I will put everybody entirely at ease," he returned; "I unhesitatingly avow the intention of this act, I disavow its expressions." M. Duchâtel again ascended the tribune. "The manifesto being neither avowed nor disavowed," exclaimed he, "is it a subject of security for us, who are charged to maintain public order? Is it a subject of security that a manifesto inciting to the violation of the laws can be openly published? a manifesto which the honorable M. Barrot dare not say that he avows?" And the minister concluded, amid applause: "The repression they talk about is simply the performance of the government's duties, the maintenance of that order and respect for law on which rest the tranquillity of the country and the safety of our institutions." In this brief skirmish the minister had indisputably gained the advantage.

The opposition deputies were visibly embarrassed. When the session broke up at five o'clock, they repaired to the house of M. Odilon Barrot, who lived at No. 2, rue Ferme-des-Mathurins, now rue Vignon. "I presided at the reunion," he says in his Memoirs. "I thought I ought not to take part in the deliberation; I had a scruple about influencing a resolution in which each man was staking his honor and possibly his life. But I was of the opinion which prevailed." They resolved on prudence. "The opposition would be senseless and culpable," exclaimed M. Thiers, "if it voluntarily exposed the capital to a sanguinary collision, if it left events to the decision of force, that wielded by the government being incomparably superior. We must submit to the law of circumstances and give way."

A deputy of the extreme left, M. Bethmont, expressed a similar opinion. M. de Lamartine vainly insisted on what he called the disgrace of backing down. He persisted in his intention of going to the banquet. "I will go," said he, "if I am accompanied by nothing but my shadow." This time he did not persuade his auditors. It was decided, by eighty votes against seventeen, that the deputies should not attend the banquet. As they were determined to do nothing without the constitutional opposition, the delegates of the central committee and of the twelfth ward proposed that it should be postponed. M. Armand Marrast himself was of this opinion. "For humanity's sake," said he, "for love of the people, give up the banquet. Let a conflict break out and the population will be crushed. Do you want to deliver them to the hatred of Louis Philippe and M. Guizot?" Informed of the decision of the deputies by a note from M. Barrot, the painter Ary Scheffer hastened with the good news to the Duchess of Orleans, who instantly imparted it to the King. "I knew very well," said he, "that if I showed firmness I would make them back down."

The military authorities were full of confidence. In his order of the day, General Jacqueminot, chief commander of the National Guard, said, not without a touch of irony: "Doubtless not many of you are disposed to let yourselves be dragged into a culpable proceeding, but I would like to spare those the regret of counting their small numbers among the eighty-five thousand National Guards of which your legions are composed." In the King's immediate circle optimism was absolute.

It is surely a whimsical result that by returning to prudential ideas and giving up the banquet the deputies of the dynastic opposition ruined the monarchy they all were anxious to support. If they had persevered in their original resolve, if they had accepted the programme of the reformist manifestation and promised to take part in it, the ministry would have planted itself vigorously on the ground of resistance, and, in all probability, would have come off victorious. Instead of that, it was unlucky enough to believe that all danger was over as soon as the deputies of the left withdrew. Accustomed to preoccupy itself solely with the country as constituted by law, it looked only at the surface of things, and did not bother itself about their depths. The ministry and the opposition were equally deceived. The false perspective of parliamentarism had obliterated their view. Not a soul in either camp had divined the ground on which the real battle would be fought. Parliamentary tactics and political strategy are two different things. A man may excel in one and be wrecked in the other.

CHAPTER XV

THE EVENING OF FEBRUARY 21

THE deputies gave up the banquet; but would the men of action give it up? That was the question people were asking on Monday evening, February 21. A reunion took place at seven o'clock, in the office of the *Réforme*, to settle on what should be done. "This journal," says M. de Lamartine in his *Histoire de la Révolution de 1848*, "represented the extreme left, the incorruptible republic, the revolution at any price. It was supposed to embody the suggestions of M. Ledru-Rollin and three or four important deputies of the Chamber. It was the tradition of the Convention, renewed fifty years after the combats and revenges of the Convention, the Mountain with its thunders and furies in a time of peace and serenity, the accents of Danton in a political academy, an imaginary terror, a systematic wrath, a Jacobinism exhumed from the soul of those who died in 1794, a misunderstanding of the future republic in wishing to create it anew in the image of the First Republic." Its principal editor was M. Flocon, "one of those primitive republicans who were obdurate in their belief in secret societies, conspiracies, and prisons." The republican sheet was far from prosperous. According to M. Garnier-Pagès, M. Flocon had asked a member of the editorial committee, the day before, for a final sum of three hundred francs, to pay the stamp duty on the issue of the 21st, the resources of the journal being entirely exhausted. Its friends in Paris and the departments could make no more sacrifices; the *Réforme*, therefore, was about to cease to appear; it would live only until Wednesday, the 23d, the morrow of the banquet, in order to die in a triumph of the democracy; it could only pay the expense of bringing out the issues of the 22d and 23d by selling off its furniture.

The gathering in the *Réforme* office lasted for several hours. The question debated was this: "Shall we, or shall we not, give the secret societies the order to march?" The most ardent, MM. Caussidière and Lagrange, for example, inclined to the affirmative. The opposite opinion was vehemently supported by MM. Louis Blanc and Ledru-Rollin. The first said that if the patriots came down into the streets the next day, they would infallibly be overwhelmed and fired at by the National Guard as well as by the army. "You will decide for insurrection if you choose," said he, "but if you do come to that decision, I shall go back home to put on mourning and weep over the ruin of the democracy." M. Ledru-Rollin used language not less categorical.

"In the first revolution," said he, "when our fathers made 'a day,' they had prepared for it long beforehand. But are we prepared? Have we arms, munitions, organized bodies of men? The government is all ready, and the troops are only waiting for a signal to crush us. My opinion is that to involve ourselves in such a predicament, in our present conditions, is simply a folly." The majority adhered to this opinion, the secret societies were requested not to move, and M. Flocon wrote the following article, which was to appear in the *Réforme* the next morning: —

"Men of the people, beware of all foolhardy enthusiasm!

"Do not supply authority with the desired occasion for a bloody success!

"Do not give this dynastic opposition, which is abandoning both itself and you, a pretext with which it would hasten to cover its own weakness!

"You perceive that these are the results of the initiative taken by those who do not belong to us.

"Patience! When it suits the democratic party to take such an initiative, we shall see whether it will draw back when it has once advanced."

Meanwhile, in the early part of the evening, the public did not know that the banquet for the next day had been abandoned. False news and contradictory rumors were circulated. Inquisitive groups got together on the boulevards, reading the proclamations of the prefect of police and the commander of the National Guard by torchlights, and commenting on them with vivacity. The evening papers were impatiently expected. There was animation and excitement on every side. At the Opera, where they were playing *Le Comte Ory*, things looked very dismal. According to Dr. Véron, a large number of influential men, some of them of high rank in the National Guard, others having business and banking affairs with manufacturers and overseers, were moving about in the corridors and the lobby. All were alarmed about the next day, and all said the same thing: "It will not be a riot but a revolution." Between ten and eleven o'clock the uneasiness diminished. The *Patrie* had just published, in a second edition, the following item: "After the session of the Chamber of Deputies the opposition met at the house of M. Odilon Barrot. Unwilling to take, either directly or indirectly, the responsibility of the consequences that may result from the new measures adopted to-day by the government, it has resolved not to attend the banquet.

"It adjures good citizens to keep away from any crowd and any manifestation which could serve as a pretext for acts of violence.

"At the same time, the whole opposition comprehends that the new resolutions of the ministry impose upon it new and serious duties which it will know how to fulfil." In spite of this vague menace, the public believed in a retreat of the opposition and a victory of the government.

At the Tuileries there was a reception. Louis Philippe was beaming. "You know," said he to the English ambassador, "all is over; I was very sure they would retreat." The instant he perceived M. de Salvandy, Minister of Public Instruction, he ran to meet him, exclaiming: "Well, Salvandy, you told us yesterday we were over a volcano; it is a fine volcano, yours! They have given up the banquet, my dear fellow; yes, they have given it up; I told you all that would end in smoke." "I was not wrong, for all that," replied the minister, "all they lacked to make a revolution was a Duke of Orleans." M. Odilon Barrot, who received these details from M. de Salvandy himself, has written in his Memoirs: "M. de Salvandy had just touched a sensitive chord; for more than once in our conversations the King had expressed the same thought, and in speaking of the abortive revolutions in Italy and Spain he had said to me: 'Bah! they won't succeed in anything; they have no Duke of Orleans!' His flattered vanity increased his excitement, and, addressing the Queen, he said: 'You just heard Salvandy, my dear Amélie; he says they have no Duke of Orleans; I think so, too; so you see they retreat.'"

Marie Amélie had been very uneasy for several days. According to M. Trognon: "All the stories she heard showed her that the popular fermentation was steadily rising." — "Things are going badly," said the Queen to a person who had her full confidence; "I expect the worst. I wanted to send you to Brussels with my diamonds and some papers, but the King was not willing." But now Marie Amélie felt reassured. She said to Admiral Baudin: "You find us much more tranquil; this morning I was very uneasy, and I wrote to my sons Joinville and d'Aumale that I greatly regretted their absence at such a moment; now I hope that all will go off well."

The whirl of gaiety went on in Paris that evening of February 21, precisely as if it were not the vigil of the most serious events. There was a ball at the house of the Duchess d'Estissac, another at the Belgian embassy, given by the Princess de Ligne. The beautiful ambassadress, a Pole by birth, was dancing the mazurka with exquisite grace, and political preoccupations did not prevent her being admired. The house of the embassy was situated on the corner of the Avenue des Champs-Elysées and the street then called the rue d'Angoulême, and now the rue de la Boëtie. The famous banquet had been prepared a few steps from there, in a piece of ground adjoining the Champs-Elysées, rue du Chemin-de-Versailles, and in order to reach the Belgian embassy carriages passed quite close to the rue de Chaillot, which conducted thither. While the ball was in progress, a group of women surrounded an aide-de-camp of the King. He reassured them to the best of his power by telling them of the military measures taken long before, and of the security of the ministers. He repeated several times that the King did not foresee the least probability of a revolution. The aide-de-camp's optimism did not appear excessive. It was a member of the provisional government, M. Garnier-Pagès, who has written: "The power of the monarchy seemed indestructible; its material means of defence were formidable; a numerous army, inured to war, and up to that time loyal, occupied the city; barracks, crenellated guard-houses, strongly built redoubts, intersected the city and connected military movements; outside the walls an enceinte and forts, the last resort of resistance and destruction; finally, the National Guard, a citizen force, desirous to uphold reform, but hostile rather than favorable to extreme democracy, would doubtless join with the army if the excitement became a riot. What could a handful of men, however determined, do against such a combination of forces?" When the democratic chiefs saw things in this light, the delusions of the friends of authority are easily comprehended. The guests of the Belgian ambassador asked nothing better than to believe the reassuring words they listened to. The ball-goers departed in high spirits. This was the last festivity of the July monarchy, the last adieu of a brilliant society about to be dispersed.

As the night wore on, confidence grew stronger in government circles. The police reports, that succeeded each other hourly at the Ministry of the Interior, were continually more reassuring. It was thought certain that the secret societies would remain quiet and that the movement had proved abortive. Then was suggested the fatal idea of the countermand, which ruined everything. It had been decided that the garrisons of Paris should assemble under arms, February 22, that the garrisons of the suburbs and the department of the Seine and Oise should arrive at the capital by six o'clock in the morning, that the artillery of Vincennes should hold itself in readiness, that the regiments of cavalry should be massed in the Avenue des Champs-Elysées and around the barrier de l'Etoile. When they learned that the rioters had given up the struggle, Count Duchâtel, the prefect of police, General Tiburce Sébastiani, commander of the garrison of Paris, and General Jacqueminot, commander of the National Guard, who were assembled at the Ministry of the Interior, were of opinion that such a display of troops had become unnecessary, might be considered a provocation and serve as an occasion for dangerous assemblages. They thought it would be better to preserve the ordinary appearance of the city and content themselves with keeping the troops in their barracks. Time pressed; it was too late to inform the ministers; even the president of the council was not forewarned; all that was done was to send General Jacqueminot to the Tuileries to take instructions from the King. Louis Philippe decided that the military preparations should be countermanded. The countermands reached their destinations between four and five o'clock in the afternoon. The insurrection might lift its head.

CHAPTER XVI

THE DAY OF FEBRUARY 22

TUESDAY, February 22, began tranquilly. A fine rain was falling. Workshops and warehouses were opened as usual. The countermand given during the night by the military authority was everywhere obeyed. There was no display of troops. The banqueting ground was almost empty. Nothing was seen there but workmen busied in taking the tables to pieces and lading wagons with the things carried there the previous evening. But this calm was deceptive, and a secret agitation speedily began to pervade the city. Toward ten o'clock several groups, chiefly composed of men in blouses, formed on the Place du Panthéon, and then marched toward the Place de la Madeleine, shouting, "Long live the Reform!" and singing the *Marseillaise*, the *Chant du Départ*, and the chorus of the *Girondins*.

At this very moment, M. Jayr, Minister of Public Works, was on his way to the King, at the Tuileries. "Well! you have come to congratulate me," said Louis Philippe, whose face was beaming; "it is a fact that the affair turned out wonderfully well.

How pleased I am with you, my dear ministers, for the way in which it has been conducted! You know they have given up the banquet. They saw, rather late it is true, that it was running too great a risk. When I think how many of our friends wanted us to give in! But this is going to strengthen the majority." M. Jayr, however, thought the situation still serious. "On my way to the château," said he, "I saw a continual stream of men in blouses going by way of the two quays to the Place de la Concorde; the faubourgs were sending their vanguard thither. If we do not have a great battle, we shall at least have a strong sedition. We must keep ready for it." "Without a doubt," returned the King, "Paris is excited; how could it be otherwise? But this excitement will quiet down of itself. After the backdown of last night, it is impossible that the disorder should assume serious proportions. Besides, you know the measures are taken."

A crowd, swelled by the curious, had gathered on Place de la Madeleine and Place de la Concorde. With a little energy the simpletons might have been easily dispersed and the evil at once cut down by the roots. It was allowed to develop with an imprudence which cost the government of July very dear. What was at first merely a tiny rivulet, soon swelled into an impetuous flood.

Many persons who were still ignorant that the deputies had resolved not to attend the banquet, stationed themselves on the lower sides of the Place de la

Concorde and on the Avenue des Champs-Elysées, as if awaiting the procession. As yet, not a soldier was in sight. The troops did not arrive until the crowd, which was growing larger every minute, started for the Chamber of Deputies.

At half-past eleven, a compact mass, of five or six thousand persons, shouting: "Long live the Reform! Down with Guizot!" arrived just in front of the Palais-Bourbon. The gate was closed. However, several of the agitators got under the colonnade. Some even entered the hall, but were promptly expelled. At this moment General Tiburce Sébastiani, commander of the 1st military division, arrived with a battalion of the 69th of the line and a squadron of the 6th dragoons. The approaches to the Chamber were cleared without resistance, and the agitators spread into the Champs-Elysées, the rue Royale, the rue Saint-Honoré, and the rue de Rivoli.

However, there seemed nothing very serious in these first disturbances. "The day of February 22," writes M. de Tocqueville, "did not at first seem to me to be of a sort to cause serious anxieties. The crowd blocked up the street, but to me it appeared to be composed of sight-seers and fault-finders rather than of seditious persons. When soldiers and citizens met they joked with each other, and I heard fewer shouts in the crowd than jests. I know it will not do to trust to appearances. Generally it is the street boys of Paris who begin the insurrections, and they generally do it gaily, like scholars going on their vacation."

The two Chambers had assembled as usual. At the opening of the session in the Chamber of Peers, the Marquis de Boissy laid down a proposition thus worded: "Seeing that the Chamber of Peers has been less personally involved in the events which prepared and led the way to the existing situation, and that it is, consequently, all the more fitting that, in this circumstance, it should take an initiative which might bring about a compromise, a reconciliation desired by all sincere and enlightened friends of the country, I have the honor to ask the Chamber's permission to interpellate the Cabinet on the present situation of the capital." The upper assembly did not take this request in earnest. It decided that there was no occasion to listen to the Marquis de Boissy. Then it took up the reports of various petitions, and broke up at the end of an hour.

The session of the Chamber of Deputies lasted from half-past one to a quarter of five. The order of the day was the prorogation of the license of the bank of Bordeaux. "On entering the Chamber," says M. de Tocqueville, "I found there an apparent impassibility, underneath which the ebullition of a myriad interior passions was perceptible. It was the only place in Paris where I had not heard loud talk that morning about the matter that was then preoccupying all France. They were listlessly discussing about a bank at Bordeaux; but, honestly, not a soul was paying any attention to the affair, except the man who was speaking from the tribune and him who was to answer what he said. M. Duchâtel told me that all was going well. He said it with an air at once confident and disturbed, which to me appeared suspicious." The session was closing, the president had already quitted his armchair, when M. Odilon Barrot rose to speak. Several voices on the left crying: "The president! the president!" M. Sauzet resumed his chair. Then M. Barrot said: "I beg the president to take up a proposition I have sent to the desk, and which is supported by a sufficiently large number of deputies, and to indicate the day when it will be debated in the committees." The Chamber fixed Thursday, February 24, as the date of this discussion, and then separated.

The proposition was signed by fifty-two deputies, among whom were three future ministers of the Emperor Napoleon III.: MM. Abbatucci, Baroche, and Drouyn de Lhuys. They called for the indictment of the ministers as guilty of having betrayed the honor and interests of France abroad, perverted representative government by systematic corruption, ruined the finances of the state, despoiled citizens of a right inherent to every free constitution, and plunged the country into profound disturbance.

M. Guizot went up to the desk, read the accusation, and smiled with disdain. "He had read much and written much history," says M. de Lamartine. "His eloquence sought for resounding occasions in the future. His glance breathed combat. He braved an accusation against which he was defended from within by a majority associated to himself, and from without by a monarchy and an army." He thus expresses himself in his Memoirs: "Of all the acts of the opposition in this heated struggle, that was the only one that had caused me any surprise. Neither the profound divergence between its ideas and ours, whether on general policy or special facts, nor the bitterness, and what I thought the injustice, of its attacks had astonished me; I had seen in them nothing but the natural course of representative government and the rude warfare of parties. But that a polemic practised during eight years amidst the most entire public liberty, tested by the most vigorous discussion in the tribune and the press, sanctioned by the adhesion of a constant majority, by several general elections, and by the accord of all the great powers of the state, free consequently from all tentative, all constitutional or illegal aspect, that such a policy, I say, was described as treason, counter-revolution, tyranny, and suddenly made the object of a judicial accusation, was a fact that went beyond my foresight." But one need be astonished at nothing on the part of party men.

Meanwhile, the day was signalized by several attempts at disorder. Barricades were started at the entrance of the rue Royale, and even in the rue de Rivoli. Some municipal guards put a very speedy end to these first experiments. According to Dr. Véron, an eyewitness, "As soon as the municipal guards left the rue de Rivoli, a band of Paris street boys, under the direction of several intelligent leaders, tore up the pavement, and began making barricades by stopping and overturning carriages. When the municipal guard was notified and returned at full gallop, the same *gamins* surrounded the officers and marshals, and offered themselves for the purpose of righting the carriages and replacing the paving stones, in a word, of repairing the disorder which was their own work. This manœuvre was kept up for several hours." There was much commotion in the neighborhood of the Tuileries, in the rue d'Alger, rue de la Sourdière, rue Saint-Hyacinthe. The crowd threw stones and broke the windows of houses. Colonel Bilfeldt, commanding at the palace of the Tuileries, as he went out with two companies, was hit in the breast by a stone, which did not prevent him from continuing his march and dispersing the perturbers of the peace.

During more than three hours the noisy crowds spread over the Place Louis XV. and the approaches of the Champs-Elysées, greatly tried the temper of the soldiery. The municipal guard in the first place, and afterwards the dragoons and chasseurs, were seen calmly receiving showers of stones rained on them by these crowds. The troops did not once use their weapons. So gentle a repression encouraged the riot. A barricade formed in the Champs-Elysées, by means of an omnibus and some chairs, was set afire by the rioters themselves, when they saw the cavalry coming. The furniture of the guard-house in the avenue Marigny was broken up and burned. Several shops were pillaged. But the struggle was not yet definitively entered on. At the sight of troops the crowd dispersed, to form anew or go somewhere else, but it nowhere offered any serious resistance. The gates of the Palais-Royal were closed at four o'clock, those of the Tuileries at five. Occupied in military fashion by the 5th regiment of light infantry, a squadron of dragoons, and a squadron of chasseurs, the Place du Carrousel resembled a bivouac. The Duke de Nemours mounted a horse and went into the ranks of the soldiery. Night was about to fall. As yet there had been no blood shed. The government, always optimistic, was not dissatisfied with the day that was about to close. It thought itself master of the situation.

CHAPTER XVII

THE EVENING OF FEBRUARY 22

ALTHOUGH the government was satisfied, the 22d of February had been a bad day from the military point of view. The troops, and in especial the municipal guard, had been uselessly fatigued, worried, and dispirited. They had been made to doubt the energy of their commanders. A dangerous contact had been established between them and the population. The rioters had been emboldened and allowed to organize the insurrection. Count de Pontécoulant has thus criticised this lack of vigor on the part of the authorities: "In those painful occasions in which he is obliged to fight against his fellow-citizens, the French soldier has need of a firm and energetic will to direct and support him; in his view, uncertainty is merely timidity, humanity only weakness, and amidst those fatal temporizings when he remains exposed to the insults of the vilest of the populace, he learns to doubt his strength, his leaders, and even the goodness of the cause he is defending. This was the great fault on the part of the authorities in February 1848."

It was a bad notion on the part of government not to make a great display of troops from the outset, instead of throwing the whole weight of repression on the municipal guard. To the rioters of Paris the municipal guards were the object of a traditional hatred, and received no thanks for the moderation they displayed. As has been remarked by M. Garnier-Pagès, "These old soldiers, assailed, bruised, wounded by the missiles of the mob, careful not to use their weapons, replying to blows from stones only with the butt-ends of their muskets and the flat of their swords, revolted against this prudence, which they began to think excessive." By determining to avoid all appearance of provocation and to remain in an attitude legally defensive, by exposing the municipal guards almost alone to the first attacks of the sedition, and not availing itself that day of the thirty-one thousand men at its disposal, by opposing a tardy and incomplete defence to a bold attack, the government had paralyzed and disorganized the resistance.

The disturbance continued in the evening. The Minister of Finance gave a great official and diplomatic dinner in the hotel of the ministry, then situated in the rue de Rivoli. The English ambassador, Lord Normanby, was one of the guests. As he had been all the afternoon in hourly receipt of very ill-omened tidings, and an incessant tumult was audible in that part of the city, the ambassador was expecting a notification that the dinner was put off, but receiving none, he ordered his carriage and set out.

On arriving within about twenty yards of the Ministry of Finance, he saw an officer of lancers approaching, who asked him to wait until the men should have relaid the pavement, adding that an attempt had just been made to raise a barricade in front of the house. The ambassador has written in his book entitled *A Year of Revolution:* "We sat down, eighteen in all, at a table laid for thirty-six persons. So many places vacant around a festive table would, under any circumstances, have impeded conversation; but at such a moment, and at the table of a minister, it seemed more suitable to avoid all allusion to the subjects we were thinking most about." In official circles, people felt bound not to display the least anxiety.

Count d'Estournel went that evening to the house of Count de Sainte-Aulaire. "They were at table," he writes in his *Souvenirs:* "I was surprised to find there the Princess de Liéven and M. Guizot, she alarmed, he confident; he relied on the measures taken, on the support given to the ministry by the majority. During the conversation, the famous plan of the occupation of Paris in case of a rising, which I had heard talked of for a fortnight, came up several times. 'Everything was foreseen long ago,' M. Guizot said to us, 'every one has his post assigned, and at this moment the movements are being executed in all quarters, and the troops are enveloping them like a net.'"

The government, after a day of hesitation, had, in

fact, resolved on a military occupation of the city, after the plan formerly elaborated by Marshal Gérard. It was that on which the ministerial council had determined on Monday morning, February 21, and which M. Duchâtel had countermanded in the night of Monday and Tuesday. M. Guizot has himself recognized the fatal effects of this countermand. He writes in his Memoirs: "King, ministers, generals, and superior agents, we were all of us, as we had been during the preceding week, still under the sway of the notion that the banquet was the great affair of the moment, and that, as it had been disorganized and adjourned, the worst strait was got over. Although we had been determined to the interdiction of the banquet by the programme of exterior and hostile manifestation added to it by the republican party, we had not been sufficiently awake to the gravity of this new fact, and the change it had brought about in the situation. Far from having diminished the movement by withdrawing from the scene, the monarchical opposition had simultaneously irritated it and freed it from all restraint." The government was at last seeing things as they really were. But it had lost an entire day, without heeding a precept which political men ought never to forget: —

Principiis obsta; sero medicina paratur.

As soon as it received orders, the army was put in motion. At nine o'clock in the evening each corps had arrived at the post it was to occupy. If this strategetical plan had been executed in the morning instead of the evening, the July monarchy would probably have been saved.

At the same moment, the leaders of the secret societies were holding a conclave in the Palais-Royal. That morning, the *Réforme*, which was to supply three members to the provisional government, had declared that the riot was a manœuvre of the police, and had dissuaded the democrats from taking part in it. In the evening, the men of action were still sceptical enough. M. Caussidière, who had witnessed that day an attempt at a barricade in the rue Saint-Honoré, had said: "All this is not clear, there is a lot of people, but that is all; it won't go so far as firing." No one believed that the time for action had yet arrived. To wait and see it come was the watchword of the Palais-Royal gathering.

In the offices of the *Réforme*, M. Flocon's journal, and of the *National*, which was M. Ledru-Rollin's, neither excitement nor confidence was displayed. In that of the *Siècle*, the sheet inspired by M. Odilon Barrot, there was gloom and discouragement. At the *Journal des Débats*, an article for the next day, describing the events of the day and evening, was in course of preparation, and some one added this conclusion to it: "We shall give our attention to the ministry at some other time; but we can say at present that there is a case in which it would have deserved to be indicted, and that is if it had tolerated the audacious insult it was desired to offer to every law of the realm, and if it had abandoned the maintenance of order and public peace into the confident hands which offered to charge themselves with it. These bands of vagabonds, whom we have to-day seen frightening the inhabitants of this great city, are the rag-tag and bob-tail of your banquets; it is the procession which ought to follow you. Go to! you ought to thank the government, which has saved you from the hands of your friends! But it was far more courageous to bring an indictment against it. The government will not recoil before these ridiculous threats, nor from the insurrection. It will do its duty, and all good citizens will also know how to do theirs." In both camps the victory of the ministers was expected, and no one as yet foresaw a revolution.

At the Tuileries, the Queen, who had great political sense, continued to see things under a gloomy aspect. But the King was fully reassured. His countenance was expressive of confidence and joy. "Parisians," said he, "are not accustomed to make revolutions in winter time. They know what they are doing; they won't truck off a throne for a banquet." The satisfaction of Louis Philippe still further increased when the prefect of police came to tell him that the heads of the secret societies persisted in keeping out of the way, and that the troops nowhere encountered any serious resistance. The ministers exclaimed that the victory was definitively gained, that the government had crushed the insurrection in the egg, that the King's infallible glance had foreseen and predicted everything, and that the alarmists must be ashamed of their fear and pusillanimity. "Never," said Louis Philippe to M. Duchâtel, "have I felt myself so strong." When he returned to his apartments he boasted.

Wherever they had shown themselves, the troops had repulsed the rioters. In places to which they did not go, there had been several disorders during the evening. Gangs had set fire to or devastated the barriers of Etoile, Roule, and Courcelles. Agitators had destroyed street lamps and cut gas pipes. At Batignolles, the rue Bourg-l'Abbé, and the rue Mauconseil there had been several affrays. But at midnight all was quiet. The districts bordering the rue Saint-Honoré, the Palais-Royal, the markets, the rues Saint-Denis and Saint-Martin, the quays, the boulevards, the Place de la Concorde, the Champs-Elysées, in a word, all the places that had been the scene of the day's disorders, were again peaceful and deserted. Some prisoners had been taken to police headquarters. All the gangs had dispersed. Nobody but patrols went about the streets. A heavy rain was falling. Bivouac fires were lighted in the squares. The riot seemed to own itself vanquished, and the military authorities felt so completely reassured that at one in the morning the regiments, with the exception of several detachments, were ordered back to their barracks. All was thought to be over, when all was just about to begin.

CHAPTER XVIII

THE MORNING OF FEBRUARY 23

WHEN the dawn broke on Wednesday, February 23, the rain was falling in torrents. Some people repeated Pétion's saying: "It rains, nothing will happen." Toward seven o'clock the troops went to take up their positions. The soldiers seemed fatigued. Some of them had bivouacked during the night, the others had taken only a brief repose in their barracks. Nevertheless, the insurrection everywhere retreated before them. The garrisons of the neighboring towns had sent reinforcements, and it seemed indisputable that the riot had received its final defeat. At the Ministry of the Interior all was thought to be over, when, toward nine o'clock, the disturbances broke out anew, concentrated this time between the rue Montmartre, the boulevards, the rue du Temple, and the quays, in the populous quarters, whose narrow and intricate streets render the action of troops particularly difficult. They might have been easily repressed, however, if the government had not conceived the fatal notion of calling out the National Guard. This guard had founded the monarchy of July, and was to destroy it. At bottom, Louis Philippe must have suspected it a little, since he had for several years refrained from passing it in review. Still, he was of the opinion that the majority of this citizen soldiery were still loyal to him. Some one having reported to him that General Jacqueminot had said: "Out of three hundred and eighty-four companies, there are six or seven badly disposed; all the rest are sincerely attached to the monarchy," the King confined himself to saying: "Six or seven bad! Oh! there are easily seventeen or eighteen." Louis Philippe relied on all the others. That is what ruined him.

For several days the question whether the troops only should be intrusted with the quelling of the disturbance had been debated in the ministerial council. Either alternative had the most serious inconveniences, as has been remarked by Count de Pontécoulant in his *Souvenirs*, and even now it would be hard to determine which of the two would have been the best. Things had come to that point when, as Cardinal de Retz said, whatever side one takes he cannot avoid faults. The summoning of the National Guard — as experience has but too abundantly proved — brought on the ruin of the monarchy, but could it have been saved if the National Guard had been set aside? It is permissible to doubt it, for it would have alleged the suspicion shown of it as an excuse for meddling in the affair in a hostile fashion, and its intervention, "in whatever manner it were brought about, could not do otherwise than favor the schemes of the revolt." At five o'clock in the afternoon of February 22 the call to arms had been beaten in several quarters; only a few of the National Guards had responded to it, and their dispositions appeared doubtful. This first trial had not been very satisfactory. Still the government, more optimistic than ever, took the resolution of convoking the whole National Guard the next day.

"Alas!" says Count de Pontmartin in his *Derniers Samedis*, "Louis Philippe, in spite of the souvenirs of the past, did not comprehend that, in an immense agglomeration like the Parisian populace, the National Guard can be nothing but an essentially revolutionary body, in which the spirit of conservatism and resistance must be intermittent; when it is too late, when the peril, instead of being near, is present; when it is a question of saving, no longer a country, institutions, and a throne, but the house and the shop; when the frightened middle class sees the lesson it wished to give power turned against itself; when, in fine, it costs more effort, more struggle, anguish, bloodshed, calls to arms, patrols in the street, and nights in the guard-house, to defend the pavements from destruction than it would have needed fillips to preserve the whole ship." On the 23d of February the government made no such reflections. It fancied that this citizen guard, which had founded the July monarchy and aided with so much zeal and courage to strengthen and consolidate it, would rally yet once more under the standard of order to put down a sedition thenceforward without a pretext. But this was to attribute reason to passions which ordinarily reason little, or badly. All that the National Guard saw in the call made upon it was a means of satisfying its spite against a ministry which displeased it. It considered itself the arbiter appointed to decide on public affairs. In claiming to change with a high hand a ministry which was acting within the law and was supported by the greatest majority ever known since 1830, it confiscated the political rights of the nation to confer them on a city. It placed itself above the government and the laws.

Yet let us observe that the National Guard, as deficient in foresight as the deputies of the constitutional opposition, still believed itself merely trying to change a Cabinet, not to bring about a revolution. It played into the hand of the Republic with an unconsciousness which was almost artless. If the spirit of imprudence and error reigned at the Tuileries, it was making equal ravages in the ranks of the opposition and the National Guard. We must be indulgent to Louis Philippe's self-deception, for everybody around him, friends and enemies, were equally self-deceived. The left was as short-sighted as the sovereign and the ministers.

There are epochs when all classes of society are simultaneously stricken with vertigo, and when Providence seems to take pleasure in frustrating all human calculations.

Early in the morning of February 23, the drums of the National Guard were beating the call to arms to convoke the twelve legions. There was a greater showing than on the previous evening. But an unfortunate symptom for the government was evident. The greater part of the conservatives of the National Guard remained at home, while all those who were in the opposition made haste to answer the call.

The troops, placed in contact with the dangerous militia and seeing its hostility to the ministry, began to be doubtful of the cause they were called on to defend. The members of the secret societies, who had been hesitating for two days whether to show themselves, perceived that they would never have a better chance of combating Louis Philippe and taking vengeance for their former defeats. The republicans alone could do nothing; joined to the Orleanist National Guards they might upset a throne. Rioters, not members of the National Guard, put on the uniform in order to carry out their revolutionary business with greater efficacity. M. Flocon came into the office of the *Réforme*, exclaiming: "Get some National Guard uniforms, quick! Hunt for them among your friends, in the second-hand clothing shops, anywhere! And as soon as you have dressed yourselves go to the mayor's offices; there, take the lead of the detachments, shout, 'Long live the reform!' and put yourselves everywhere between the troops and the people." The government had fancied that the National Guard, associated to the army for the maintenance of order, would usefully take its place in the strategetic plan for the occupation of Paris, and prevent the erection of barricades in places where the troops could not go. Instead of that, it simply paralyzed resistance.

Between ten and eleven o'clock in the morning the greater part of the legions began to move.

The first (quarters of the Champs-Elysées and the Place Vendôme) was the only one which, as a whole, preserved an attitude favorable to the government. Not merely did it refrain from shouting, "Long live the reform!" but it hissed when passing the deputies of the left.

The second (Palais-Royal, Chaussée d'Antin, and faubourg Montmartre) sang the *Marseillaise* under the windows of the Marsan pavilion.

The third (Montmartre quarter and faubourg Poissonière) declared to its colonel that it would not lay down arms until the ministers had been dismissed. Charged with defending the Bank, it forced the municipal guards to withdraw, and crossed bayonets against the cuirassiers, crying: "Down with Guizot!"

The fourth (Louvre quarter) signed a petition intended for the Chamber of Deputies, and worded as follows: "We, all of us belonging to the militia of Paris, and protectors of public order, mean to go wherever we are sent, in order to prevent or put a stop to bloodshed; but, at the same time, protectors of liberty, we declare that our reunion is in no wise intended to approve the ministerial policy, either at home or abroad, nor to give any manner of support to a ministry which, on the contrary, we censure with all the energy of good citizens."

The petition ended by demanding the dismissal of the ministers and their impeachment. It was carried to the Chamber by a number of National Guards, who, being stopped on the quay by a conservative battalion, delivered it to some deputies of the left.

The fifth legion (Bonne-Nouvelle quarter and faubourg Saint-Denis) prevented the municipal guards from charging on the riot.

The sixth (Temple quarter) assembled on the Place de la Bastille to sing the *Marseillaise*.

The seventh (the quarters bordering on the Hôtel-de-Ville) called on the prefect of the Seine to acquaint the King that if he did not instantly yield, no human force could prevent a collision between the National Guard and the troops. Several guards belonging to this legion gave their weapons to the insurgents.

The tenth (faubourg Saint-Germain) was divided. One part protected the approaches to the Chamber of Deputies, another attached itself to the reform movement and refused to obey its colonel.

One can easily understand what a painful surprise must have been occasioned to the King by such tidings. What! this National Guard of Paris, his native city, this National Guard to which he had always testified such kindly sentiments, this National Guard whose uniform it pleased him to wear at all public celebrations, this National Guard to which he owed so much and which owed so much to him, would abandon and betray him! He had admitted it to the first ranks in his royal fêtes, he had treated its mere privates as comrades, he had reigned for this citizen militia, whose interests seemed to be linked forever to those of his dynasty! And behold, the hands he had so often pressed in his were raised against him! And behold the habitual supporters of his throne, behold his best friends, suddenly becoming his most ruthless adversaries! What was to be done? Could he give the command to fire on men who had so often defended him against the blows of anarchists and assassins?

And, on the other hand, if the National Guard were allowed to continue acting as vanguard and buckler to the insurrection, if one acceded to petitions presented at the end of its bayonets, how could the cause of order be protected?

At the time when the hostile manifestations began, M. Dupin was at the Tuileries. "I regard the danger as imminent," said he to the King, "because the struggle is prolonged, but especially because a part of the National Guard is not simply not with the government, but is declaring for the dismissal of the ministry, and shouting: "Long live the reform! Down with Guizot!" As Louis Philippe expressed the hope that order would soon be restored, M. Dupin said: "That is a delusion, Sire; the evil is increasing; it is profound, and may possibly assume the character of a social strife." — "But do you believe they will go so far as to think of supplanting me?" "Sire, I have heard no pretender named, and no one has said anything of the sort to me, but when a struggle with the extreme democracy breaks out, if it gets the upper hand but one chief is probable, — it is the republic or anarchy."

In this interview the King allowed nothing to be seen which might give the idea that he thought of changing his ministry. An aide-de-camp came to tell him he was waited for at the council. "He rose," writes M. Dupin in his Memoirs, "and gave me his hand, which I pressed respectfully. Alas! it was for the last time; I have never seen him since!"

Meanwhile all the legions, with the exception of the first and a part of the tenth, had declared against the government. In the quarters where the insurrection was concentrated, men armed with sticks and crowbars went over every story of the houses, demanding the muskets of the National Guards in imperative tones. The frightened women made haste to obey these threatening summons, and some one chalked "*Arms given*" over the doors. What was nothing but a wretched squabble the day before was to become a terrible contest. A dilemma presented itself: either to fight the National Guard or capitulate to the riot.

L

CHAPTER XIX

THE FALL OF THE MINISTRY

THE Chambers assembled as usual on February 23. At the opening of the session in the Chamber of Peers, the Marquis de Boissy made the following motion: "Seeing that blood flowed yesterday in several parts of the capital; that to-day, again, the Parisian population is menaced with death and conflagration, with death by sixty howitzers, provided partly with grape-shot, partly with cannon-balls; with devastation and fire by forty petards, all hastily transported from Vincennes to the Military School, I have the honor to ask the Chamber to address interpellations to the Cabinet on the situation of the capital."

The Chancellor. — "Is this motion seconded by two peers?"

Count d'Alton-Shée. — "I second it."

The Chancellor. — "As this motion is not seconded by two peers, the Chamber is not called upon to notice it."

The upper assembly afterwards debated a project of law relating to compulsory expropriation in the colonies, and separated at a quarter to four, without suspecting that it had held its last session.

The Chamber of Deputies opened its session at half-past one o'clock. The order of the day, about which the president cared greatly, was the continuation of the discussion about the privilege of the Bank of Bordeaux. But the assembly had not the courage to occupy itself with such a question in the midst of so formidable a crisis. M. Vavin, deputy of the Seine, was about to demand the interpellation of the ministers on the situation, but as Count Duchâtel, Minister of the Interior, had not yet taken his seat, it was decided to suspend the session until his arrival.

At this very moment, M. Duchâtel was at the Tuileries, holding a very important conversation with the King.

The King. — "Well! how are we getting on now?"

M. Duchâtel. — "Sire, the affair is more serious than it was yesterday, the horizon is more overcast; but if the resistance is energetic we shall pull through."

The King. — "That is my sentiment also. They are advising me on all sides to put an end to the crisis by changing the Cabinet, but I will not lend myself to that."

M. Duchâtel. — "The King knows very well that, for my own part, I do not cling to power, and that it would not cost me much to renounce it; but concessions torn by violence from all the lawful authorities are not a means of safety; a first defeat would soon lead to a second; it was not long, in the Revolution, from June 20 to August 10, and to-day things move quicker than they did then; events go by steam, as well as travellers."

The King. — "I think as you do that we must remain firm; but chat with the Queen a moment, she is very much alarmed. I desire that you should talk to her."

For several days past Marie Amélie had had no illusions as to the extreme gravity of the crisis. As M. Guizot has written: "The great soul of the Queen, always heroic in the time of trial, was as impassioned as it was noble, and she could sometimes be keenly anxious beforehand about the situation of her husband and children." Marie Amélie knew that Louis Philippe's horror of bloodshed would prevent his resorting to rigorous repression. From the moment that the King refused to allow his troops to fire on the National Guard, a change of ministers became inevitable. The Queen, followed by the Duke de Montpensier, entered the King's Cabinet; she seemed greatly excited, and the conversation continued: —

The Queen. — "Monsieur Duchâtel, I know M. Guizot's devotion to the King and to France; if he takes counsel of it he will not remain in power an instant."

M. Duchâtel. — "Madame, M. Guizot, like all his colleagues, is ready to shed his last drop of blood for the King; but he does not claim to impose himself on him against his will. The King is the master and can give or withdraw his confidence accordingly as he judges it convenient for the interests of his crown."

The King. — "Do not say such things, my dear; if M. Guizot knew it!"

The Queen. — "I ask nothing better than that he should know it; I will say it to him myself; I esteem him sufficiently for that; he is a man of honor and will comprehend me."

M. Duchâtel. — "I am bound to tell the King that it would be impossible for me not to communicate to M. Guizot all I have just heard. It is an important element of the situation; I could not conceal it from him either as colleague or friend."

The King. — "There might be a chance to convoke the council immediately."

M. Duchâtel. — "I think there might be some inconvenience about a sudden convocation of the council; the Chamber is in session and could not be left without ministers. The King would do better, it seems to me, to talk with M. Guizot first."

The King. — "You are right; go and find M. Guizot without a minute's loss of time, and bring him to me."

M. Duchâtel hastened to the Palais-Bourbon, where, without entering the Chamber himself, he had M. Guizot called out and drove with him to the Tuileries. On the way he told him what the King and Queen had just been saying. The two ministers agreed that they could not remain in power under such conditions. They reached the château at half-past two o'clock and found the King and Queen, and the Dukes de Nemours and de Montpensier sitting together. The King dwelt upon the gravity of the circumstances, adding that he would rather abdicate than part with his ministers.

The Queen. — "You cannot say that, my dear, you owe yourself to France; you are not your own."

The King. — "That is true; I am more unfortunate than the ministers, I cannot send in my resignation."

M. Guizot. — "It is for Your Majesty to decide; the Cabinet is ready either to defend the King and our conservative policy to the last, or to accept without complaint the King's action in calling other men to power. There is no room for self-deception, Sire; such a question is settled by the very fact that it is put at such a moment. At present the Cabinet, in order to maintain the struggle with any chance of success, needs the decided support of the King more than ever before. It is inevitable that the public know of the King's hesitation, and when it does so the Cabinet would lose all moral force and be incapable of accomplishing its task."

The King. — "It is with very bitter regret that I part with you; but necessity and the safety of the monarchy require this sacrifice."

The Duke de Montpensier (addressing himself to

M. Guizot). — "My conviction must have been very profound when it could outweigh the gratitude I owe you."

The King. — "I am thinking of M. Molé. What do you think about it?"

M. Guizot and M. Duchâtel making no objection, Louis Philippe resumed, "Then I shall have him summoned."

The Queen. — "You will always be the King's friends; you will support him."

Weeping, Louis Philippe embraced the two ministers, and as they were departing he said to them: "You are happier than I am."

During this time the Chamber of Deputies, which had suspended its labors, was in a state of constantly increasing anxiety. "At a certain moment," says M. de Tocqueville, "we heard a great blowing of trumpets on the outside, and presently learned that the cuirassiers on guard were sounding fanfares by way of amusement. The triumphant and joyous sounds of the instruments were so painfully incongruous with the thoughts secretly disturbing us, that this indiscreet and inconvenient music was speedily silenced."

At a quarter past three o'clock, M. Guizot, followed by M. Duchâtel, entered the hall with his firmest step and loftiest air. At last open mention was to be made of what the Chamber had been whispering about for several hours.

M. Vavin ascended the tribune. "Gentlemen,"

said he, "I ask permission of the Chamber to address certain interpellations to the ministry, on the part of the deputation of the Seine, especially. For more than twenty-four hours grave disturbances have been afflicting the capital. Yesterday, the population remarked the absence of the National Guard with painful surprise; this surprise was greater and more painful because they knew that the order to call it out had been given on Monday evening. It must be true, then, that during the night this order had been revoked. It was not until five o'clock last evening that the call to arms was beaten in several quarters to assemble some of the National Guards; during the day the people of Paris had been left to the dangers surrounding them (*violent murmurs from the centre*), without the protection of their civic guard. Fatal collisions took place, perhaps we should not now have occasion to deplore them if, when the troubles began, this National Guard, whose device is 'Public order and liberty,' had been seen in our streets and squares. I beg the ministers to give us some explanation of these grave and unfortunate facts."

It was M. Guizot's turn to speak. Slowly, majestically, the president of the council ascended the steps of the tribune, throwing back his head lest he might seem to lower it.

M. Guizot (profound silence). — "Gentlemen, I think it will neither be conformable to public interests, nor apropos for the Chamber, to begin at this moment any debate upon these interpellations" (*violent murmurs*).

Numerous voices on the left. — "Hear! hear!"

M. Guizot. — "I say that will be conformable to neither the dignity nor the interest of the Chamber to enter at this moment upon any debate relative to the interpellations just addressed to us by the honorable M. Vavin. The King is about to summon Count de Molé to intrust him . . ." (*prolonged bravos on the left*).

M. Odilon Barrot. — "The Chamber should preserve its dignity."

M. Guizot. — "The interruption just made will not cause me either to add or to retrench anything from my words. The King is about to summon Count de Molé for the purpose of intrusting him with the formation of a new Cabinet. So long as the present Cabinet is at the head of affairs it will maintain or re-establish order, and cause the laws to be respected, according to its conscience, as it has done up to the present."

Never had such a dramatic stroke occurred within the memory of Parliament. M. de Tocqueville has described it in these terms: "The opposition remains in its seats, the crowd of its members uttering shouts of victory and satisfied revenge; its leaders alone remain silent, busied in silently reflecting what use they will make of the triumph, and already careful not to insult a majority which they may presently need to call to their aid. The latter, stricken by a blow so unforeseen, is curiously agitated for an instant, like an oscillating mass which seems as ready to fall one way as another; then its members come down noisily into the semicircle; some throng around the ministers to ask explanations or pay them their final respects, some to rise against them in noisy and insulting vociferations."

Different voices. — "It is a piece of cowardice. . . . It is dishonoring! We shall see how they will manage that."

A great tumult prevailed in the hall. Animated groups collected on all sides.

Numerous voices in the centre. — "Let us go to the King! Let us go to the King! Raise the session, Mr. President."

"The despair of the partisans of the ministry," M. de Tocqueville has said again, "will surprise no one who reflects that the majority of these men felt themselves attacked, not merely in their political opinions, but their private interests. . . . I saw this undulating crowd from my bench; I perceived surprise, wrath, fear, cupidity, disturbed before they had been well filled, blending their different traits on these affrighted faces, and, for my own part, compared all these legislators to a pack of dogs torn away from their quarry with their chops still full."

In the midst of this tumult M. Guizot retained his imperturbable coolness. The doctrinaire fell, but with dignity, and without having sacrificed his doctrines. He believed, in his conscience, that the only culpable person was the King, who was abandoning his ministry in the thick of the struggle, and who might have saved it by putting forth a little energy. As haughty as on the previous day, he accused himself of nothing, he retracted nothing. *Impavidum ferient ruinæ.*

M. Odilon Barrot thought the notion of impeaching the ministers no longer opportune. It was to have been discussed the next day; he proposed another order of the day. M. Dupin expressed himself in the same sense. "Ought we," said he, "to introduce at this moment irritating deliberations, deliberations about impeachment, which, however solved, will certainly militate against the end you ought to seek, that of the tranquillization of the public mind and the restoration of order? I hope the day will not end without our attaining this result. I think it would be best to adhere to the demand for an adjournment, which I heartily support."

M. Guizot. — "Gentlemen, I said just now that, so long as the Cabinet should have the honor of remaining at the head of affairs, it would maintain or re-establish order and cause the laws to be respected. The Cabinet, for its own part, sees no reason why any business before the Chamber should be interrupted, or any questions raised in it fail to receive their solution. The Crown is exercising its prerogative; the prerogative of the Crown should be fully respected; but, so long as the Cabinet remains at the head of affairs, so long as it sits on these benches, nothing can be interrupted in the labors or deliberations of the great public powers. The Cabinet is ready to respond to all questions, to enter into all debates; it is for the Chamber to decide as it sees fit." Such were M. Guizot's final words. He was never again to ascend any tribune.

M. Dupin again insisted, but in vain. In vain he exclaimed: "In spite of you, gentlemen of the ministry, in spite of the majority, I call for an adjournment." The Chamber, obedient once more to a ministry which had been in power for seven years and a half, decided that no change should be made in the programme for the next day, and then separated. It was four o'clock in the afternoon.

CHAPTER XX

THE FIRING ON THE BOULEVARD

AT the close of the session of the Chamber of Deputies, all the ministers repaired to the Tuileries. The King had already been informed of the stupor and indignation which their downfall caused among their partisans. Visibly disturbed, he began to wonder whether he had done well in acceding to the demands of the rioters, and would have liked to persuade himself that the ministry had spontaneously offered its resignation. M. Guizot writes, in his Memoirs: "I reaffirmed, in positive terms, what I had already said to the King during our first interview. 'We were ready and determined,' I said to him again, 'to maintain to the last the policy of order and legal resistance, which we found to be the only good one; but the King showed that he was inclined to think he ought to change his ministry. To put such a question, at such a moment, was to answer it.' The King did not insist further. MM. Hébert, de Salvandy, and Jayr plainly expressed their disapprobation of his resolution. We left the Tuileries, intending, until the formation of a new Cabinet, to concern ourselves simply with the defence of order, which was everywhere violently attacked."

At the same moment, M. de Montalivet was saying to the mounted National Guards: "Go through Paris, and announce everywhere that the King is changing his ministry and consents to a reasonable reform." Horsemen dispersed in all directions to scatter the news. The wealthy quarters received it with transports of joy. Men embraced each other in the streets. People shouted: "Illuminate! Illuminate!" (The air of the *lampions*, borrowed from the rhythm of the National Guard's call to arms, did not come until several days later.) Houses were lighted up as for a festival. Lamps, tapers, candles, were set in the windows. On the Boulevard des Italiens, the Grand-Balcon café was dazzling, with sheaves of flame. Aides-de-camp and officers of the royal artillery came to tell the King that his prudent decision had pacified the public mind and restored entire tranquillity. The Duchess of Orleans wept for joy, and exclaimed, as she embraced the Count of Paris: "Poor child, they put your crown in great danger, but heaven restores it to you." M. de Lamartine writes, in his *Histoire de la Révolution de 1848:* "All citizens were deeply penetrated with a sentiment of peace and inward joy. It was like a mute proclamation of reconciliation and concord, after an abortive quarrel between King and people." It had not yet occurred to Louis Philippe that he might lose his throne.

There was a grand dinner that evening at the Ministry of the Interior. Count Duchâtel had not thought it his duty to recall invitations given before these events occurred. M. Guizot and most of the other ministers were among the guests. The future Cabinet and the difficulties of its situation were discussed. After dinner, some deputies and peers came in. Whist tables were arranged. It might have been mistaken for an ordinary ministerial reception.

At the house of M. Thiers, in the Place Saint-Georges, people were exultant. All the clientèle, parliamentary and extra-parliamentary, of the left centre, thronged around the man whom they considered the coming minister. The place was blocked up by an enormous crowd. M. Thiers was standing just behind the locked gate, exchanging congratulations and promises with the populace.

At the house of M. Odilon Barrot, there was still greater animation. "My house," he has said, "had become a sort of headquarters where popular excitement came to a focus, and whence political directions were sent out. Sometimes a mass of the common people, armed with flambeaux, came and asked to see me; sometimes delegations from the schools or the National Guard, who wanted to confer with us; sometimes there were resolutions to take, which involved peace or war, the overthrow of the monarchy or its preservation. Hence we might have been said to be in permanent session in my salon, for the purpose of considering all the incidents which succeeded each other with such rapidity." A crowd, carrying torches, made its way into the court, which was overlooked by a small open gallery on the first story. There M. Barrot, attended by several deputies of the left, placed himself, and made a liberal speech, full of confidence and enthusiasm.

And yet the satisfaction in Paris lacked a good deal of being unanimous. Conservatives and revolutionists were equally discontented. The first were distressed by a tardy concession, which to them seemed a dangerous capitulation. The others said that, as yet, there had been no precise act affording serious guarantees, that M. Molé's name was insufficient, and that the King was perhaps deceiving the people. Many liberals, more perspicacious than their party, made no secret of their fears. "I keenly desired the downfall of the Cabinet," said M. Jules de Lasteyrie to Count Duchâtel, "but I would much rather have seen you remain in power ten years longer than going out by this door." M. de Tocqueville went to call on M. de Beaumont. "There," says he, "I found all hearts rejoicing. I was far from sharing this joy, and, to those with whom I could speak freely, I gave my reasons for it. 'The National Guard of Paris,' I said to them, 'has just destroyed a Cabinet; then it is by its good pleasure that the new ministers are going to direct affairs. You are delighted because the ministry is over-

UNIV. OF
CALIFORNIA

thrown; but don't you perceive that it is power itself which is laid low?'" The Duke de Nemours, who had taken no part in the dismissal of the Cabinet, met M. de Montalivet at the staff-office. "Well, my dear Count," he said to him, "you ought to be contented; M. Guizot is no longer minister." "Far from that, Monseigneur," returned M. de Montalivet, "I am most profoundly grieved about it. It is either too late or too early. You can't change a general in the thick of a battle."

The battle! a great many people thought it ended. It was to break out again suddenly, and in a terrible way.

There was great disorder throughout the city, and the republicans were determined to profit by it. In spite of its promise, the ministry no longer governed. Fatigued, badly fed, worn out by watching, the troops stationed on the boulevards and in the streets were uneasy and bewildered. Not knowing whether they ought to resist or give way, they allowed the agitators to free the prisoners who had been put in the barracks. A column of manifestants, composed of National Guards, rioters, and street-boys, and carrying flags, lanterns, and torches, had formed upon the Place de la Bastille. It crossed the boulevards without being halted by the troops. At the Château d'Eau there was some artillery, and cannons occupied the roadway. Making haste to open the passage, the artillery-men themselves displaced the pieces, amidst the applause of the crowd, and the

M

procession continued its march without impediment as far as the Boulevard des Capucines.

Here things wore another aspect. Precise instructions had nowhere been given to the troops, except in front of M. Guizot's residence, the Ministry of Foreign Affairs. This house, which had already been threatened more than once by the insurrection, occupied on the boulevard, at the corner of the rue Neuve-des-Capucines, the site now filled by the shops of the former Giroux firm. Its garden, which, like the house itself, has disappeared, extended all along the boulevard. While M. Guizot was dining at the Ministry of the Interior, the Ministry of Foreign Affairs and its approaches were occupied by dragoons, line infantry, and National Guards. It was the only spot in Paris where free passage was forbidden. The house was dark. Its obscurity contrasted with the daylight brilliancy of the neighboring windows, whose illuminations, dancing on the helmets of the dragoons, made them almost seem alive. A battalion of the 14th of the line, commanded by Lieutenant-Colonel Courand, with the regimental band, was drawn up opposite the ministry, and had in front of it, under the orders of M. Talabot, Colonel of the 2d legion, a battalion of the National Guard, so placed in order to prevent all contact between the troops and the manifestants. Unluckily, an unforeseen circumstance caused this battalion of the 2d legion to leave the position it had taken. A group of rioters had collected in front of the Ministry of Justice, in the Place Vendôme, shouting: "Down with Hébert!" demanding the illumination of the house, and threatening to burn it down if the injunction were not obeyed. A detachment from the post on duty at staff headquarters was defending the Ministry of Justice. It called on M. Talabot for re-enforcements, and he hastened thither at the head of his battalion. A few minutes later, the column from the Bastille arrived opposite the Ministry of Foreign Affairs, where it was confronted by the foot-soldiers of the 14th of the line, with dragoons behind them.

The orders given to Lieutenant-Colonel Courand were formal. He was to protect the house of the Ministry of Foreign Affairs, and to cut off all circulation on the Boulevard des Capucines. This was the origin of the catastrophe. A shot was fired, which gave the signal for the downfall of the throne.

It was long believed that the firing on the Boulevard des Capucines was provoked by a pistol-shot, discharged with premeditation by an ardent democrat, M. Lagrange. It now seems established that this account is fabulous. In his *Souvenirs de l'année 1848* M. Maxime Du Camp has thought himself enabled to affirm that the first shot was fired, under the following circumstances, by a sergeant of the 14th of the line, a Corsican named Giacomoni.

It is half-past nine in the evening. The column, coming from the Place de la Bastille, finds itself face to face with the soldiers, who close up their ranks and get into position. At the cry, "No one can pass!" the band halts. Colonel Courand advances alone, and says: "What do you want?" "We want the Minister of Foreign Affairs to illuminate." — "That does not concern me!" "Let us pass!" — "My children, I am a soldier and must obey; I have received instructions to let nobody pass, and you shall not pass. If you want to go further, take the rue Basse-du-Rempart [*cries of Long live the line!*]. I am much affected by your sympathy; but I am obliged to execute superior orders, and I cannot let you pass."

A Rioter (carrying a torch). — "You are nothing but scoundrels, the whole lot of you; I tell you we will pass; we have a right to."

The Colonel. — "I don't know what your right is, but I do know what is our duty, and I shall not fail in it."

The Rioter. — "You're nothing but a greenhorn, and I'm going to scorch your moustache."

Here the rioter put his torch to the face of the Colonel, who threw his head back very quickly. Sergeant Giacomoni sprang forward and took aim at the man who held the torch.

Captain de Ventiny (addressing the Sergeant). — "Are you mad? What are you doing?"

Giacomoni. — "If some one tries to hurt the Colonel, it is my business to defend him, isn't it?"

The Captain. — "Keep quiet."

Spectators on the pavements. — "They will pass!

They won't pass! Down with Guizot! Long live the Reform! Long live the line! Illuminate! Illuminate!"

The Rioter. — "For the last time, will you let us pass?"

The Colonel. — "No! Grenadiers, cross bayonets!"

Sergeant Giacomoni fires on the man holding the torch, who falls dead at once. Thinking themselves menaced, two companies also begin firing, and kill or wound fifty-two persons.

The tumult is indescribable. The crowd utter shouts of horror and affright. The foot-soldiers disband and hasten into adjacent streets. The dragoons gallop off at full speed toward the Madeleine. The causeway of the Boulevard is emptied. It is a pool of blood.

Here is a situation on which the revolutionary genius pounces in an instant. A wagon, loaded with the baggage of travellers about to take the train for Rouen, was just passing by. On this were piled the corpses of the sixteen victims of the firing, and by the light of torches, illumining the livid and blood-stained bodies, and to cries of "Vengeance! Treason!" the fatal tumbrel began its march. Such a spectacle is the most striking, the most sinister, the most decisive, of all revolutionary propagandas.

Is there a scene in Lamartine's *Histoire des Girondins* which surpasses this in horror? The crowd shouts: "They are cutting the people's throats. To arms! To the barricades!" And until two o'clock in the morning the funereal procession, in the midst of violent public exasperation, goes travelling about the boulevards and the most populous quarters, without any one daring to stop it.

CHAPTER XXI

THE NIGHT OF FEBRUARY 23-24

NOTWITHSTANDING the firing on the Boulevard des Capucines, no one as yet suspected that this night of February 23-24, begun by the splendors of an illumination, would be the last night of royalty. M. Guizot, who had dined at the Ministry of the Interior, with several of his colleagues and political friends, was still there when he learned what had happened in front of the Ministry of Foreign Affairs. He instantly repaired to the Tuileries, accompanied by M. Dumon, to impress upon the King the urgent necessity of putting Marshal Bugeaud at the head of both the army and the National Guard.

Created Duke of Isly and appointed Marshal of France by Louis Philippe, the celebrated soldier had been living in a sort of retreat since he ceased to be Governor-General of Algeria. His biographer, Count d'Ideville, writes: "More than any other conservative deputy, Marshal Bugeaud was subjected to the malevolent and unjust attacks of the opposition; and the great citizen who had given Algeria to France beheld himself almost disdained, and viewed with suspicion. He, whose lofty personality should have made him one of the firmest supports of the throne, had been attacked with such rage and perfidy that he lost somewhat in popular esteem. In short, every political empiric who talked about assisting the throne by snatching up the inheritance of M. Guizot, rejected the assistance of the Marshal as compromising and unpopular. As to him, strong in his own rectitude and the consciousness of duty done, he was in Paris, modestly fulfilling his functions as deputy, when the Revolution broke out." Much beloved by the troops, the Marshal had excited lively animosities among legitimists and republicans. The first bitterly reproached him with having been governor of the citadel of Blaye during the captivity of the Duchess of Berry; the second never pardoned the energy with which he had repressed the insurrection of April, 1834, and accused him of the affair of the rue Transnonain, with which he had had nothing whatever to do.

No sooner had M. Guizot uttered the Marshal's name, than the King said it was his intention to give him command of all the forces, but that it would be necessary to await the formation of the new Cabinet. M. Guizot left the Tuileries before anything had been decided.

During several hours, Count de Molé had been trying to form a ministry. According to M. de Lamartine, the Count was "a man of political temperament, used to crises, agreeable to courts, esteemed by conservatives, liked by the upper middle class,— one of those autocrats by birth and character whose superiority is so natural that the most jealous democracy honors itself by recognizing and loving them." And M. de Lamartine adds, in his *Histoire de la Révolution de 1848:* "Had M. Molé, who was all prudence and moderation, but begun the task three days sooner, he could doubtless have found means of conciliating what was necessary for the conservation of the monarchical principle, to which he had been attached all his life, with what was demanded by the irritations of parliamentary opinion." But on the 23d of February it was too late. MM. Dufaure, Passy, Billault (the future Minister of Napoleon III.), whom M. Molé desired as colleagues, having agreed that nothing could be done without the assistance of M. Thiers, M. Molé went to the Place Saint-Georges and had a long interview with M. Thiers, at the close of which he gave up the attempt to form a Cabinet. The King was informed of this toward midnight.

Between midnight and one o'clock, M. Guizot was summoned to the Tuileries. Louis Philippe said to him: "M. Molé cannot succeed in forming a ministry. I have called M. Thiers, but meanwhile the disturbance is growing more serious; a military chief is wanted on the instant, whose authority and capacity are proven, and who can bear the burden until the installation of the new Cabinet. I ask you for the immediate nomination of Marshal Bugeaud to the command of the National Guard and the army. Perhaps M. Thiers would not nominate him; but he will accept him, I have no doubt, if he finds him appointed and installed. It is in the name of the monarchy that I make this appeal to the devotion of my former ministers." M. Guizot replied: "The King knows we are all ready to accomplish his desire." Louis Philippe then sent for M. Duchâtel and General Trézel, whose signatures were necessary for the double appointment. Both arrived in great haste, and countersigned the royal decree.

In a letter addressed to M. Léonce de Lavergne, October 19, 1848, the Marshal thus relates the manner in which he was invested with the command: "It was two o'clock in the morning when one of the King's aides-de-camp came to summon me to the château. I hurried thither. I was offered the command of the troops and of the National Guard. I understood perfectly that it was too late, but I thought it unworthy of me to refuse. The former ministers were sent for to countersign the decrees appointing me. All this took far too much time, and it was not until toward three o'clock that I could place myself in contact with the troops, on the Place du Carrousel and in the court of the Tuileries. I quickly assembled the officers and non-commissioned officers; I made them a speech, which was certainly energetic. . . . All the detached troops at the Bastille, the Hôtel-de-Ville, on the Boulevards, at the Panthéon, had received orders to fall back around the Tuileries at daybreak. I made haste to order them to remain firm at their post, assuring them that some columns would move toward them at daybreak, and that then we would take the offensive."

M. Thiers, whom an aide-de-camp had been looking for, and who must have had to cross a good many barricades to get to the Tuileries from the Place Saint-Georges, reached the King at half-past two in the morning. As soon as he saw him, Louis Philippe said: "Ah! it is you, M. Thiers. I thank you for having come. You know I have been forced, to my great regret, to part with my ministers. I had summoned M. Molé. He has just given me back his powers. I have need of you, then, and I beg you to form a Cabinet for me." M. Thiers responded: "Sire, under existing circumstances, that is a very difficult mission. Nevertheless, I am at the King's orders; but, before anything else, we ought to come to an understanding about men and things." Louis Philippe and M. Thiers then had a long conversation. In spite of his repugnance, Louis Philippe agreed that M. Odilon Barrot should enter the ministry. But on the question of the dissolution of the Chamber, he was intractable. "The dissolution of the Chamber!" he exclaimed. "I do not consent to that; I will never consent to it." He then announced that he had put Marshal Bugeaud at the head of the armed force. "He is your friend," said he, "you will understand each other admirably." And as M. Thiers, somewhat embarrassed, complained that so serious a step should have been taken without consulting the new Cabinet, the King rejoined: "What would you have? I need a man to defend me, and Bugeaud is the only one in whom I have confidence. . . . Besides, what can they say to you? It is not you who nominated him, it is Duchâtel. Go and find the Marshal, and consult with him." Louis Philippe went to bed toward four o'clock in the morning, having invited M. Thiers to return to the Tuileries at eight with the men who were to form the ministry.

The King was not at all discouraged. "His battlefield," M. de Lamartine has said, "had always been opinion. It was on that he wanted to act. He desired to reconcile himself with it speedily by means of concessions. Only, like a thrifty and prudent politician, he bargained with both opinion and himself, in order to obtain this reconciliation with the least possible detriment to his system and his dignity. He supposed he had still many steps of popularity to descend before reaching those of the throne. The rest of the night appeared to him more than time enough for eluding the emergencies of the situation with which he was threatened by the day."

M. Guizot has likewise expressed the conviction that the King's self-confidence did not fail him even in the night of February 23-24. "Neither perseverance nor hope," he says, "were extinct in the soul of King Louis Philippe. Whether by nature, or through his experience of the vicissitudes and reactions that succeed each other in revolutions, he was one of those who think that to recover good opportunities and good luck, it is enough to know how to survive and wait. I am convinced that, amidst his miscalculations and discouragement, he was far from despairing of his own future, and that, even while accepting the laws of the constitutional régime, he counted on regaining the influence he thought necessary in order to give legal ascendency to the policy he believed indispensable to the welfare of his country and the safety of his throne. Men did not leave him time for it; God did not grant him grace."

After leaving the King, Thiers went to staff headquarters, Place du Carrousel, where he found Marshal Bugeaud installed and giving orders. As soon as he caught sight of him, the latter exclaimed: "Well, my dear Thiers, I am charmed to see you. I am commander-in-chief; you are prime minister. Between us, we shall make a good job of it. . . . It would doubtless be very unfortunate if the National Guard should refuse to march. But if things should turn out that way, tell them plainly that that will not be reason enough to make me throw up my hand (*pour me faire jeter ma langue au chat*)."

Born in 1784, the victor of Isly had lost none of his moral or physical activity. No young man had higher spirits or greater vigor. He had just said to M. Guizot, who had been asking what he thought about the next day: "It is a trifle late, but I have never been beaten, and I shall not begin to-morrow.

Give me my head and let me fire; there will be bloodshed; but by to-morrow night force will be on the side of law, and the seditious will have got their deserts." To M. Thiers he expressed an equal confidence. "I allowed no occasion to escape," he writes, in the letter we have already cited, "of raising the moral tone of all who surrounded me. Nor was I unsuccessful; I saw countenances, at first very dejected, gradually become animated as they saw what measures I was taking. I had around me at least one hundred and fifty staff-officers of the army and the National Guard; a crowd of generals came to offer me their services. There were too many, in fact, every one trying to attract my attention and make protestations, and causing me to lose precious time. Besides this, they were bringing me a hundred items of news at a time and demanding a hundred orders."

M. Thiers went next to the house of M. Odilon Barrot. "It was between three and four o'clock in the morning," writes the latter in his Memoirs, "when I was awakened by my servant, who announced to me that M. Thiers, accompanied by MM. de Rémusat and Duvergier de Hauranne, was waiting for me in the salon. I dressed in a hurry, and M. Thiers informed me that the King had summoned us to form a new ministry. I replied that I was ready to report myself at the Tuileries, and was greatly annoyed when I heard of the delay imposed by the King." While Louis Philippe was taking a few hours' repose, and his new ministers trying to come to an understanding, the insurgents were organizing the struggle, casting bullets, ringing the tocsin, assembling the secret societies, covering the streets with barricades.

To put down such an insurrection, Marshal Bugeaud should have been allowed to follow the pitiless tactics of Bonaparte on the 13th Vendémiaire, and let the big voice of cannon speak on every side. "There was in the Marshal's exterior," says M. de Lamartine, "in his style, in the curt speech which cut without wounding, a judicious rusticity, a military frankness, and an authority of power, which awakened attention in the masses, confidence in the troops, and terror in the enemy. Such a man, placed at the head of the army of Paris on the previous day, would have rendered the victory of the people either impossible or bloody. Summoned at the moment when the government was weakening, his name was inconsistent with concessions. It made them suspicious on the side of royalty, inacceptable on the side of the people." The nomination of the Marshal could have had no justification unless Louis Philippe and his new ministers had definitively adopted the policy of resistance.

All the rest of the night, the victor of Isly was pressing forward the military preparations. He decided to form the troops he had at hand into four columns, which, taking the offensive, should drive the insurgents before them and destroy the barricades. The first, commanded by General Tiburce Sébastiani, was to go by way of the Bank toward the Hôtel-de-Ville. The second, under the orders of General Bedeau, was to reach the Bastille by way of the Bourse and the boulevards. The third was to come behind the first two, in order to prevent the barricades from being put up again. The fourth was to rejoin General Renault at the Panthéon. The reserves were to remain on the Place du Carrousel. In this plan, no part had been assigned to the National Guard, which the Marshal had so many reasons to suspect. "At half-past five in the morning," he has written, "the four columns started from the Place du Carrousel, in good spirits, but ill-provided with munitions for a long conflict. The heads of these columns, and a good many of the officers, had received instructions in which I had rapidly indicated the manner of attacking barricades and compact masses, of entering houses, etc. Confidence was visible on all faces, and, as I thought the war already well started, I did not doubt that the combat would begin immediately."

But the Marshal was not aware that neither the King nor the new ministers cared about fighting. Their pacific intentions were in glaring contrast with the bellicose measures taken by the valiant warrior. On one side there was an olive branch, on the other a sword. M. Thiers and M. Barrot were about to destroy, in one instant, the results already obtained by the Marshal.

CHAPTER XXII

THE MORNING OF FEBRUARY 24

WHEN dawn broke on February 24, Marshal Bugeaud still expected to be master of the situation. The first column, made up of the 30th of the line, a battalion of the 34th, a battalion of the 69th, a squadron of cuirassiers, and two pieces of artillery, under the command of General Tiburce Sébastiani, had arrived at the Hôtel-de-Ville at seven o'clock in the morning. The fourth, formed of the 15th of the line and two companies of the 14th, under the orders of Colonel Brunet, had rejoined General Renault at the Panthéon.

The second, commanded by General Bedeau and destined for the Place de la Bastille, had been stopped on the way. Its effective force was about eighteen hundred men. It comprised two battalions of the 1st light troops, two of the 21st, a detachment of light infantry from the 6th battalion, a squadron of the 8th dragoons, and two pieces of artillery. After destroying several empty barricades in the rues Neuve-des-Petits-Champs, Vivienne, and Feydeau, the column was entering the boulevard, when the platoon in advance was fired upon by some men who were defending the barricades erected at the extremity of the rue Montmartre. Two soldiers were wounded; the platoon returned fire, and a rush was made on the barricades, which were immediately destroyed.

The column then turned in the direction of the Bastille. General Bedeau has said that he expected a combat and was prepared for it. But he soon experienced extreme surprise on learning, from officers of the National Guard and some inoffensive and unarmed citizens, that the popular exasperation arose from ignorance of the change in the ministry and a belief that the unfortunate event on the Boulevard des Capucines had been premeditated by the ministers for the purpose of intimidating the population. "If it is true that there has been a change in the ministry," cried the officers of the National Guard, "quiet will be soon restored; but give us time to spread the news, for a great many National Guards are behind the barricades." "In face of this unexpected situation," General Bedeau has written, "was it my duty to march on, and by a continued attack give confirmation to the lie skilfully propagated by the partisans of the insurrection? I did not think so. I halted my column on this side of the Gymnase Theatre, and sent an account of the situation to the superior authority."

The pencilled note which the General forwarded to General Bugeaud was worded thus: "I am in presence of a population *unarmed*, inoffensive, and deceived. It does not believe there has been a change in the ministry; it is shouting: 'Long live the Reform!' Pray send me some proclamations. I have come to a halt in order to facilitate the reunion of the National Guard." The General had, in fact, sent a detachment of infantry to escort the drummers of the National Guard, who were beating the call to arms in the neighboring streets.

The Marshal sent this billet in reply: "I approve of what you have done. I am sending you some proclamations; have them distributed by every means in your power, for it is of the utmost importance that this news should be known. But it remains understood that, if the rioters show themselves, they must be summoned to disperse, and force energetically resorted to, as we agreed this morning." General Bedeau hoped that all was about to quiet down. At eight o'clock in the morning nobody was shouting, "Long live the Republic!" on the Boulevard Bonne-Nouvelle, where his column had just halted. The longer the immobility of his troops lasted, the greater grew the crowd around them, hoping that they would not force their way through. A merchant of the neighborhood, M. Fauvelle-Delabarre, offered to go and acquaint Marshal Bugeaud with the situation and bring back his definitive orders. General Bedeau promised to make no attack until this should be done.

On arriving at the staff headquarters, Place du

Carrousel, M. Fauvelle-Delabarre said to Marshal Bugeaud: "If the troops fire a shot, all is lost; all mediation becomes impossible, and Paris is drenched in blood." The Marshal allowed himself to be convinced by the merchant, whose advice was supported by a great number of persons, and who was, moreover, of the same opinion as the King and his new ministers. The Marshal, who seemed inflexible two hours before, was no longer so energetic. He was thinking of conciliating opinion rather than of waging a sanguinary conflict, and considering the possibility of entering the liberal Cabinet as Minister of War. At the very moment when he was sending out the columns of the attack, he had written to M. Thiers: "I have long foreseen that you and I would be called on to save the monarchy. . . . When I shall have put down the riot, — and we shall put it down, for inertia and refusal to assist on the part of the National Guard will not stop me, — I will gladly enter into the formation of a new Cabinet with you, as Minister of War, unless the pretended unpopularity they accuse me of should prove an insurmountable obstacle. In that case, I would not hesitate to advise you to take Bedeau, a distinguished officer, and to associate with him, as under-secretary of state, M. Magne, deputy, whose rare capacity I am personally acquainted with."

So, then, there was no Minister of War. The *Moniteur* had just come out. In its official news appeared the nomination of Marshal Bugeaud as commander-in-chief of the army and the National Guard. But M. Thiers and M. Odilon Barrot were not mentioned, except in its unofficial department. The *Journal des Débats* seemed wholly occupied with the formation of a Molé ministry. Under such circumstances, is not the public confusion easy to comprehend?

A year later, Marshal Bugeaud, meeting M. Fauvelle-Delabarre in an official salon, said to him: "I recognize you, sir; you did a great deal of harm. Instead of listening, I ought to have driven you out of my presence, and, deaf to the lamentations of your citizens and your National Guard, defended my King in his Tuileries, and shot you all down without mercy. Louis Philippe would still be on the throne, and you would now be lauding me to the skies. But what would you have? I was tormented, stupefied, by a lot of poltroons and toadies. They had made me as imbecile as themselves." In a letter dated October 19, 1848, the Marshal has written: "An unheard-of combination of circumstances had paralyzed me; I could make no use of my experience and the military faculties that nature had given me. I had nothing but the shadow of authority. Everything hampered me."

Yielding to the solicitations of M. Fauvelle-Delabarre, the Marshal sent the following instructions to General Bedeau: —

"My dear General, my arrangements are modified.

Announce everywhere that the firing is to stop, and that the National Guard will assume police duty. Make them listen to words of conciliation.

"The Marshal Duke of Isly.

"P.S. Fall back upon the Carrousel."

According to M. Garnier-Pagès, this billet was written from the Marshal's dictation by Captain Fabar, and the postscript by Major Trochu, the future governor of Paris.

The Marshal's billet was carried to General Bedeau by M. Fauvelle-Delabarre. As soon as it was received, the General wheeled his troops, put himself at their head, and set off in the direction of the Madeleine.

Now let us see what had become of the new ministers. Toward half-past seven o'clock, M. Thiers, accompanied by the politicians of whom he intended to compose his ministry, MM. Odilon Barrot, Duvergier de Hauranne, de Rémusat, de Malleville, Abbatucci, and General de Lamoricière, had started to walk from his house in Place Saint-Georges to the Tuileries. They had to cross several barricades on their way, and once narrowly escaped being caught between two fires. As they passed, many National Guards asked what they had to do. "The very simplest thing," replied M. Barrot; "get together, cover the city with your uniforms and your arms; the pavement of Paris ought to belong to the National Guard; otherwise, all is lost." When M.

Thiers and his colleagues arrived at the gate of the Tuileries, they saw the keepers of the château, who were returning the shots fired from the roofs of the opposite houses. A few soldiers, or firemen in case of necessity, would have been sufficient to dislodge these sharp-shooters. No such attempt had been made. An unpleasant symptom.

When the new ministers were in Louis Philippe's presence, he said: "I am glad to see you, M. Odilon Barrot; I do not doubt your devotion." M. Barrot responded that precious time had been lost already, and that it was essential to get into communication with the people by every possible means, in order to separate the reformist from the revolutionary element; that everything else would be easy when this separation was once effected. It was then proposed to the King to give General de Lamoricière command of the National Guard, under the superior direction of Marshal Bugeaud. After several objections, the King ended by saying: "Very well! arrange that with the Marshal." Then said M. Thiers: "There is another thing we must insist on, and that is that Your Majesty shall give us a formal promise to dissolve the Chamber, if not immediately, at least very soon." "Oh! on that point," replied Louis Philippe, "I do not intend to make any compromise." — "But, Sire," said M. Duvergier de Hauranne, "can Your Majesty understand how we can assume power with a majority which has just treated us as blind men or enemies?" "What!" said the King, "you have your reform, and you are not satisfied?"

"M. Thiers and I," writes M. Odilon Barrot in his Memoirs, "persisted in declaring that it would be impossible for us to assume power unless we were assured of being able to dissolve the Chamber. 'No! no!' obstinately reiterated the King; and, withdrawing toward his study, where M. Guizot was, he shut the door in our faces. Much surprise has been expressed at M. Guizot's presence at such a moment; for my part, I think it very natural; so long as the new ministry was not formed,— and, as one may see, it was far enough from being so,— the place of the former ministers was with the King." M. Guizot was at the Tuileries merely for the purpose of taking final leave of the sovereign. He never saw him again, except at Claremont.

Availing themselves of Louis Philippe's half-consent, MM. Thiers and Barrot went to staff headquarters with General de Lamoricière. "Gentlemen," cried the Marshal, "I tell you it is impossible to govern if there is freedom of the press." "M. Marshal," returned M. Barrot, "we will discuss that, if you like, at a more convenient season. Just now, there is not a minute to be lost. Are you willing, yes or no, that General de Lamoricière shall command the National Guard of Paris?" "Oh! well, do as you please," replied the Marshal.

The General was in citizen's dress. "Take the first uniform you can find," M. Barrot said to him, "and rejoin me on the Boulevards, where I am going." As he was descending the staircase, M. Barrot met Horace Vernet, the painter, who, as colonel of the staff of the National Guard, had just been visiting the posts in the neighboring quarters. The following dialogue ensued: —

"What is going on?"

"I have just informed the post of the Théâtre-Français that M. Thiers has been asked to form a Cabinet. Seeing that this did not produce the effect I hoped for, I mentioned you, and they would not believe me. 'Odilon Barrot and Marshal Bugeaud!' they exclaimed; 'absurd! they can't go together; they are making game of us.'"

"Very well! since they won't believe you, I will go and talk to them myself."

M. Thiers wished to accompany M. Barrot. "No," said the latter. "Stay here. If there is any likelihood of being shot, it is useless for all of us to be exposed. Besides, the King will need your counsels. Simply defend yourself here while I try to make the people listen to reason." "The truth is," writes M. Barrot in his Memoirs, "M. Thiers would have been rather a hindrance than a help in the campaign I was about to make on the barricades. He remained near the King, with MM. de Rémusat and Duvergier de Hauranne, until the dénouement; I did not see him again that day. On this I started out through the gate of the rue de Rivoli, with MM. Abbatucci, Quinette, de Beaumont, Chambolle,

Havin, Horace Vernet. It was then about half-past nine o'clock."

Two or three hundred paces from the gate of the rue de Rivoli, M. Barrot found a barricade, on the rue de l'Echelle. He gave his name and was allowed to pass. In the Boulevard des Capucines he encountered a regiment of infantry, which, instead of conducting itself in military fashion, was mixed up with the crowd. "As soon as it had been decided to give way," he writes, "it was certainly well to avoid everything likely to exasperate the populace anew; but then, the troops should have been withdrawn, not left in a forced inaction and in contact with the people at the very time when the National Guard had been called on to replace them. The misfortune of that day was that no one knew how to make either peace or war."

The further M. Barrot advanced on the Boulevards, the less favorable did he find the temper of the crowds. They were shouting: "Down with Bugeaud! Down with Thiers!" At the end of the rue Saint-Denis rose an enormous barricade, surmounted by a red flag. The rioters defending it gave a very cool reception to M. Barrot and his friends. "What was to be done?" he writes; "should we cross the barricade and enter the rue Saint-Denis, in order to reach the Hôtel-de-Ville? But, after having let us pass, would these men in front of us, who evidently wanted something more than a simple reform, let us go further on, and would they not, in any case, prevent our return? And, in that case, would not all action, all influence, on our part, be paralyzed? These reflections speedily decided us to go back."

On their return, as the National Guards surrounding M. Barrot were powerless to repress the crowd, he was induced to mount a horse, and several cordons of National Guards, holding each other firmly by the arms, formed a sort of dike to protect them from the mass of men that followed. Near the rue de la Paix he met General de Lamoricière, whose pacific tour of inspection had succeeded no better than his own As they arrived together at the Place Vendôme, the crowd was shouting: "To the Tuileries! to the Tuileries!" Let us allow M. Barrot himself to describe what happened: "This formidable cry suddenly enlightened me concerning the situation; I saw the consequences of my reappearance at the Tuileries at the head of this armed multitude. Leaving the King's Cabinet with a mission to appease the insurrection, I could not, without loss of honor, return at the head of that very insurrection, to impose abdication on Louis Philippe; and it was this, at least, that the crowd would have exacted. I bent toward the National Guards who were leading my horse, and said vehemently, 'No, no, my friends, not to the Tuileries; you see for yourselves that I am exhausted; and, besides, I must go back home to reassure my wife!' These good fellows understood me, and, turning my horse round, instead of crossing the Place Vendôme, they led it by the rue des Capucines, toward the rue de la Ferme-des-Mathurins, where I lived. Part of the crowd took the same direction, and, after inundating my street like an avalanche, made their way into my house. A woman preceded them, carrying a tricolored flag, which she planted at one of my windows, while some men, with the aid of a ladder, were suspending at the beginning of the street that placard which was still to be seen there several months later, and which bore the inscription: *Street of the Father of the People.* Melancholy testimony of a popular favor which lasted several minutes!"

While M. Barrot had been making his unlucky excursion on the Boulevards, the retreat of General Bedeau and his column had been not less unhappily effected. The General has given the details of it in a letter of April 4, 1851, which we have already cited. Before quitting his position on the Boulevard Bonne-Nouvelle, he ordered a company of the National Guard to precede his column, in order to facilitate the opening of the barricades he had to cross, and also to avert more surely any misunderstanding with the people. At the top of the rue Montmartre he found an immense crowd, blocking up the alleys and the roadway of the boulevard. The real news had not been disseminated. At every step it was necessary to declare the change in the ministry, in order to allay public excitement. Nevertheless, the General did not hear a single cry from which one could infer an intention to overthrow the government. On the Boulevard des Italiens, he encountered M. Odilon Barrot, who, at this moment, was still being cheered on every side. "This meeting," says the General, "made me understand still better than the order I had received, what pacific intentions had directed the policy of the government." The column marched with difficulty through a constantly increasing crowd. In front of a barricade erected at the upper end of the rue de Choiseul, it abandoned its two pieces of artillery, and several soldiers laid down their arms. The General was not apprised of these two facts until the moment when he arrived in the rue Royale with the head of his column. Mixed up with the people in a tumultuous rabble, his troops had an aspect that made the twenty municipal guards of the station in the Avenue Gabriel, corner of the rue des Champs-Elysées (now rue Boissy-d'Anglas), think that the rioters had arrived, and they put themselves on the defensive. Attacked, or believing themselves attacked, by the people, they fired. The crowd returned the fire. "At this moment," says the General, "I was so convinced of the government's intention to avert all conflict, that I thought the best thing I could do was to throw myself between the two fires and try to stop them. I did not succeed, in spite of the very meritorious efforts of several National Guards and the promises made to me. At the moment when the municipal guards came out of the guard-house, some sprang forward to shield and others to attack them. There were twenty guards; two were killed, several wounded, and others sheltered, three of them by me, in this deplorable affray." An instant later, in the middle of the Place de la Concorde, at the railing called du Pont-Tournant, the guard, deceived by another alarm, also fired a discharge, which killed three persons, among them a conservative deputy, M. Jollivet, who was struck at the very moment when he was making the most generous efforts to save the life of a municipal guard who was pursued by the crowd.

After these disastrous incidents, General Bedeau succeeded in rallying his troops and bringing them into position on the Place de la Concorde, at the side of those already there. It was about half-past ten in the morning. At this moment the General perceived M. de Tocqueville. "He jumped off his horse," the latter has written, "and shook my hand in a way that showed me how greatly he was disturbed. . . . Bedeau was a just man, moderate, liberal, humane, modest, moral, delicate, and even religious. It certainly was not faint-heartedness which made him do some things which might seem to indicate as much, for he had a courage equal to every test; still less was treason his incentive. . . . His sole misfortune was to be mixed up in events too great for him, to have nothing but merit where genius was essential, and especially that particular genius of revolutions, which chiefly consists in regulating one's actions by facts alone, and in knowing when to disobey." The General was just saying to his interlocutor that the duty of the opposition was to descend in a body to the street, in order to allay the popular excitement, when a crowd of people, stealing in and out between the trees of the Champs-Elysées, advanced toward the Place de la Concorde. "As soon as he perceived this," adds M. de Tocqueville, "Bedeau dragged me toward them, on foot, at least a hundred paces from his squadrons, and began to harangue them; for he had a greater taste for haranguing than I ever saw in any other man who carried a sword. While he was discoursing, the circle of his auditors was spreading out, and would soon have hemmed us in. Some one said: 'It is Bugeaud!' I whispered to him: 'Take my word for it and get back to your horse this instant; for if you stay here, you will be killed or taken within five minutes.' He did believe me, and he did well."

Marshal Bugeaud had not been more successful than his lieutenant, in his attempts at pacification. He had several times shown himself to the National Guards ranged on the Place du Carrousel, but without result. In vain had he said to them: "Friends, comrades, all is over. Orders have just been sent to the troops, and the safety of Paris has been confided to the patriotism of the National Guard." In vain had he gone into the rue de Rivoli and ordered a battalion of the 2d legion to break into sections and follow him. Not a soul had obeyed him. The entire government was at last beginning to comprehend that, as Marshal Bugeaud himself has written, the enemy cannot be discouraged by a retreat nor tumultuous masses by concessions.

CHAPTER XXIII

THE LAST REVIEW

LOUIS PHILIPPE, still believing that the disturbance was merely a riot, foresaw neither his abdication nor the proclamation of the Republic. When he sat down to breakfast with his family, at half-past ten o'clock, in the gallery of Diana, he did not suspect that he was about to eat his last meal in the Tuileries. As yet he knew nothing, except the fortunate beginning of M. Odilon Barrot's excursion on the boulevards, and had heard not a word of General Bedeau's disastrous retreat. No sign of discouragement was visible on the countenance of the old King. Had he not seen more terrible tempests in the course of his perturbed career? As to the Queen, although ready to display the same energy as her ancestress, the great Empress Maria Theresa, she was under no illusion concerning the gravity of the peril; she knew that the hour of the last crisis had arrived. The night just ended had been to her a night of anguish. Pious and resigned as she was, she had been scarcely able to hold the prayer-book in which she was seeking consolation.

The Duchess of Orleans had spent a part of this painful night beside her. "We had not even strength to pray," has said the Duchess.

The breakfast of the royal family had just begun. MM. Thiers, Duvergier de Hauranne, and de Rémusat were present at it. Suddenly a door opened. A captain of the staff, M. de Laubespin, entered, bringing the worst of tidings. He had just seen how the retreat of General Bedeau's troops had been effected, and he thought the King no longer in safety at the Tuileries. M. Thiers at once proposed a retreat to Saint-Cloud. He said afterwards: "Sixty thousand men could have been assembled at Saint-Cloud the following day, and with that army we could have marched on Paris by the 26th of February. . . . The citizens, after having been in the hands of the republicans for two days, would have become our devoted friends. We should have been obliged to destroy the Hôtel-de-Ville, and to employ cannon for that purpose; but I would destroy ten such palaces to put down a revolution." M. Thiers' proposition was rejected.

After M. de Laubespin's arrival, some officers had been sent to the Place du Carrousel for news. On returning, they declared that the situation was improving, as General Bedeau had rallied his troops, and that there was no further danger of an attack on the Tuileries from that side.

It now occurred to Louis Philippe to examine for himself the forces defending him on the Place du

Carrousel. In great haste, and for the last time, he put on the uniform of a general of the National Guard, and held a review, like that held by Louis XVI. on the morning of August 10, 1792, before quitting the Tuileries forever. Many of the National Guards broke their ranks, and coming down from the terrace surrounding the lake in the garden, crowded about Louis XVI. as he passed, with noisy threats. At that sight Marie Antoinette wept. "The review," she cried, "has done more harm than good." It was to be the same way with Louis Philippe's last review, and Marie Amélie was to experience the same impressions and the same anguish as her aunt.

Toward eleven o'clock Louis Philippe mounted a horse, accompanied by the Dukes de Nemours and Montpensier, Marshal Bugeaud, General de Lamoricière, and several other generals. M. Thiers and M. de Rémusat followed on foot. People were amazed to see General de Lamoricière on the King's left, muffled up in a rough great-coat with the epaulettes of a general of the National Guard, and wearing an old cap, both of which seemed to have been unexpectedly thrust upon him, since they fitted neither his figure nor his head. This circumstance was a confirmation of the news, learned only a few minutes earlier, that the National Guard, having declined Marshal Bugeaud as their commander, he had been replaced by the General.

Four thousand soldiers, with sixteen pieces of

artillery, were drawn up on the Place du Carrousel. The National Guard was represented by a detachment of cavalry, under the orders of Count de Montalivet; by some fractions of the 10th legion, resting against the Hôtel de Nantes, a detached dwelling on the place, near the rue de Rohan; by a battalion of the 1st legion, backed against the railing separating the Carrousel from the Tuileries; and, finally, by the equivalent of a battalion of the 4th, composed of men from all the companies of the legion. This battalion, circulating around the quays, had forced its leader to conduct it toward the Tuileries through the gate of the bridge des Saints-Pères, and, entering the Place du Carrousel, had drawn up in battle array before the château, in utter disregard of the objections made by several superior officers of the line.

From the windows, the Queen, the Duchess of Orleans and her son, the Duchess de Nemours, and the Duchess de Montpensier, were anxiously watching the King. It was the Queen who had counselled this review. It was she who sought to inspire energetic and virile resolutions. "The countenance of this beloved wife, this mother, who had so long been happy," says M. de Lamartine, "was animated by the energy of her double sentiment for her husband and her children. All her tenderness for them was concentrated, and became impassioned in solicitude for their honor. Their life took the second place in her love. Her white locks, contrasting with the fire of her eyes and the ruddy animation of her cheeks, imprinted on her countenance something tragical and holy." The opening of the review made her heart throb with hope. On entering the Carrousel, Louis Philippe met first the National Guards of the 1st legion, who gave him a cordial welcome, and cried: "Long live the King!" as well as: "Long live the reform!"

"You shall have the reform, my friends," said he. "There is no longer any pretext for disturbance." The attitude of the National Guards of the 10th legion was equally good. But those of the 4th gave the sovereign a totally different reception. Making a violent clamor and brandishing their arms, they furiously shouted: "Long live the reform! Down with the system! Down with Guizot!" The unhappy King tried in vain to pacify them. Their shouts redoubled. This threatening behavior on the part of men whom he had been accustomed to consider his friends, his defenders, and the best supporters of his throne, smote Louis Philippe with dull amazement. Paying no attention to the troops, who were expecting to be reviewed also, he turned back, dismounted from his horse at the pavilion of Flora, and re-entered the château, which he was to leave forever within another hour. He sank into an armchair and remained for some time motionless and silent, with his head in his hands.

Meanwhile, the insurrection, already in possession of the Hôtel-de-Ville, where General Sébastiani's column had been ordered to stop firing, was making the most astonishing headway. The prefecture of police was threatened, the Panthéon blockaded. Barricades were multiplying with frightful rapidity. Rioters were burning toll-gates, bridges, and guard-houses, occupying barracks, seizing arms, and stealing munitions.

At the very moment when the King's review came to an end, a band of common people and National Guards, armed with sabres, muskets, and bars of iron, advanced through the little streets which at that time existed between the Palais-Royal and the Place du Carrousel, and debouched on that place. Marshal Bugeaud, on horseback, went to meet the column, and harangued them with pathetic energy. "The proof that I succeeded," he has written himself (letter of October 19, 1848), "is that they sprang toward me, holding out their hands. One man only, dressed as a National Guard, said to me: —

"'Are you Marshal Bugeaud?'

"'Yes, I am.'

"'You butchered our brethren in the rue Transnonain.'

"'You lie; for I was not there.'

"The man made a movement with his musket. I pressed closer to him, in order to seize his weapon; but his neighbors silenced him and began to shout: 'Long live Marshal Bugeaud! Honor to military glory!' Major Trochu, Colonel Sercey, and Captain of Artillery Fabar were near me at the time. After shaking a thousand hands, I induced this column to retrace their steps. A great many of those composing it promised me to go to their own quarter and try to restore order."

This last glimmer of hope, which, feeble as it was amidst the gathering storm, still shone upon the Marshal, was speedily extinguished. Already the château of the Tuileries, that palace of disasters, was presenting a deplorable spectacle. The guard-houses were dismantled, the sentries departed, the doors open. Officers, deputies, journalists, men known and unknown, were entering wherever they chose, even into the salons adjoining the Cabinet of the King. The moment was at hand when the unfortunate sovereign was about to accede to pusillanimous counsels, instead of adopting the energetic resolutions suggested by Marie Amélie, whose courage increased in proportion with the danger.

CHAPTER XXIV

THE ABDICATION

LOUIS PHILIPPE is in his study on the ground-floor of the château of the Tuileries. After the review that has just taken place, he is sad and seems plunged in gloomy reflections. But he does not dream as yet of abdicating. The Queen and the princesses are in an adjacent room. The Duchess of Orleans, whom malevolent persons accuse of ambitious views, wishes to be near the King at this supreme moment. She has breakfasted with him. She has seen him hold his last review. She is there with her two sons. Some member of her household says to her: "What are they going to do? What will Madame do?" "I do not know what will be done," she answers; "all I know is that my place is near the King; I ought not to quit him; I will not quit him." The Queen never loses her head for a moment. Worthy granddaughter of the Empress Maria Theresa, she is resolute, energetic, ready to face the greatest dangers without blenching. Knowing thoroughly the history of the celebrated Days of the Revolution, she means that her courage shall prevent another 10th of August. If the men near her had her presence of mind and coolness, the throne might yet be saved; but on this lamentable day it is only the women who have virile sentiments.

Everything had been lost from the moment when a change of ministry was decided upon in the thick of a riot, and the troops forbidden to fire. At the château the disorder is complete; all the barriers of etiquette have fallen; people go in and out as if it were a tavern.

M. Crémieux (introduced by the Duke de Montpensier). — "Sire, I have just been passing through several quarters; the game may yet be won. Only, the people want a minister who will frankly belong to the left; M. Thiers' presence is an anomaly; he must be replaced by M. Odilon Barrot. At this price I think I can guarantee the re-establishment of order. If the King delays, all is lost."

Louis Philippe (turning toward M. Thiers). — "Eh! my dear Minister, so you are unpopular in your turn! It is not I, you observe, who repudiate your services."

M. Crémieux. — "The people are irritated against Marshal Bugeaud. He must be replaced by Marshal Gérard."

Marshal Bugeaud enters.

The King. — "My dear Marshal, they want me to part with you."

Like M. Thiers, the Marshal offers no objection to his displacement.

The King calls for his secretary, Baron Fain, and tells him to prepare the decrees, which ought to be countersigned by the former Minister of War, General Trézel. In the existing state of trouble there will be no time for these formalities.

General de Lamoricière (who has just been announcing to the crowd the concessions that have been made). — "Sire, they are not contented with what I have promised in the name of Your Majesty; they demand something more."

The King. — "Something more? That must be my abdication, and as I will not give it, except with my life, they will not get it."

A noise of firing is heard. On the Place du Palais-Royal there is a large guard-house, the entire lower story of which is occupied by a grotto of pebbles and a jet of water. It is what is called the water-château of the Palais-Royal. The windows of this guard-house are protected by very solid iron bars. A detachment of the 14th of the line is established there. Assailed by the insurrection, it refuses to surrender. A sustained firing begins. The soldiers shoot from behind the window gratings; the insurgents reply from behind the columns of the Palais-Royal.

M. Emile de Girardin enters the King's Cabinet, holding a paper in his hand. It is noon-day.

The King. — "What is the matter?"

M. de Girardin. — "The matter is, Sire, that they have been making Your Majesty lose precious time.

If another minute is wasted, within an hour there will be neither king nor royalty in France."

The King. — "What is to be done?"

M. de Girardin. — "Abdicate, Sire! Abdicate in favor of the regency of Madame the Duchess of Orleans. They will not have the Duke de Nemours. Here is the proclamation, all ready; it was given to the printers in order to save the seconds that are escaping us: —

"'Abdication of the King.

"'Regency of Madame the Duchess of Orleans.

"'Dissolution of the Chamber.

"'General amnesty.'"

The Duke de Montpensier. — "Since things are as M. de Girardin affirms them to be, Sire, do not hesitate! Abdicate!"

The Queen. — "No, no, my friend, you will not do that! They are trying to tear away your sceptre. There is no one but you who has strength to wield it. Rather die here than escape through that door! Mount a horse, the army will follow you! . . . I cannot understand any one abandoning the King at such a moment! . . . You will all repent of it. . . . You do not deserve so good a King."

The Duchess of Orleans (at Louis Philippe's knees). — "Sire, I entreat you, do not abdicate!"

M. Piscatory. — "No, Sire! do not abdicate. I have just been all over Paris. If you can maintain yourself four hours behind the walls and gratings of the Tuileries, — and you can do it with the troops surrounding you,— I am convinced that all will be saved. But if, in spite of our prayers, you have resolved to yield, it is not here that you should abdicate, but at Vincennes or Mont-Valérien."

The King. — "I have signed nothing yet."

Marshal Soult is there; he does not speak.

The noise of musket-firing seems coming nearer.

The Duke de Montpensier. — "There is not a minute to lose. The balls are whistling even in the court."

The King. — "Is it true that all defence would be impossible?"

Several voices. — "Impossible! impossible!"

M. Piscatory tries to make another appeal.

The Queen (to M. Piscatory). — "Thanks, but you have done enough, do not say another word; there are traitors here."

The Duchess of Orleans. — "Sire, no one is prepared to see me regent, and I less than any one else. And it is on a feeble woman they would throw, at such a crisis, a weight which you judge too heavy for your shoulders!"

The King. — "I am a pacific sovereign; since all defence is impossible, I will not shed French blood uselessly; I abdicate."

Count de Pontécoulant has said in his *Souvenirs:* "Of all imaginable means, none was more certain to conduct the state to a catastrophe than that which was selected, and the riot might have had devoted partisans even in the very Cabinet of the King, who would not have served it better than such imprudent counsellors."

Let us cite also this passage from the Memoirs of M. Dupin: "When the entire army was still firm and faithful, when the two Chambers showed themselves devoted to the King, whe all the authorities were at their posts, ought the defection of several companies of National Guards to have brought about so unexpected a discouragement, a self-abandonment so instantaneous and complete? . . . By what means were they able to persuade the King that it was right for him to despoil himself at once of power, in the midst of danger, for the sake of investing a child with it? Who was it that counselled so desperate an act? Certainly it was not Marie Amélie, who on that day, as wife and mother, and especially as queen, displayed (as everybody is continually saying) a dignity equal to her rank and a firmness superior to her sex."

Fearless for himself, Louis Philippe is timid for his family. His imagination, filled with souvenirs of the Revolution, which did not spare women, reminds him of Marie Antoinette, Madame Elisabeth, and many another innocent victim. On the other hand, the philanthropic King, the pacific King, has a horror of bloodshed. When young, he had several times succeeded in conquering this repugnance and putting down an insurrection. But now that he is old, he cannot persuade himself to fire upon his people, to kill those National Guards who for so long have been his friends and defenders. He believes, moreover, that in abdicating he is sacrificing no one but himself, and he thinks that this sacrifice, far from destroying his dynasty, will save it. He hopes in this way to avert suspicions, allay excitement, and render the establishment of the regency easy and substantial.

Marshal Gérard enters the Cabinet of the King. He is asked to announce the abdication to the people.

The Queen. — "My good Marshal, save what can still be saved."

The Marshal is in civilian's dress. Without giving him time to put on a uniform, he is set on a horse in the court of the château, and a green branch put in his hand as a token of peace; just as he is passing through the gate, some one calls his attention to the fact that he has no paper declarative of the abdication. "That is true," says he, and keeping straight on toward the Palais-Royal, where the fighting continues, he begs two persons to go and ask for this paper.

Not until then does the King decide to sign. He arranges his pen and paper slowly.

Several voices. — "Quicker! Quicker!"

The King. — "I am doing it as quickly as I can, gentlemen."

The Duke de Montpensier. — "Sire, I implore you to make haste."

The King. — "I have always written slowly; this is not the moment to change my habit."

And with a firm hand, and in large script, the unfortunate sovereign traces these lines: —

"I abdicate this crown, which the national voice had called on me to wear, in favor of my grandson, the Count of Paris.

"May he succeed in the great task which falls to his lot this day!

"This February 24, 1848.

"LOUIS PHILIPPE."

An Unknown (standing behind the King). — "At last we have it."

The Queen. — "Who are you, sir?"

The Unknown. — "Madame, I am a provincial magistrate."

The Queen. — "Well, yes! you have it, and you will repent it. Oh! my God, they will regret it!"

M. Crémieux and several other persons complain that Louis Philippe has not named the Duchess of Orleans regent, in the act of abdication.

The King. — "Others will do it if they think it necessary; but, for my part, I will not. It is contrary to law. Thanks to God, I have never yet violated a law, and I will not begin at such a moment."

The majority of those who had invaded the King's Cabinet now disperse.

A young man goes to carry the act of abdication to Marshal Gérard, but does not succeed in reaching him, and the paper falls into the hands of the insurgents. The Marshal's attempt at pacification has failed. A trumpeter preceded him, and two men led his horse by the bridle, crying: "Make way! Make way!" At the end of a few minutes they had been obliged to retrace their steps.

The soldiers shut up in the guard-house are still being sacrificed. A charge of the cuirassiers and dragoons massed in the Carrousel could have cleared the Place du Palais-Royal and given these brave foot-soldiers a chance to effect their retreat. But not a troop comes to their assistance. General de Lamoricière tries in vain to interpose between the combatants and stop the firing. His horse falls, struck by a ball, and he himself, wounded by a bayonet-thrust, becomes the prisoner of the insurgents. The latter go to rue Saint-Thomas-du-Louvre, to search the King's stables for vehicles and hay-carts; these they push against the guard-house and set them on fire.

Meantime, Louis Philippe is making ready to leave the Tuileries. But he does not suppose that he is departing into exile. In his view, it is merely a journey to the Château d'Eu, where he will be left to repose in peace while the regency installs itself at Paris. Assisted by the Queen, he takes off his uniform, resumes civilian's dress, and gets together several objects which he proposes to carry with him. He sends to the royal stables for two four-horse berlines for the journey. But just as they are coming out by the rue Saint-Thomas-du-Louvre, they are seized by the insurgents, and the huntsman, Hairon, is killed.

The Duchess of Orleans (who sees the preparations for departure). — "Ah! Sire, do not abandon me. I am only a poor woman; what shall I do without your advice and protection?"

The King. — "My dear child, you owe yourself to your son and to France; you must remain."

The failure of Marshal Gérard's mission, and the progress of the riot that threatens the Place du Carrousel, is announced.

M. Crémieux. — "Sire, there is not an instant to lose. The people are coming. In a few minutes they will be at the Tuileries."

The moment of departure has arrived. It is half-past twelve o'clock.

The fugitives walk through the grand alley of the garden of the Tuileries. The King gives his arm to the Queen. Behind them come the Duke de Montpensier, the Duchess de Nemours, with her three children (the Count d'Eu, born in 1842; the Duke d'Alençon, born in 1844; and the Princess Marguerite, born in in 1846), the Duke Auguste of Saxe-Coburg-Gotha, and his wife, the Princess Clémentine of Orleans, with their three children (Princes Philippe and Auguste, the one born in 1844 and the other in 1845, and Princess Clotilde, born in 1846); then MM. Crémieux, Ary Scheffer, and General Dumas; people in waiting; and, as escort, several

National Guards on horseback, commanded by Count de Montalivet.

The sad procession recalls that of Louis XVI. and his family, quitting the Tuileries, August 10, 1792, to go to the legislative assembly, and find no asylum there except the reporters' box. Behold the fugitives arriving at the gate that opens on the Place de la Concorde, and which is still called the gate du Pont-Tournant, on account of a drawbridge which was formerly thrown across the moats of the château. Here they had expected to find the two large travelling carriages which had been sent for from the royal stables in the rue Saint-Thomas-du-Louvre. But the carriages are not there. As we have just said, they have been taken by the insurgents and delivered to the flames. Another resource remains. At the moment when the royal family was quitting the Tuileries, there were in the court of the château two small one-horse carriages called broughams, and a two-wheeled cabriolet, all of them belonging to the King's establishment and intended for the use of the aides-de-camp, and persons in service who might have errands in the city. The Duke de Nemours had sufficient presence of mind to reflect that, although these vehicles, constructed to hold three persons only, were certainly insufficient, yet they might receive several members of the family; and he had them taken through the gate of the court and the still unimpeded quay, to that point in the Place de la Concorde where the berlines were to have

awaited them. Fifteen persons crowd into these
three vehicles. The King looks at the spot where
his father's scaffold had been erected, and then enters
one of the broughams, with the Queen, the two
young princes of Coburg, and the little Duke d'Alençon. M. Basire, a stock-broker, and captain of the
staff of the National Guard, who has followed the
royal family from the château, takes the driver's
seat. The Duchess de Nemours, the daughter of
the Princess Clémentine, and three women of her
suite, enter the second brougham. The Duke de
Montpensier, General Dumas, and one of the Queen's
women get into the cabriolet. As to the Princess
Clémentine, she takes her husband's arm, and, instead of departing, mingles with the crowd. The
three carriages, escorted by National Guards and two
squadrons of the 2d cuirassiers, commanded by Colonel Rewbell, set off at a gallop in the direction of
Saint-Cloud.

CHAPTER XXV

THE DUKE DE NEMOURS

DISORDER is at its height after the abdication of Louis Philippe. There is no longer either a ministry or a commander-in-chief of the troops and the National Guard. No signed document confers authority on M. Thiers or M. Odilon Barrot, nor does any declare that Marshal Bugeaud has been replaced. Legally, there are but two things subsisting: the royalty of the Count de Paris and the regency of the Duke de Nemours. The King himself, in abdicating, could not dispossess this prince of a right belonging to him in virtue of the law of August 30, 1842, and of which, by Article 3, he came into possession from the moment of the accession. The will of Louis Philippe, and even the renunciation of the Duke de Nemours, would not have sufficed to modify this law. A new law, passed not only by the Chamber of Deputies, but also by the Chamber of Peers, would have been required. It has been wrongly stated that, during the scene of the abdication, the Duke had himself pronounced for the regency of the Duchess of Orleans. The

Duke had neither asserted nor abandoned his right. Observe this remark in M. Odilon Barrot's Memoirs: "At the moment when the King was departing, the Duchess of Orleans, having asked him for orders, received this reply: 'I have no orders to give. The Duke de Nemours is regent; you must address yourself to him.'"

As soon as Louis Philippe had left the Tuileries, the Princess, taking her two sons by the hand, passed through the long galleries which led to her apartments in the pavilion of Marsan. In her salon there was a full-length portrait of her husband, by Ingres. She remembered having written, in 1843: "It is under this portrait that all my important actions should be performed;" and stopping there, she said with calmness: "We must die here." Then she ordered all the doors to be opened, without fearing the rioters, whose cries she could already hear.

During this time, the Duke de Nemours had mounted a horse, and, taking command, in order to assure the King's safety, had deployed two battalions of the line in the court of the château, posted two others at the windows of the first story, and made the cuirassiers enter the garden through the vestibule of the Horloge pavilion. At this moment, he thought the Duchess of Orleans had gone with the royal family. But as soon as he learned that the Princess was still in the palace, he sent several officers to tell her to leave it at once, and go through the Tuileries garden to the gate of the Pont-Tournant, where he would rejoin her.

M. Dupin and another deputy, the Marquis de Grammont, had just arrived at the Marsan pavilion. They found the Princess alone there, with her two sons and one of her ladies, Madame de Wion de Peysac. She was standing opposite her husband's portrait in the salon, the shutters of the windows opening on the rue de Rivoli having been closed so that the balls of the rioters might not enter. "Oh! M. Dupin," she exclaimed, "you are the first to come to me." Then she told the Count de Paris to give his hand to the two deputies, which the young Prince did with much grace. Presently came a messenger, who told the Duchess that the King was waiting for her at the gate of the Pont-Tournant. Thereupon she decided to depart. Giving her left arm to M. Dupin, she took the Count de Paris by the right hand. M. de Grammont gave his left hand to the little King. The Duke de Chartres, who was slightly ill, was carried by Dr. Blache. They crossed the court of the château and the Horloge pavilion, and entered the garden, taking the same path that Louis Philippe had gone through a few minutes earlier. As they were entering the grand alley, an adjutant came galloping up to ask the Princess to walk faster. M. Dupin replied that they were going as fast as possible, considering the illness of one of the children. The cavalier departed at once. Just as they were approaching the great

octagonal reservoir, he came back to say that the
King could not remain any longer, and had gone on
toward Saint-Cloud without waiting for M. Odilon
Barrot, who had not yet arrived.

At the same instant, the Duke de Nemours, who,
after giving his last instructions to the troops for
the retreat, had just crossed the vestibule of the
Horloge pavilion, on horseback, rejoined his sister-
in-law between the octagonal reservoir and the gate
of the Pont-Tournant. "Hélène," he said to her,
"the position is no longer tenable in Paris, but it
may still be so elsewhere. I have a half-battery of
artillery yonder. Get on an artillery wagon with
your children. It shall be my affair to take you to
Mont Valérien." The Princess making no objection, the Duke rode in haste to the Place de la Concorde to consult with the different commanders of
companies.

Meanwhile, two emissaries of M. Odilon Barrot,
MM. Havin and Biesta, approached the Princess,
and announced that M. Barrot had expressly recommended that she should not be taken to the Chamber
of Deputies. "I felt," the latter has written, "that
this Chamber, being still more unpopular than the
ministry itself, could defend nobody; and unfortunately I was not mistaken." After insisting upon
M. Barrot's recommendation, M. Biesta added: "Do
you know how to ride, Madame?" "Certainly,"
replied the Princess, "and if a woman's saddle cannot be found, let them unseat a dragoon, and I will

mount his horse." "All this is folly," cried M. Dupin; "your place, Madame, is at the Chamber, where your regency is about to be proclaimed."

M. Dupin has himself avowed, in his Memoirs, that the idea of this proclamation by the Chamber had not occurred to him until the last moment. "If M. Barrot had been there," he writes, "and Madame the Duchess of Orleans could have obtained an open carriage, I have no doubt she would have entered it and been courageous enough to show herself to the people and drive over the boulevards with the young King. But all means of action were lacking at once, and as there was no possibility of going back, there seemed nothing to be done but to go to the Chamber of Deputies, a thing we had not so much as thought of at the moment of departure."

It was necessary to come to some decision. The eyes of the soldiers on duty and those of the crowd gathering around the gate of the Pont-Tournant were fixed upon the Duchess of Orleans and her sons. Taking off his hat, M. Dupin shouted: "Long live the Count de Paris, King of the French people! Long live the Duchess of Orleans, regent!" This cry was repeated by the crowd. Then the National Guard and the people made way for the Princess and her sons, from the gate as far as the Pont de la Concorde. Accepting M. Dupin's advice, the Princess had determined to go to the Chamber.

The Duke de Nemours counted for nothing in this determination. Until these latter times, the details

of the part played by the Duke on that terrible
24th of February were imperfectly known. But
the Prince had taken care personally to supply
M. Thureau-Dangin with the information which the
eminent historian has recorded in his masterly work.
From this, it becomes evident that the Duke de
Nemours by no means expected his sister-in-law's
departure for the Chamber of Deputies. At the time
when she was going toward the Pont de la Concorde, he was still intending to carry her to Mont
Valérien on an artillery wagon, and was taking
measures for that purpose. He had a regiment of
cuirassiers, who were to surround the battery; the
infantry would march on either side and behind; the
troops, about to evacuate the Tuileries, would form
the rear-guard, and prevent pursuit. "Thus com-
bined," says M. Thureau-Dangin, "the operation
was militarily infallible. Politically, was it not the
best thing to be done? It could be seen on the road
whether it were better to go to Saint-Cloud or to Mont
Valérien. The essential thing was to gain some
hours, in which to find out how things stood, to put
an end to the disorder, to manage to assemble considerable forces, to give France time to intervene
and Paris time to reflect. . . . Might not this scene,
of a princess riding with her two children on an
artillery wagon, be the very thing which would fortunately impress the popular imagination?"

Great was the Duke's surprise,—and great likewise
his sorrow,— when, just as he was giving his orders

in the middle of the Place de la Concorde, he was told that his sister-in-law, instead of waiting for him, as he expected, was on her way to the Chamber of Deputies. Amidst the general confusion had she failed to hear him, or had she misunderstood his words? He felt that nothing could be more perilous for her than her appearance at the Palais-Bourbon, where there was nothing in readiness to support her. He determined to hasten after her, try to stop her if she had not yet entered the Chamber, or, if she were already there, to make her leave it. Unable to admit the idea that a woman, his sister-in-law, confided to his care by the last will of his brother, the Duke of Orleans, should incur dangers while he was not present to defend her, the Duke de Nemours went in all haste to her assistance. All sentiment of personal ambition was foreign to this brave and loyal prince, who, as a republican, M. Garnier-Pagès, avows, "by his self-abnegation, his fraternal piety, and his self-sacrifice, merits a place in the esteem of all good men."

The July monarchy, nevertheless, must have regretted that the Duke de Nemours did not remain on his horse in the Place de la Concorde. The troops of General Bedeau and those which General Ruhlières had just brought back from the Carrousel were drawn up there in good order, and, under the Prince's personal supervision, might easily have prevented the invasion of the Chamber. According to all probability, the faint-heartedness of the two generals would not have occurred, and the throne of the Count de Paris might have been saved. But it was impossible for the Prince to suppose that the troops could be so badly commanded that they would leave the way clear for a handful of insurgents. He counted on the energy of General Bedeau and General Ruhlières. The latter being the older of the two, the Duke de Nemours enjoined him to take command of all the forces assembled on the Place de la Concorde, giving him special orders to guard the approaches to the Chamber. He sent a like order to the general commanding on the left bank, and then set off on a gallop in the direction just taken by the Duchess of Orleans. When he arrived at the gate of the Palais-Bourbon, the Princess had already gone inside. The Duke dismounted, and went to rejoin her who now engrossed his whole attention.

All the way from the Tuileries to the Chamber of Deputies, the Duchess of Orleans had shown herself courageous. M. Dupin, who did not leave her for a single instant, pays her the following tribute: —

"On entering the apartments of this heroic woman, I found her tranquil, firm, undaunted;

"Ready to follow the King even to Saint-Cloud, if she could have rejoined him in time;

"Capable, if she had had a carriage to get into, a minister to aid her, of showing herself to the people, like another Maria Theresa, and of braving the turbulence of the insurgent masses;

"Full of confidence when it became necessary to

repair to the midst of the Chamber of Deputies in order to present her son to the representatives of the nation.

"Throughout the whole way thither not a gesture, not a word which betrayed trouble, vexation, weakness, or hesitation. Far from that, what was noticeable in her was a calm dignity, an intrepid resolution, an imperturbable coolness."

CHAPTER XXVI

THE DUCHESS OF ORLEANS IN THE CHAMBER

IT is half-past one o'clock when the Duchess of Orleans and her two sons cross the threshold of the Chamber of Deputies. Confusion there is at its height. As has been said by M. Victor du Bled, in his remarkable *Histoire de la monarchie de Juillet:* "The government has addressed no communication to the Chamber, nor established any relations with it. Its dissolution has been publicly announced, and it is already treated as if it were dissolved. The government appears to be ignorant that there is a Chamber, just as the latter does not yet know whether there is any government, where it is, or what it is." The order of the day provided: a reunion in the government offices to discuss the proposition of an impeachment of the ministers; a public session at three o'clock; a discussion of the privilege of the Bank of Bordeaux. But the order of the day has not been followed. The reunion in the government offices has been suppressed, and at half-past twelve President Sauzet is in the chair. No one dreams of opening a discussion on the Bank of Bordeaux. The ministerial bench is empty. The Assembly displays a keen anxiety. It has been said that M. Odilon Barrot had just been appointed president of the Council, and his absence creates astonishment. There had been a rumor that the King had abdicated, but as yet nothing has confirmed the news. M. Thiers had put in a brief appearance in the Conference room. Troubled by the hostile manifestations of the public he had encountered on the Place de la Concorde, alarmed, fearing for his life, and unaware, moreover, that the Duchess of Orleans intended coming to the Chamber, his sole idea was to escape as soon as possible; according to an eyewitness, the Count de Falloux, he asked by what door he could go out, when that door stood wide open in front of him. At the moment when the Duchess of Orleans was entering the Chamber, he had already vanished, and gone back to his own house, deranged and desperate, and taking the most circuitous route, in order not to be noticed by the crowds.

It is announced that the Count de Paris and his mother are to be present at the session. At the same instant, Madame the Duchess of Orleans, leading the Count de Paris by one hand and the Duke de Chartres by the other, enters the hall. It resounds with acclamations. A great many deputies shout: "Long live the Duchess of Orleans! Long live the Count de Paris! Long live the King! Long live the regent!" Seats are speedily brought into the semicircle below the tribune, in which the Duchess, her two sons, and the Duke de Nemours place themselves.

M. Lacrosse (amidst the racket). — "I ask leave to speak for M. Dupin, who has just brought Monsieur the Count de Paris to the Chamber."

M. Dupin. — "I have not asked for it."

Many voices. — "Speak! Speak!"

M. Dupin (in the tribune). — "Gentlemen, you know the situation of the capital and the manifestations that have taken place. The result of them has been the abdication of His Majesty Louis Philippe, who has declared that he lays down power, and that he freely transmits it to the Count de Paris, under the regency of Madame the Duchess of Orleans."

Later on M. Dupin will write: "I spoke of this only from hearsay, not having seen the act of abdication." And M. Barrot will say, in his Memoirs: "An official lie," the King having formally maintained the regency of the Duke de Nemours.

Numerous shouts. — "Long live the King! Long live the Count de Paris! Long live the regent!"

M. Dupin. — "Gentlemen, your acclamations, so precious to the new King and to Madame the regent, are not the first that have greeted her; she has walked through the Tuileries and the Place de la Concorde, escorted by the people and the National Guard [*bravo! bravo!*], expressing her heartfelt determination to administer solely with a view to the public interest and the glory and prosperity of France." (*More bravos.*)

M. Dupin resumed his seat.

Several members. — "M. Barrot! M. Barrot to the tribune!"

Other members. — "He is absent."

M. Dupin, from his place. — "It appears to me that the Chamber by its unanimous acclamations has just expressed an unequivocal sentiment which ought to be authenticated."

Many voices. — "Yes! yes!"

Different voices from the left and the extreme left. — "No! no! wait for M. Barrot! A provisional government!"

M. Dupin. — "I ask that, while waiting for the arrival of the act of abdication, which will probably be brought by M. Barrot, the Chamber shall have recorded in the minutes the acclamations which accompanied hither and saluted in this hall the Count de Paris as king of the French people, and Madame the Duchess of Orleans as regent, under the guarantee of the national will." (*Yes! yes! bravo! No! General excitement.*)

The President. — "Gentlemen, it seems to me that the Chamber, by its unanimous acclamations . . .*" (*Approbation from the centre; objections from left and right, and from spectators who have entered the lobbies.*)

M. Dupin. — "I verify first of all the acclamations of the people and the National Guard."

LEDRU-ROLLIN

UMA
CRITICA

M. Marie asks leave to speak, and ascends the tribune. The noise and disturbance prevent his making himself heard.

M. de Lamartine is about to come on the scene, and his part will be decisive. Let us first examine what he had been doing since the morning. He has taken pains to let us know just what it was. "Lamartine," he says in his *Histoire de la Révolution de 1848* (in which he never speaks of himself but in the third person), "Lamartine, unaware of any sort of conspiracy against the monarchy, had gone to sleep the night before, dismayed by the bloodshed on the boulevard, but firmly convinced that the night, which had put a truce to the conflict, and the day, which would illuminate new concessions from royalty, would pacify the movement. Without a party in the Chamber, without an accomplice in the street, detained by an indisposition, he did not dream of rising from his repose. Why should he be present in the Assembly merely to listen to the names and the programme of a new ministry? . . . However, at half-past ten o'clock one of his friends hurried in to tell him that they feared the Chamber of Deputies would be invaded by the people. Lamartine rose on hearing this, although he did not greatly believe in such impotency on the part of the fifty thousand troops supposed to be concentrated in Paris. But it was his duty to share the danger that might be foreseen for his colleagues." However, when he reached the Chamber, he regarded the crisis as terminated. Seven or eight persons were waiting for him in the vestibule. They were opposition journalists and republicans; among others, MM. Bastide, Armand Marrast, Hetzel, and Bocage, the actor. They drew him into one of the committee rooms and asked him to choose between the regency and the republic. A royalist a few minutes before, he becomes a republican. The agreement is concluded. The republicans will give Lamartine power, and Lamartine will give the republicans the republic.

The presence of the Duchess of Orleans in the Chamber embarrasses the great poet. He fears lest he shall be mastered by an involuntary tenderness. He dreads his emotion and his pity. It is he himself who thus describes the arrival of the Princess in the Assembly room: " A woman appears; it is the Duchess of Orleans. She is dressed in mourning. Her half-lifted veil allows one to see her face, marked by an emotion and a sadness which heighten its youth and beauty. Her pale cheeks bear traces of a widow's tears and a mother's anxieties. It is impossible for a man's eyes to rest upon those features without emotion. All resentment against the monarchy evaporates in the heart. The blue eyes of the Princess turn hither and thither in the void which has dazzled them for a moment, to ask assistance from every glance she meets. Her frail and slender figure inclines toward the tumultuous applause which greets her. A faint red, the glimmer of hope amid disaster, of joy in sadness, colors her cheeks.

Her grateful smile shines through her tears. It is plain that she feels herself surrounded by friends. With her right hand she holds the young King, who stumbles up the steps, and with her left, her other son, the little Duke de Chartres, — children for whom their own catastrophe is a spectacle. They both wear short jackets of black cloth, over which fall white collarettes; they are living Van Dyck portraits, issuing from the picture of the children of Charles I."

All the partisans of the Duchess of Orleans feel confidence in M. de Lamartine. He, the quondam body-guard of royalty, the knightly poet, who testified so much enthusiasm for the Princess, who, in spite of her, had in 1842 so vigorously supported her maternal right to the regency; he, the bard of women, is doubtless about to lift his voice for the noble widow of the unfortunate Duke of Orleans, for the courageous mother of an infant king.

The danger is growing greater very minute. The Chamber is not yet completely invaded by the multitude. But men, armed and unarmed, are coming into the lobbies, and the semicircle also. They are like the first wavelets of the advancing tide, which is going to submerge everything. M. de Tocqueville thinks that Lamartine is the only man who can set a barrier to it, and, perceiving him standing by his bench, he makes his way thither through the crowd. "We are being ruined," he says to him in a hasty whisper; "no one but you can get a hearing at this supreme moment; go up into the tribune and make a speech." Lamartine seems absorbed in contemplation. He merely points toward the Princess and says: "I will not speak while that woman and that child are there." That woman and that child, in fact, touch him with remorse. Perhaps he is already reproaching himself with having abandoned the cause of the widow and the orphan.

While M. Marie, from the tribune, is vainly trying to make himself heard, M. de Lamartine says, from his place: "I ask the President to suspend the session on account of the respect inspired by the presence among the national representatives of the august Princess now before us."

Deceived by this apparently sympathetic language, the President does not see the trap laid for him, and he announces that the Chamber is about to suspend its session until Madame the Duchess of Orleans and the new King shall have withdrawn.

Several deputies approach the Duchess and seem trying to induce her to withdraw. The Duchess refuses, and keeps her place.

M. Lherbette, addressing the President. — "Madame the Duchess of Orleans wishes to remain here."

The President. — "Every one, no matter what his opinions may be, must understand that in presence of an august princess and her son silence and respect are due from all." (*Various noises.*)

The Duchess and her sons remain standing in the semicircle, surrounded by many deputies.

General Oudinot. — "I request a moment's attention from the Chamber. [*Hear! hear!*] An appeal has been made to all generous sentiments. You have been told that the Princess has traversed the Tuileries and the Place de la Concorde, afoot and alone, with her children, amid public acclamations. If she desires to withdraw, let the exits be opened for her, and our respect surround her as she was just now surrounded by the respect of the city of Paris. Let us accompany her wherever she wishes to go. If she asks to remain in this hall, let her stay, and she will be in the right; for she will be protected by our devotion." (*Very good!*)

The President. — "The first measure to adopt is to invite all persons unconnected with the Chamber to leave the hall. [*No! no! in the lobbies.*] The Chamber cannot deliberate. Gentlemen, out of respect for the Chamber and the Constitution, will you be kind enough to retire?" (*No! no!*)

The tide rises incessantly. The noble woman defends herself against it, inch by inch. She withdraws only because her children would be stifled should she remain where she is. Preceded by the Duke de Nemours and followed by the Count de Paris and the Duke de Chartres, she ascends the steps of the hall through the centre lobby, which leads to the door underneath the clock. But she is absolutely bent on remaining in the hall. On reaching the back benches of the left centre, she seats herself, with her sons and the Duke de Nemours, amidst the acclamations of nearly the whole Chamber.

M. de Lamartine already feels a certain satisfaction. Though the Princess has not quitted the hall, she is at all events no longer at the foot of the tribune, and when he begins to speak this woman will not be close to him.

The number of National Guards and persons unconnected with the Chamber constantly increases. The man who is incurring the greatest danger is the Duke de Nemours. Against him the insurgents have a special grudge, because they fear him more than any one else. His uniform attracts attention. The Prince remains unmoved. Convinced that his post is beside his sister-in-law, he is determined not to leave her upon any pretext. As M. de Lamartine has written, "the countenance of this Prince, ennobled by misfortune, breathes the courageous but modest satisfaction of a duty fulfilled at the risk of his ambition and his life."

M. Marie. — "Gentlemen, in the existing condition of Paris, you have not a moment to lose before taking measures which will be authoritative as soon as they are announced. . . . The regency of Madame the Duchess of Orleans has just been proclaimed. You have a law which appoints the Duke de Nemours regent. You cannot create a regency to-day, for it is certain that you must obey the law. Nevertheless, we must consider; we need, in the first place, an imposing government at the head of the capital, as well as at the head of the whole kingdom. I ask that a provisional government be constituted." (*Bravos in the galleries.*)

M. Crémieux. — "At such a moment it is impossible that all should agree on proclaiming Madame the Duchess of Orleans regent and the Count de Paris king; the population cannot immediately accept this proposition. We were very much hurried in 1830, and here we are, in 1848, obliged to begin over again [*bravo! bravo!*]. Gentlemen, we will not hurry ourselves in 1848; we will proceed regularly, legally, firmly. As for myself, I declare that I have the profoundest respect for Madame the Duchess of Orleans [*bravo! bravo! these bravos are stifled by shouts and the tumult in the galleries*], and I but just now had the melancholy honor of conducting the royal family to the carriages which are taking them on their journey; I have not failed in this duty, and, I will add, that all along the route of the unhappy King and his unhappy family the people received them perfectly well. [*Tumultuous murmurs.*] But now, gentlemen, the generality of the Parisian population, the loyal National Guard, have manifested their legal opinion. . . . Let us appoint a provisional government. . . . We have arrived to-day at what the Revolution of July ought to give us; let us try to profit by events and not leave to our sons the task of renewing that Revolution." (*Approbation on the left and in the galleries. This intervention of the galleries is not repressed. No order is given to empty them. No injunction to the ushers! No intervention from the questors.*)

M. de Genoude (*legitimist, advocate of the appeal to the people*). — "You can create neither a provisional government nor a regency. The nation must be convoked. You have something to do. Nothing exists without the consent of the people. It is just as it was in 1830, you have not appealed to the nation; you see what has happened to you; it will be the same thing again, and you will see greater troubles arise than those you are producing now."

M. Odilon Barrot, impatiently awaited by the Princess and the Chamber, at last comes into the hall. He may be reproached with having been the dupe of many illusions, but he cannot be accused of having failed in loyalty, devotion, and courage. He has multiplied himself since morning in his efforts to save the dynasty of July. He has made an excursion over the boulevards to preach pacification, even in the midst of the barricades. He has been to take possession of the Ministry of the Interior, left vacant by the departure of Count Duchâtel. He arrived there with MM. Garnier-Pagès, Havin, Abbatucci, Biesta, Pagnerre, and Degouve-Denuncques, either in his carriage or on the outside of it, all of whom called themselves partisans of the Duchess of Orleans, and added that, if they had the Republic in their hands, they would take good care not to open them. From there he hastened to the Tuileries to look for the Princess, and, not finding her, he returned to the Ministry of the Interior, whence, in order to reassure the departments, he issued telegrams announcing that "order, momentarily disturbed in Paris, is about to be restored, thanks to the concurrence of all good citizens." Doubtless he would have done better to go at once to the Chamber of Deputies. But he did not even yet know that the Duchess of Orleans was there, and, in the beginning, no one suspected the importance which the Chamber would have in the course of the day. Somebody having said to M. de Beaumont, who had come from the Ministry of the Interior with M. Barrot, "Have you taken any precautions for the defence of the Chamber?" M. de Beaumont had replied: "Who thinks about the Chamber? Of what use can it be, and what harm can it do in this state of affairs?" M. de Beaumont was wrong. As M. de Tocqueville has remarked, "he forgot that it is especially in times of revolution that the least organs of legal right, and still more the exterior objects themselves which recall men's minds to the idea of law, assume the greatest importance; for it is principally in the midst of this anarchy and universal disturbance that people feel the necessity of recurring to some emblem of tradition and authority, in order to save what remains of a half-destroyed constitution or to complete its destruction. If the deputies could have proclaimed the regency, perhaps it might in the end have prevailed, notwithstanding their unpopularity; and, on the other hand, it cannot be denied that the

Provisional Government owed much to the chance which gave it birth inside the four walls so long inhabited by the national representatives."

Here is M. Barrot in the hall. He has already mounted some of the steps of the stairway leading to the tribune, when a number of his friends drag him almost by force into a committee room, where there are some republicans, among others MM. Arago, Bastide, and Clément Thomas.

"What are you going to do, M. Barrot?" they say to him.

"Proclaim, this very instant, the accession of the Count de Paris and the regency of his mother."

"It is too late; things have been moving; they have outstripped the regency; a provisional government has been proposed already. Support that proposition, be a part of the government; you will have influence there."

"What you propose is a folly and a crime! Don't you see that to create a provisional government is to begin a revolution and plunge France into the horrors of civil war? I would far rather die than take part in it."

"But you are refusing to recognize the rights of the sovereign people."

"The real people, those who desired and still desire the establishment of July, will commend me."

M. Barrot, instead of lingering in the room, has not even sat down there. Throwing off the hands which seek to retain him, he hastily re-enters the hall. He is in the tribune.

M. Barrot.— (*Hear! hear!*) "Gentlemen, never have we had more need of coolness and prudence. I hope you may all be united in the same sentiment, that of saving the country from the most detestable of all plagues, civil war. [*Very good!*] Nations do not die, it is true, but they may be weakened by intestine convulsions, and France has never had more need of preserving all her force and grandeur. Our duty is clearly defined; fortunately, it has that simplicity which impresses a whole nation; it appeals to its most generous, most innate sentiments, — its courage and its honor! The crown of July rests henceforward on the head of a woman and a child." (*Hearty applause from the centre.*)

The Duchess rises and salutes the Assembly. She invites the Count de Paris to imitate her, and he does so. M. Barrot pauses, the instant that he sees her rising, in order that she may speak, but those who are beside her make her resume her seat.

M. Barrot. — "It is in the name of liberty, of order, and, above all, in order to preserve our union amidst such difficult circumstances, that I ask my country to rally around this woman and this child, noble representatives of the Revolution of July. The more grandeur and generosity there is in thus protecting and elevating purity and innocence, the more will France devote itself courageously to the task. For my part, I shall be happy to devote every faculty I possess to the triumph of this cause; for it is that of liberty."

The Marquis de La Rochejaquelein. — "I ask leave to speak."

M. Barrot. — "Can it be by any chance that any one should pretend to call again in question what we decided by the Revolution of July? [*Very good!*] Gentlemen, I admit that the circumstance is difficult, but there are such elements of grandeur, generosity, and good sense in this country, that I am convinced it is only necessary to appeal to them in order to induce the whole population to rise and salute its standard. [*Yes! yes!*] If there is any one here who would have the courage to assume the responsibility of civil war, I declare him guilty, in the highest degree, toward liberty, France, and the whole world. For my part, I cannot take that responsibility. The regency of the Duchess of Orleans, a ministry representing the most approved opinions, will give a fuller guarantee to liberty than any other combination. Then the country can be consulted, and will give its decision freely and without being led astray by rival pretensions, from which war would inevitably result."

M. Barrot comes down from the platform and regains his seat. The republicans, feeling themselves in a minority, go out to look for reinforcements.

M. de La Rochejaquelein. — "Gentlemen, perhaps it properly belongs to those who in the past have always served the kings to talk now of the country and the people. [*Several voices: Very good! very good!*] To-day, you are nothing here; you are no longer anything!" (*From the centre: What's that! what's that!*)

M. de Morny. — "We cannot accept that."

The President. — "I call you to order."

M. de La Rochejaquelein. — "Allow me to speak. When I said you were nothing, I truly did not expect to raise a storm. It is not I, a deputy, who will tell you that the Chamber of Deputies exists no longer as a Chamber. The nation must be convoked, and then . . . ."

At this moment the Chamber is invaded.

CHAPTER XXVII

THE INVASION OF THE CHAMBER

A CROWD of armed men, National Guards and workmen, make an irruption into the hall and even reach the semicircle. They are some insurgents, who, after having devastated the palace of the Tuileries, ran about shouting: "Down with the regency! Put the deposition to vote! No more Bourbons! Down with the traitors! Down with the Chamber!" The troops on the Place de la Concorde, commanded by Generals Ruhlières and Bedeau, allowed them to pass, in spite of the orders sent to the two generals by the Duke de Nemours. A violent commotion ensues in the Assembly. The greater part of the members occupying seats in the centre retreat to the upper benches. One of the invaders, M. Dumoulin, commander of the Hôtel-de-Ville in 1830, and a known Bonapartist, climbs up to the tribune and deposits on the marble the staff of a flag. "The people," he cries, "have reconquered their liberty and independence to-day, as they did in 1830. The throne has just been broken in the Tuileries, and thrown out of the window." M. Ledru-

Rollin and M. de Lamartine both ascend the tribune at the same time. The commotion in the hall increases, and M. de Lamartine finds great difficulty in making himself heard. "Better acquainted than I was with his intentions," M. Barrot has written, "the republicans knew beforehand what he was about to say; for me, remaining at the foot of the tribune, I had, I confess, a moment of complete illusion; I remembered his speech in favor of the regency of the Duchess of Orleans, and I fancied that, finding an occasion to draw the conclusions from that speech, he was naturally going to seize it, and for once, at least, show himself consistent." President Sauzet was under the same illusion. "One hope remained to me," he has said in his account of the session; "M. de Lamartine had asked permission to speak. . . . The idea of seeing this poetic and chivalrous nature spurning with his foot the suppliant mother and the royal child, besieged in the last asylum offered by the devotion of the national representatives; of hearing that noble and harmonious voice employed as the organ, and almost the herald, of these lawless bands, who simultaneously applauded the orator, insulted his colleagues, and menaced the Assembly with their weapons,— such an idea had not occurred to M. de Lamartine's most inveterate enemies."

The illustrious poet, in his *Histoire de la Révolution de 1848*, has himself worded the speech which he might have addressed to the Duchess of Orleans and her sons. "'Stand up!' he might have said to them. 'You are the widow of that Duke of Orleans whose death and memory the people have crowned in you! You are the children deprived of that father and adopted by the nation! You are the innocent victims of the faults of the throne, the guests and suppliants of the people! You are escaping from the throne in a revolution! This revolution is just; it is generous; it is French. It does not fight with women and children; it does not inherit from widows and orphans; it does not despoil its prisoners and its guests. Go and reign! It restores to you through compassion the throne forfeited by faults of which you are merely the victims. The ministers of your grandfather have squandered your inheritance; the people restore it to you, it adopts you, it will itself be your ancestor. You had only a prince for a tutor; you will have a mother and a nation.'" M. de Lamartine has claimed that if he had delivered such a speech, he could have had the regency proclaimed and brought back the Duchess and her sons in triumph to the Tuileries. That, doubtless, is an error of his fertile imagination. The crowd applauded him only because he was its tool.

Nevertheless, the opening of his discourse raised some expectations in the partisans of the Duchess. "Gentlemen," said he, "I share as profoundly as any one among you the double sentiment which has just agitated this assembly on beholding one of the most touching spectacles which human annals can present, that of an august princess defending herself, along with her innocent son, and coming from the midst of a deserted palace to throw herself into the midst of the representatives of the people." The Duchess and her sons were still on the upper row of benches opposite the tribune. As their friends exhibited some satisfaction in listening to the poet's exordium, the Duchess, with a sweet but melancholy smile, indicated by a slight movement of the finger that she did not share their illusion.

M. de Lamartine made haste to reassure the republicans. "Gentlemen," said he, "if I share the emotion inspired by the spectacle of the greatest human catastrophes; if I share the respect which animates every man in this hall, no matter what his opinions may be, I do not less share your respect for that glorious people which for three days has been striving to chastise a perfidious government, and to reestablish the empire of order and liberty on a basis that shall henceforth be immovable. I ask, in right of the public peace, in right of the blood that has flowed, in right of this people, famished by the glorious task it has been accomplishing for three days, I ask that a provisional government be instituted,—a government which prejudges nothing, neither our resentments nor our rages, our rights nor our sympathies,—with that definitive government which it shall please the country to give itself when it shall have been consulted." The crowd applauded. "The names," it shouted, "the names of the members of the provisional government!" M. de Lamartine resumed: "Wait! The mission of this provisional government, in my view, will be: 1. To establish the indispensable truce, the public peace between citizens; 2. to prepare instantly the necessary measures for convoking the whole country, all whose title as men carries with it the rights of citizenship. One last word: The powers which have succeeded each other for fifty years . . ." At the very moment when the orator is beginning this sentence, a violent knocking is heard outside of the doors of one of the public galleries. The doors speedily yield to blows from the butt-end of muskets. Men of the people, mingled with National Guards, penetrate into all the galleries, shouting: "Down with the Chamber! No deputies!" A rioter, setting his foot on the inner cornice, turns his musket toward President Sauzet and M. de Lamartine, whose speech has just been interrupted by the tumult. Other insurgents make a show of aiming at members of the Assembly. Some one cries: "Don't fire! It is M. de Lamartine who is speaking." Yielding to the entreaties of his comrades, the man who is aiming at the orator raises his musket, but the confusion becomes indescribable. Threatening vociferations, furiously demanding the proclamation of the provisional government, make one dread that a bloody affray may break out at any moment if the President persists in not putting this revolutionary proposition to vote.

Listen to an eyewitness, M. de Tocqueville: "This was the time when all imaginations were bedaubed by the gross colors which Lamartine had just been spreading over his *Girondins*. The men of the first Revolution were living in all minds, their acts and words were present to all memories. All that I saw on that day bore the visible imprint of those souvenirs; it always seemed to me that they were imitating the French Revolution rather than continuing it."

The President, still in his chair, rings his bell violently and calls for silence. Vain efforts! The tumult merely redoubles. Thereupon, M. Sauzet, after having said, "Since I cannot obtain silence, I declare the session adjourned," leaves the chair. The other officials leave the hall with him, through a private door behind the tribune, and are followed by a majority of the deputies. The crowd loll on the centre benches, shouting: "Take the traitors' places!" The insurgents level their muskets this way and that, until they catch sight of the Duchess of Orleans and her sons at the head of the upper benches of the semicircle. Between this group and the balls there is nothing except a number of loyal deputies, who make a rampart of their bodies for the Princess and the two young princes. "What do you advise me to do?" says the Princess, still calm in this supreme crisis. Some one answers: "Madame, the deputies are no longer here, it is necessary to go to the Presidency to rally the Chamber."

"But how am I to get there?" she returns. To retreat through a crowd which howls and threatens, is both difficult and dangerous. Above the benches of the deputies there is a circular lobby provided with several doors, which open upon as many staircases, conducting to the lower corridor of the hall. The Duchess, pushed with her sons and the Duke de Nemours toward the door over the benches of the extreme left, takes staircase A, which ends in a dark and narrow little lobby, closed by a glass door, near the Salle des Pas-Perdus. The throng is so compact, the crowd so tumultuous, that, before she reaches the lobby, the Duchess is violently separated from her children, whom she was holding by the hand. Thrown down, picked up again, dragged this way and that, calling on his mother with shrieks of terror, the Count de Paris is rescued only by the energetic intervention of Usher Desportes, but he remains separated from his mother, whose uneasiness and anguish are at their height. M. César Lipmann, brother of the usher of that name, carries the Duke de Chartres in his arms away from the conference hall. M. Dupin runs before him and opens the doors which lead through this hall and the cloak-room, to the staircase running not only down into the rue de Bourgogne, but up into the servants' apartments, one of which is occupied by Usher Lipmann. In this the young Prince is set down, by the brother of this usher. At the same time the Duchess, in the lobby near the Salle des Pas-Perdus, is crushed, bruised against the walls, and thrown against the glass door. One pane breaks into splinters. The door does not yield for all that; the stronger the pressure is, the more the leaf resists, since it opens from without. This obstacle is at last overcome. The Duchess passes through the door, crosses the Salle des Pas-Perdus, and arrives at the Presidency, but without her children, for whom she pitifully entreats.

A few minutes later, the Count de Paris is carried into the Salle des Pas-Perdus. Two National Guards jump from the third window of this hall into the Presidency garden, receive the child in their arms, run toward the first window on the ground-floor of the house, break a pane, and enter the room where the Duchess of Orleans is, and give her back her eldest son, safe and sound. But what has become of the Duke de Chartres? The unhappy mother does not know, even at the moment when, in order to secure her from some sudden attack, they force her, as quickly as possible, into a carriage which takes her and the Count de Paris to the Hôtel des Invalides.

At the same time, the Duke de Nemours, who has just shown so much devotion to his sister-in-law and incurred the greatest dangers, is drawn into the Salle des Pas-Perdus; there, behind a rampart of loyal breasts, he takes off the general's uniform, which he could not have retained without certain death, and is then led into a room usually occupied by the committee on the budget. Here he puts on the uniform of a private of the National Guard, in which he is not recognized when he goes out of the Presidency, mixes with a group of National Guards, and goes to the Hôtel des Invalides, to rejoin the Duchess of Orleans and the Count de Paris, of the triumph of whose cause he does not even yet despair.

Now let us see what has happened in the session-room of the Chamber since the deputies left the place free to the multitude.

CHAPTER XXVIII

THE PROVISIONAL GOVERNMENT

THERE is no longer a session in the Chamber, but a club, a popular assembly, a sort of forum of the riot, a violent tumult, an indescribable mob. All the deputies have disappeared except a dozen or so belonging to the extreme left, who are making terms with the invaders. The populace is mistress. M. Dupont (de l'Eure), a veteran of liberalism, is called on to take the President's chair. He does so, in order to give an appearance of deliberation to the fantasies of the crowd. Among the innumerable persons in the semicircle, one notes the celebrated novelist Alexandre Dumas and two actors, Bocage and Raucourt. M. de Lamartine is still on the platform, between two insurgents who brandish flags. From all sides, men are shouting for a vote on the provisional government. Then M. de Lamartine manages to get this remark listened to: "Gentlemen, the proposition which has been made, and which you have consecrated by your acclamations to this tribune, is accomplished. A provisional government is about to be proclaimed by name."

M. Dupont (de l'Eure). — "Here are the names: Arago, Lamartine, Dupont (de l'Eure), Crémieux." (*Noise and disturbance.*)

M. de Lamartine. — "Silence, gentlemen! if you wish the members of the provisional government to accept the mission you have confided to them, it is at least necessary that it should be proclaimed. Our honorable friend cannot make himself heard amidst this noise."

A citizen. — "Make them understand that the people will not have a monarchy. The Republic!"

Several voices. — "Let us deliberate immediately."

Other voices. — "Sitting! Sitting! Sit down! Let us take the traitors' places."

Other voices. — "The bribe-takers!"

Still other voices. — "The pot-bellies!"[1]

At this moment, some men of the people, students, pupils of the Polytechnic School and National Guards, who, until now, have been standing in the semicircle or close against the steps of the tribune and the committee room, sit down, laughing and shouting, on the benches of the ministry and the deputies of the centre, as if to proceed to a regular debate.

A citizen (shaking a flag). — "No more Bourbons! The Republic!"

A man of the people. — "Down with the Bourbons! the young as well as the old!"

---

[1] *Des ventrus!* a sneering title for the members of the centre in a legislative body,

Another man of the people. — "Ah! the pretty young ones!"

The Marquis de La Rochejaquelein. — "They did not steal it. It is a loan returned."

A voice. — "A moment of silence; if not, we shall come to nothing."

Another voice. — "We demand that the Republic shall be proclaimed."

M. Dupont (de l'Eure) reads the following names, which are repeated in a loud voice by several reporters and seem to be accepted by the majority of the crowd: Lamartine, Ledru-Rollin, Arago, Dupont (de l'Eure), Marie.

A voice. — "The members of the provisional government must cry: 'Long live the Republic!' before being nominated and accepted."

Another voice. — "The provisional government must be conducted to the Hôtel-de-Ville. We want a prudent, moderate government; no bloodshed, but we will have the Republic."

M. Bocage. — "To the Hôtel-de-Ville, Lamartine at the head!"

M. de Lamartine, deferring to this injunction, leaves the hall with M. Dupont (de l'Eure), and a great part of the crowd. The other part remains scattered about the benches of the Chamber, in the semicircle, and the lobbies. The tumult continues. M. Ledru-Rollin, already, perhaps, the rival of M. de Lamartine, had determined to remain behind him in the hall so that he also might play a part.

"Citizens," says he, "you comprehend that you are performing a very serious action in nominating a provisional government."

Different voices. — "We don't want one! — Yes! yes! We must have one!"

M. Ledru-Rollin. — "We are going to do something serious. Objections have been made already. A provisional government cannot be nominated lightly. Permit me to read you the names which seem to have been proclaimed by the majority. [*Silence! hear! hear!*] Now, as I read the names, accordingly as they please or displease you, you will cry out, yes or no [*Very good! Hear!*], and to do things in an official way, I beg the stenographers of the *Moniteur* to take down the names as I pronounce them, because we cannot present to France names which have not been approved by you. I read: Dupont (de l'Eure) [*Yes! yes!*], Arago [*Yes! yes!*], Lamartine [*Yes! yes!*], Ledru-Rollin [*Yes! yes!*], Garnier-Pagès [*Yes! yes! no!*], Crémieux." (*Yes! yes!*)

A voice (in the crowd). — "Crémieux, yes, but not Garnier-Pagès." (*Yes! yes! No! He is dead, the good man!*)

Other voices. — "Keep still! Order!"

Ledru-Rollin. — "Let those who are unwilling, raise their hands. [*No! no! Yes! yes!*] I wish to add one word. Permit me, gentlemen! The provisional government which has just been nominated has great, has immense, duties to fulfil. We are about to raise the session in order to repair to the centre of government and take all necessary measures to put a stop to bloodshed, so that the rights of the people may be consecrated."

Numerous voices. — "Yes! yes! to the Hôtel-de-Ville."

A pupil of the Polytechnic School. — "Not one of the members of your provisional government wants the Republic. We shall be betrayed as we were in 1830."

Several voices. — "Long live the Republic! Long live Ledru-Rollin! To the Hôtel-de-Ville!"

A young man. — "The centre of government is not at the Hôtel-de-Ville; it is here."

The election of the members of the provisional government — this nomination by auction, as M. Dupin has said — being accomplished, M. Ledru-Rollin thinks it useless to remain in the hall any longer, and he also repairs to the Hôtel-de-Ville. M. de Lamartine will be Minister of Foreign Affairs, but he will be Minister of the Interior.

The crowd decreases after his departure, but the tumult and the vociferations still continue.

A young man (in the tribune). — "No more civil list!"

Another. — "No more royalty!"

Some one directs the attention of the crowd to the large picture hung over the table behind the presidential chair. It represents King Louis Philippe taking the oath of royalty to the Charter. "It must be destroyed!" shouts somebody. Men standing on the table make ready to lacerate it with sabres. A workman, carrying a musket, who is in the semicircle, cries: "Wait! I am going to fire on Louis Philippe." Two musket-shots are heard. Another workman springs up the tribune steps, and says: "Respect the monuments! respect the properties! Why should we destroy? Why fire muskets at this picture? We have shown that the people must not be maltreated; now let us show that the people know how to respect monuments and honor their own victory!" These words are greeted with applause, and a crowd gathers round the man who has just uttered them, to ask his name. He calls himself Theodore Six, a working upholsterer. Then the hall is emptied. It is four o'clock in the afternoon.

M. de Tocqueville relates in his *Souvenirs* that at the moment when M. Ledru-Rollin had just quitted the hall, he also left the Chamber; but, unwilling to be dragged along by the crowd that was marching toward the Hôtel-de-Ville, he took a different road, and began to descend the staircase leading to the inner court of the Palais-Bourbon. Then he beheld coming toward him a column of armed National Guards, who ran up the same staircase, with fixed bayonets. Two men in citizen's dress appeared to be leading them, shouting lustily: "Long live the Duchess of Orleans! Long live the regency!" One of these was General Oudinot and the other M. Andryane, the prisoner of Spielberg, the author of memoirs resembling those of Silvio Pellico. Seizing M. de Tocqueville by the arm, M. Andryane said to him: "Sir, you must join us in order to rescue the Duchess of Orleans and save the monarchy." "The intention is good," responded M. de Tocqueville, "but you come too late; the Duchess of Orleans has vanished, and the Chamber has dispersed." And, in his account, he adds: "Where was this mettlesome defender of the monarchy that same evening? In M. Ledru-Rollin's Cabinet, administering, in the name of the Republic, as Secretary-General of the Ministry of the Interior. . . . To please the column he was leading, I joined it, although I hoped nothing from its efforts. Obeying, mechanically, the movement that had been given it, it advanced as far as the doors of the Chamber; there, the men composing it saw what had just taken place; they turned back on themselves for a moment, and then disbanded in all directions. Half an hour earlier, this handful of National Guards might have changed the destinies of France, as they did on the following 15th of May. I allowed this new crowd to slip past me, and then resumed, alone and very thoughtful, the road to my own house, not without turning a last look toward that now silent and deserted hall, where, for the last nine years, I had listened to so many eloquent and ineffectual speeches."

The general sentiment was one of stupefaction. Listen to a legitimist deputy, Count de Falloux. "I reached the Place du Palais-Bourbon," he says, "by the little door opening on the rue de Bourgogne. Everything there was as quiet as usual. I had walked only a few steps when I was accosted by the Marquis de Gontaut Saint-Blancard. 'Well! well!' said he, briskly, 'what is going on?' 'A revolution is going on,' said I, 'or, rather, a revolution has just gone on toward the Hôtel-de-Ville;'—and I gave him, in a few words, the details of our session. While still listening to me, he said: 'But I can't realize it!' I, who had just seen it, I could not either!"

At the same time, M. de Lamartine, cheered by the crowd, was walking from the Chamber of Deputies to the Hôtel-de-Ville. On the way he stopped in front of the cavalry barracks on the quay d'Orsay. The dragoons had closed the gate of it. "Soldiers," the poet said to them, "a glass of wine!" The glass was brought to him. "Friends," he cried, making an allusion to the different banquets which had been the prelude to this *journée*, "friends, this is the banquet. Let the people and the soldiers fraternize in it with me." And he drank. The Revolution was accomplished.

Less than four months later,—May 15,—the dragoons of the 2d regiment, having received the necessary orders, will issue from these very barracks of the quay d'Orsay, to drive out the rioters who have invaded the Chamber.

CHAPTER XXIX

THE SACK OF THE TUILERIES

AT the moment when the Place du Carrousel and the approaches to the Tuileries had been evacuated by the troops, the court of the château was almost entirely empty. But it soon began to fill up with individuals thoroughly amazed at the facility with which their ingress was effected. They entered the palace without its occurring to any one to offer them the least resistance. Among them were two men of letters who have become famous, Gustave Flaubert and Maxime du Camp. The latter shall describe the scene: "In a dining-room, lighted from the garden and situated on the ground-floor, we saw a table set; on the large, white table-cloth were bowls of milk, silver coffee-pots, with the King's monogram, and rolls in baskets. Some of the men sat down and began eating; one of them cried: 'This is our reform banquet.' The joke took, and caused a good deal of laughter. We went up to the first floor; I looked at the time by a clock placed on a very beautiful mantelpiece of sea-green marble incrusted with cameos; it was ten minutes past one." There were no great excesses committed at this beginning of the invasion. Curiosity was more keen than anger. But one portrait, that of Marshal Bugeaud, was slashed in the hall of the Marshals. The men put their bayonets back into the scabbards lest they might break the chandeliers or tear the hangings. There were not more than two hundred invaders in the apartments. At this moment everything was still respected, except the throne. A rather well-dressed man ascended the steps of it, sat down, and gravely saluted the crowd. "Gentlemen," said he, "it is always with a new pleasure that I find myself among you." This was a phrase which had frequently served as exordium to the speech from the throne, and the petty journals were in the habit of deriding it. There was a burst of laughter.

The iconoclasts, the vandals, were approaching. The lanes which then surrounded the Palais-Royal and did not disappear until the completion of the Louvre by Napoleon III., vomited forth in an instant a crowd of prostitutes and pillagers, who rushed upon the palace as their prey. Some insurgents who had been fighting at the water château in the Place du Palais-Royal also came running up.

The populace first invaded the apartments of Madame Adelaide, on the ground-floor, which had been closed ever since the death of that Princess. The great shutters were torn open, and through the vast windows, whose panes flew into splinters, the motley crowd might be seen, when the noise of platoon firing was suddenly heard. It was a company, forgotten on the Place du Carrousel, who were discharging their muskets in the air. The crowd thought they had fallen into a snare. There was a general stampede. The invaders of the ground-floor jumped into the moats, which then bordered the château on the garden side. The same panic seized the masses who were arriving by the quay du Carrousel. They rushed madly into the Seine barges, flinging down sabres and muskets, sticks and spits in front of them. After a few minutes it was plain that there had been a false alarm, and the devastation of the château began.

The ground-floor was the first one to be pillaged, — the King's study, his bedroom, and the salons of the Queen. Then they went up to the first story. Listen once more to M. Maxime du Camp: "An enormous uproar, composed of vociferations and the clashing of arms, rose toward us; we ran to the head of the great staircase and found ourselves in presence of a mass of men, who were climbing the steps and uttering shouts of death and victory. It was a ground-swell. The balusters were giving way under the lateral pressure against them. As fast as this violent rabble could reach the landing, they precipitated themselves into the apartments. We heard several detonations; they were breaking the mirrors by firing at them. The genius of destruction, who torments children and victors, had made his entry into the palace."

The riot can finish the breakfast begun that morning by the royal family. A mass of precious objects covers the floor; broken busts, mirrors flying to pieces, torn hangings, are rolling in the dust. An urchin hoists himself up to the summit of the Horloge pavilion and tears down the flag floating over the dome of the palace. Strong hands detach the hammer from the clock. Aided by this heavy piece of iron, there are no secretaries, no commodes, no wardrobes, that cannot be broken. In the interior, vast fireplaces are fed with registers, portfolios, letters of all descriptions. In the garden, in immense brasiers underneath the casements, people are burning books and letters thrown out of the windows. Even the kitchens and cellars are invaded. Three thousand bottles of different wines are drunk, carried away, or broken.

Some one proposes that the throne shall be taken through the city, and afterwards burned on the Place de la Bastille, at the foot of the column of July. This idea is adopted with enthusiasm. Standards, dais, armchair, are carried out and piled on a cart, which, followed by an immense procession, at last reaches the revolutionary Place, where the throne is delivered to the flames.

Meanwhile the sack of the Tuileries continued. No one remained there except thieves, old-clothes dealers, and receivers of stolen goods; many honest people had been attracted by mere curiosity; others had come with the sole desire of saving as many things as possible and restoring them to the royal family.

Yet, even in the midst of the devastation, there were honorable actions. Near the apartment of the Queen there was a room which had been the studio of Princess Marie. The window, which opened on the court of the château, was ornamented with stained glass, like an oratory. On pedestals of the utmost simplicity stood the models of sculptured statues by the ideal princess, who died so young and so regretted: the *Jeanne d'Arc of Versailles*, the *Jeanne d'Arc quitting her village*, the *Angels praying*, which were executed in marble for the Saint-Ferdinand chapel, aux Ternes. All of these objects were respected; still there was one rascal who pleased himself by firing at and breaking the arm of one of the angels.

A noble homage was paid to the memory of the Duke of Orleans. Vandalism came to a halt before the apartments of this popular prince, whose tragic death had impressed the public imagination, and who might, perhaps, have been able to prevent the Revolution of February.

In his work entitled the *Dernières heures d'une Monarchie*, M. Fernand de Montréal has narrated how the apartments of the Duke and Duchess were saved from profanation. A band of insurgents, who doubtless came to do some shooting on the Place du Carrousel, arrived under the leadership of a man of colossal figure and a heavy red beard streaked with white (possibly a former combatant of July), wearing an old otter-skin cap without a visor, his arms bare, his hands blackened with powder, and carrying a musket. With his armed band he made his way to the pavilion of Marsan, just after the Duchess of Orleans had left for the Chamber of Deputies. The apartments of the Princess were still open. Those of her husband had been closed ever since July 13, 1842. The leader of the band attempted to open the Duke's door. Finding it resist, he gave it a violent blow with the butt-end of his musket, and, turning toward an old servant who had remained at his post: "Open it for us," said he; "who lived there?"

"They are the apartments of the late Duke of Orleans, which have been closed since his death."

"Silence . . . and respect, you fellows! . . . Let no one touch a thing. We are entering the rooms of the Duke of Orleans."

The windows of the cabinet of the Duke of Orleans, his bedchamber, and the large room preceding them, opened on the court of the château. The bedchamber communicated with the large salon containing Ingres' *Stratonice*, Paul Delaroche's *Meurtre du Duc de Guise*, Ary Scheffer's *Françoise de Rimini*, and the *Joseph vendu par ses frères* of Decamps. The band passed through all of these rooms without touching a single object they contained. They were affected on crossing the bedchamber of the Prince, that chamber which he left to die by a carriage accident on the road of the Révolte, near

Neuilly. The chamber had remained in the same state as on that fatal day. Even the water had not been thrown out of the basin in which he had washed his hands before starting. On the white marble of the two commodes were two hats, a black one and a white one, with gloves spread out on the brims, and a plate containing some grapes, which the Prince had seeded; in a large armchair near the mantelpiece, the *Journal des Débats* of July 13, 1842, lay open; on a bureau were pens and pencils; on the silken hangings landscapes by Huet and Corot, portraits of the Duchess of Orleans and the Count de Paris, engraved from Winterhalter's pictures; beside the unmade bed several small boxes and a trunk prepared for the journey. In the salon of the Duchess, between the bureau and the mantelpiece, there was a round table covered with books and papers. These papers were the exercises of the Count de Paris and the Duke de Chartres, translations made by them and corrected by their mother. Among the books was a volume of M. de Lamartine's *Histoire des Girondins*, with an ivory knife placed by the Duchess at the head of a chapter she was about to begin. On perceiving in the salon a life-size portrait of the Duke of Orleans, by Ingres, the leader of the band paused, and, lifting his otter-skin cap, he said: "Poor young man, go!" After this respectful visit, the apartments of the Duke were closed again.

Nor was the chapel of the château desecrated. The invaders paused on the threshold, took off their hats, and, obeying the suggestion of a pupil of the Polytechnic School, marched silently toward the altar, detached the crucifix, withdrew the sacred vessels from the tabernacle, and escorted them respectfully to the church of Saint-Roch, where they delivered them to the clergy. The time was not one of sacrilege and impiety, as in 1830.

But if religion was respected by the Revolution of 1848, with what outrages was not royalty overwhelmed! There were other devastations besides that of the Tuileries. People sacked with equal fury the former residence of the Orleans family, the cradle of the July monarchy, that once popular Palais-Royal, whence Louis Philippe had issued, July 31, 1830, cheered by the crowd, to go and seek investiture from Lafayette at the Hôtel-de-Ville. During thirty years, as prince or king, he had embellished this, his favorite residence. It became the prey of a horde of vandals. Buildings, objects of art, pictures, furniture, stables, cellars, — all were pillaged. An eyewitness, M. Maxime du Camp, has written: "We penetrated into the court of the Palais-Royal, between the Orleans gallery and the palace. People pillaged and burned. What a performance, as stupid as useless! Five large fires were kindled, and furniture, mirrors, china, all flung into them; nothing was spared. I caught sight of a silver cup adorned with antique medals of important value and great beauty. I picked it up and asked exemption for a work of art so precious on many accounts; they very briskly took aim at me, and I threw the cup into the flames. I addressed myself to a pupil of the Polytechnic School, who was promenading his elegant uniform among wide-open shirts and tattered blouses, and explained to him that there were rare pictures in the palace, signed by illustrious names, and that some effort should be made to save them from certain destruction. The poor youth listened without understanding me. Lifting his arms at last with a gesture of discouragement, he said: 'What do you want me to do about it?'" One hundred and eighty pictures from the gallery, situated in the left or Montpensier wing, were destroyed; among others: *Cardinal Richelieu disant la messe*, by Eugène Delacroix; portraits of Louis Philippe and Marie Amélie, by Gérard; *le Duc d'Orléans proclamé roi*, by Heim; *la Duchesse de Bourgogne et ses Enfants*, by Mignard; *Henri IV.*, by Parlus; *l'Hospice du Mont Saint-Gothard* and *le Duc d'Orléans passant une revue*, by Horace Vernet.

Not only did the people devastate the apartments, but they forced an entrance to the cellars; after drinking, they kindled a fire. The firemen came running up and began pumping water on the incipient fire, and even on the drinkers. "I remember," says M. Maxime du Camp, "one of the insurgents, with sleeves rolled up, drunk and staggering, who was making desperate efforts to upset the pumps; he was thrust back without too much violence, for he was armed. This completely besotted victor took a grudge against the pipes, which he whacked lustily with his sabre; but the leather pipes, inflated with water, were very unyielding; the weapon rebounded, and so well that it hit the forehead of the drunkard, who began to shout: 'The assassin!' Some of his comrades took pity on him and laid him down in a corner, where he went to sleep." In the Orleans gallery, erected on the site of the famous wooden galleries, an ambulance had been improvised, for which the cushions of the royal sofas served as a mattress, while the wounded were covered with red velvet curtains bordered with gold fringe.

The château of Neuilly was treated still worse than the Tuileries and the Palais-Royal. It was set on fire and destroyed from top to bottom. Thus disappeared that beautiful and charming residence where the royal family so delighted to repose, where the young princes had passed such pleasant hours, and which the companion of their sports, Alfred de Musset, has celebrated in his stanzas on the Thirteenth of July.

"Neuilly! charmant séjour, triste et doux souvenir !
Illusions d'enfants, à jamais envolées !
Lorsqu'au seuil du palais, dans les vertes allées,
La reine, en souriant, nous regardait courir,
Qui nous eût dit qu'un jour il faudrait revenir
Pour y trouver la mort et des têtes voilées ! "[1]

[1] Neuilly! charming abode, sad and sweet remembrance! — Illusions of children, forever flown! — When from the palace threshold, in the green alleys, — The smiling queen beheld us running, — Who would have told us that one day we should return, — To find death there and veiled heads!

CHAPTER XXX

THE EVENING OF FEBRUARY 24

AFTER a day so troubled and so strange, night came to overspread the city. The dominant sentiment among the population was neither joy nor anger, but surprise. M. Garnier-Pagès, a member of the provisional government, has written: "Since my reason has been conscious of itself, I have desired the Republic; but, like Paris and the entire republican party, I would have been contented, on February 23, with the fall of the ministry, the dissolution of the Chamber, and electoral and parliamentary reform. By the morning of February 24, I had accepted the deposition of the King, and the regency." A republican journal, the *National*, published this avowal in its evening issue, February 24: "Never has a revolution been so unforeseen. This morning, at seven o'clock, the call to arms of the National Guard was beaten in all the quarters. What was to be the dénouement? At that time it was impossible to conjecture." Lastly, the chief founder of the Second Republic, M. de Lamartine, has written, in his criticism of the *Histoire des*

Girondins: "Although more implicated than any one in the movements, things, and men of the Revolution of 1848, I have found it impossible to discover the least glimmer of verity, or even of probability, on the causes, acts, and plans of this resort to arms of the 22d, 23d, and 24th of February against the royalty of July. I have emerged from this historic inquiry without finding either conspiracy, plan, or leader of this inexplicable event. . . . There are events which come out of the ground, like the craters of a volcano, without having been kindled by any hand, or which come from the sky, like meteors, without any one being able to say whence they came, what they are going to strike, or where they will become extinct. The most notorious republicans have said to me: 'We came down into the street because we saw our friends there, but we do not know by whom the blaze was kindled.' There is more chance than people think for in revolutions; they have more mysteries than secrets."

Stupefied with their victory, in the evening of February 24 the republicans feared that royalty would take its revenge the following day. The partisans of Louis Philippe thought themselves the sport of a dream, an hallucination, and could not become accustomed to the idea that a throne which had appeared so firm but a few hours before, could have fallen to pieces so easily and quickly. Never had any change of scene been so rapid, never any catastrophe so startling. No one knew what had become of the King. It was known that he had gone in the direction of Saint-Cloud. But had he stayed there? Would he concentrate around him the troops that still remained faithful? Was the army about to return and take the offensive? Would the provinces accept the accomplished facts?

According to M. Maxime du Camp, "there was profound stupor in the sane and industrious portion of the Parisian population, and many believed that the National Guards, on coming to themselves after an unheard-of error, would spontaneously reunite for the purpose of going to meet Louis Philippe, who was said to have withdrawn to the environs of Paris."

The fate of the Duchess of Orleans was likewise veiled in mystery. It was not known that on leaving the Chamber of Deputies she had betaken herself to the Hôtel des Invalides, where she hoped at least for a temporary asylum in which she could deliberate on the part that now remained for her to take. Having found a carriage at the door of the presidency of the Chamber, she had entered it with the Count de Paris and two National Guards. M. de Lasteyrie, on the seat, had taken the reins from the coachman, in order to hasten the departure. The Marquis de Mornay, who followed them afoot and running, arrived at the gate of the Invalides almost as soon as the carriage. The Duchess went hastily upstairs to the apartment of the governor, Marshal Molitor, who, being ill, was unable to leave his chamber. Having only a few old soldiers at his disposal, he feared lest these veterans might refuse obedience to persons whom they did not know. "Let orders be given in my name," said the Duchess; and as the Marshal said he was unable to protect her: "No matter," she exclaimed, "this is a good place to die in, if we have no morrow; to stay in, if we cannot defend ourselves." On learning that the riot was drawing nearer, she had not a moment of weakness. "Is there any one here," said she, "who advises me to remain? So long as there is one person, only one, who is of that opinion, I shall stay. I care more for my son's life than for the Crown; but if his life is necessary to France, a king, even a king but nine years old, should know how to die."

At six o'clock in the evening, M. Odilon Barrot arrived at the Invalides. He briefly described the situation to the Duchess. "All means of resistance," said he, "fail us at the same time in Paris; the troops are dispersed and demoralized, the National Guard divided, and the old Invalides themselves are complaining; under such circumstances, a conflict with the advancing insurgents ought not to be risked."

"Very well," said the Princess, "what is to be done?"

"Leave Paris for a time, and yet stay within reach of what may happen; it seems to me that when the population of Paris quiets down and measures the depth of the abyss into which it is being dragged, it cannot escape a reaction. Moreover, the conquerors of to-day are divided among themselves; there is the *National* faction and the *Tribune* faction, which are fighting each other to-day and may fight again to-morrow."

The Duke de Nemours, who had rejoined his sister-in-law, was listening. He closed the interview by these words, "Very well, we must go." Some one having proposed to the Princess that she should leave the Hôtel des Invalides secretly and conceal herself in the neighborhood, so as to return there in the morning if any means of defence had been organized, she refused to expose the old soldiers to any dangers she did not share. "I will stay altogether or go altogether," said she. When they had finally persuaded her to depart, she was entreated to disguise herself. She rejected this idea with energy. "If I am taken," she cried, "I will be taken as a princess," and all she could be induced to do was to tear off the lace that covered her dress.

M. Odilon Barrot then took leave of the Duchess. "I had saluted her on her arrival in France," he has said, "when the people of Paris greeted her with enthusiastic applause, and now the same people were forcing her to flee." The Duchess was not recognized during the short passage from the Invalides to the rue de Monsieur, a transit which she made on foot, leaning on the arm of the Marquis de Mornay, Marshal Soult's son-in-law. The Count de Paris walked a few steps behind her, holding M. de

Lasteyrie's hand. The Duke de Nemours followed her to the house of the Viscount Léon de Montesquiou, son of General Anatole de Montesquiou, in the rue de Monsieur. Yielding to the urgent entreaties of the Prince, she consented to leave this house and depart from Paris without delay, but only on condition that she should await the chances of the following day in a neighboring château. "At a word," said she, as she entered the carriage, "I will return here, whether it is to-morrow or ten years from now." Some insurgents, suspecting her presence, shouted for the carriage to stop, and took aim at the driver, but he whipped up his horses, and they arrived without hindrance at the château de Bligny, belonging to the Viscount Léon de Montesquiou, and situated near Limours, in the department of Seine and Oise. As to the Duke de Nemours, he accepted the hospitality of M. Biesta, rue de Madame, and occupied the chamber in which a republican, M. Pagnerre, had sought shelter the night before.

M. Odilon Barrot returned home, "his body worn out with fatigue," as he has said himself, "his heart distressed and full of the most melancholy presentiments concerning the future of the country." He speaks with bitterness, in his Memoirs, of this Revolution, to which he had contributed without willing or knowing it: "What is to be said of these madmen, who find that the government of July had not been sufficiently legitimated by the national consent, and who, without consulting France and amidst a veritable orgy, impose on it a radical revolution entirely of their own motion? What is to be said of these lunatics, who, having a very good house, which they had founded themselves eighteen years before, and which, at most, needed only a few repairs, raze it to its foundations without so much as knowing under what roof they shall shelter themselves next day? What is to be said of these pretended liberals, who, after plotting for a simple reform, create a violent and radical revolution? What is to be said of these pretended votaries of the grand principle of national sovereignty, who violate that sovereignty with arms in their hands, and impose on a whole nation a form of government which it repels? What could result from such an orgy? The ruin of the very men who had taken part in it, or else an atrocious civil war, and, finally, military despotism. All those who promoted the Revolution on that fatal day have been disappointed in their expectations; it might justly be styled the *Day of Dupes.*"

Night had not succeeded in calming the anxieties of the population. Count d'Estournel wrote in his *Souvenirs*, in the evening of February 24: "My nephew returned from his guard at the Military School. There is no figure of speech in saying that we are over a volcano; in spite of all that could be said to them, he has seen drunken armed men penetrate into the artillery magazines, smoke there, and discharge their guns in the middle of the powder. It will be great luck if there is not some frightful explosion. Moreover, it is expected that there will be pillaging to-night. I go to the Sardinian Embassy, whose excellent hosts have given shelter to my sister-in-law. I venture into the streets, which have a less disturbed look than I should have thought possible in the evening of such a day. On the Pont Royal, a man says to me: 'I am cold, you ought to give me your cloak.' I answer: 'If you are cold, go and warm yourself; there is a good fire at the gate of the Tuileries.' They were, in fact, burning tables and chairs from the château there."

It was constantly dreaded that the lighted brasiers might communicate their flames to the incomparable museum of the Louvre, and destroy the finest masterpieces of art by a sacrilegious conflagration. Out of hatred for royalty, the rioters had conceived the idea of burning the Tuileries, as they had already burned the throne, and perhaps the act of vandalism of 1871 might have been accomplished on February 24, 1848, if some one had not conceived the ingenious notion of saving the palace of the kings by placing on it this inscription: *Hospital for invalid citizens.*

Transformed partly into a hospital, partly into a popular ball-room, the château assumed a very strange aspect that evening. More than twelve hundred individuals had installed themselves there, as in a bivouac, organizing by societies in each of the apartments. They slept in their clothes and fully armed, on the divans and carpets. Some made soup on the hearths of the marble chimneypieces. They ate off of Sevres and Dresden plates. Women, escaped from the prison of Saint-Lazare, had come to join those who were already occupying the palace as its mistresses. Lamps and chandeliers had been lighted. Dr. Véron recounts in his *Mémoires d'un Bourgeois de Paris*, "that a young man, elegantly dressed, of a great name,— a name especially celebrated in all the historic annals of the close of the eighteenth century, and the beginning of the nineteenth,— was at the piano, and played by turns, to the applause of this drunken crowd, the *Marseillaise*, galops, and polkas. The entire feminine personnel of the squares and streets had seized the robes of princesses, ladies of honor, and of the Queen herself; they cut off the corsages of these, threw them in the fire, and secreted magnificent skirts of silk and velvet under the tatters they wore on coming out of prison." Comical sights and dismal ones were blent together. In the apartments of the princes a caged paroquet had been found, which said in the most distinct manner: "Down with Guizot!" This opposition bird had an immense success. It was gorged with sugar and dainties. Some pretended that Prince de Joinville had been its political instructor.

On this boisterous evening the Hôtel-de-Ville presented a not less animated appearance than the Tuileries. An immense crowd encumbered courts and stairways, halls and lobbies. As has been said by M. de Lamartine: "The flood of the daytime had tossed up and the night had left at the Hôtel-de-Ville a part of that scum of the vicious population of great capitals which commotions stir up and keep afloat on the surface for several days, until it falls back into its native sewers. . . . Fanaticism, delirium, fever, drunkenness, uttered at random sinister or absurd notions, caught up here and there by confused acclamations, only to sink down under the disgust of the multitude, which treated them with horror or contempt at the suggestion of a good citizen."

According to one of them, M. Garnier-Pagès, the members of the provisional government had great difficulty, amidst all this agitation, in obtaining a little bread and cheese; all they had to drink was water; a broken sugar bowl served as a goblet for each and all of them. And yet the men who were making this frugal repast had already more courtiers than a king. The multitude of solicitors was at their heels. Power, born but a few hours since, had already made many malcontents. Plaints and recriminations were beginning. The most violent passions — hatred, anger, ambition — were boiling at the Hôtel-de-Ville as in a caldron. Night came at last, to give repose to the population of Paris. But the founders of the Second Republic took no time for sleep. They were making appointments, drawing up proclamations, organizing a government, with dizzying rapidity.

CHAPTER XXXI

DREUX

WE left the King, the Queen, and a part of their family on the Place de la Concorde, at about one o'clock in the afternoon of February 24, at the moment when they had just entered their carriages to drive toward Saint-Cloud. There was still something royal in this departure. The sovereign was surrounded by royal troops. General Regnault de Saint-Jean-d'Angély, commander of the brigade of cavalry concentrated on the place, had placed himself at the head of the escort, which was composed of two squadrons of the 2d cuirassiers under the orders of Colonel Rewbell, and of mounted National Guards commanded by Count de Montalivet, one of the King's most devoted adherents. At the doors of his carriage Louis Philippe had two of his aides-de-camp, General Dumas and Count Friant, and two of his orderlies, MM. Perrot de Chazelles and de Pauligue, as well as M. Fiereck, an orderly of the Duke de Montpensier. The three carriages were completely surrounded by the escort. They took the road of the Cours-la-Reine. In front of the bridge of the Invalides a group of rioters, who had sacked and burned the guard-house, made a pretence of stopping the cortège, but the cavalry of the escort had no trouble in preventing them. They reached Saint-Cloud, without encountering any impediment, at about two o'clock in the afternoon. Louis Philippe remembered that on July 31, 1830, this château had been the point of departure for Charles X. on his way to exile. The King of the French made but a short halt there. Before quitting forever this domain of his ancestors, he bade farewell to the cuirassiers and National Guards by whom he had been escorted, and thanked them for their good sentiments.

As yet Louis Philippe believed neither in the fall of his dynasty nor the proclamation of the Republic. Imagining that he could install himself tranquilly in his château of Eu, one of his favorite residences, he did not consider himself a fugitive, still less a proscript. Nevertheless, there were certainly difficulties about the continuation of his journey. The party had left the Tuileries with such haste that there had been no time to bring along the needful money. The Queen's purse was the best provided, but even that contained merely a few twenty-franc pieces. They could not remain at Saint-Cloud without running the risk of an invasion of the Parisian population. The fortress of Mont-Valérien would have been an easy asylum to defend, but it was feared that a retreat to this impregnable place might seem like a provocation. At three o'clock they took the Versailles road, in two omnibuses hired by General Dumas at Saint-Cloud. A second halt was made at the Grand Trianon, which had been the first stopping-place of Charles X. on his way to Cherbourg. It is said that when Louis Philippe likewise halted for a few moments in the château of Louis XIV., he remembered his cousin, and two or three times exclaimed sadly: "Like Charles X.! Like Charles X.!"

Trianon also was too near to Paris to be a safe resting-place. There the party found Princess Clémentine and her husband, Duke Auguste of Saxe-Cobourg-Gotha, who, as we have said already, had left the royal family on the Place de la Concorde, and, after mingling with the crowd, had taken the train to Versailles. General Dumas, having borrowed twelve hundred francs from a friend, and hired two berlines at Versailles, it was decided that the journey should be made in two distinct groups. One of the berlines was reserved for the Duke and Duchess of Saxe-Cobourg-Gotha and their three children. This detachment, directed by M. Aubernon, prefect of Versailles, reached Eu in safety, whence it started for Boulogne. The other members of the royal family occupied the second berline, which conducted them to Dreux, where they passed the night. They arrived there in the evening.

The King and Queen had made their last visit to Dreux on January 5, when they came to be present at the obsequies of Madame Adelaide, interred in the vaults of this Saint-Denis of the Orleans family. Louis Philippe's heart was wrung on that day, for he had just lost a sister who was like the half of his own soul; but if the private man was then plunged in grief, the sovereign still possessed great satisfactions. He believed that the success of his work was assured and France preserved from revolution. What changes had been wrought in a few weeks! How the wheel of fortune had revolved! And yet, when he arrived at Dreux in the evening of February 24, Louis Philippe was still far from comprehending the whole extent of the catastrophe, and fancied that he would arrive at the château of Eu without difficulty, and that no one would come thither to disturb the tranquillity of his retreat.

He wrote this letter, the *fac-simile* of which has been reproduced by Dr. Véron in the *Mémoires d'un Bourgeois de Paris*, to M. de Montalivet, before going to bed: —

"DREUX, Thursday, February 24, 1848.

"My dear Count, having departed without a farthing, it became necessary to borrow at Versailles the wherewithal for our wretched journey. We arrived here very comfortably at eleven o'clock this evening. It was best. At present we must make arrangements for our journey to Eu as quickly as possible. We must have carriages, and it would please me to have you get into one of them and bring me the money for which I remit orders, so that I can concert with you the horrible and alarming arrangements of my new position; I hope that you can come. Good evening."

To this letter were joined the following documents: —

"I authorize Count de Montalivet to have the sum of thirty thousand francs credited to my private account.

"I authorize M. de Verbois to remit to me at Dreux, where I am this evening, the sum of thirty thousand francs, which I have just authorized Count de Montalivet to credit to my private account.

"DREUX, February 24, 1848."

The whole was written in a firm hand, which proves that Louis Philippe had lost none of his coolness.

At the same moment, General Dumas was writing this letter to M. de Montalivet, which proves the illusions still prevalent in the circle surrounding the unfortunate sovereign: —

"DREUX, February 24, 1848,
11 o'clock in the evening.

"The King has arrived at Dreux. His Majesty intends to await your answer here; afterwards, he proposes to go to Eu.

"The King has been able, and was obliged, to travel to-day completely incognito. In future it cannot be so. To this end, His Majesty desires that you should concert with the government the measures necessary for the entire security and convenience of his journey.

"The King further charges me to beg you to have his travelling carriages sent to Dreux immediately. There should be three, sufficiently commodious to contain some luggage. The others will be sent to Eu with the King's baggage wagons.

"The King wishes you to come to Dreux in one of his carriages.

"You well understand how important it is that the King's intentions should be promptly carried out; His Majesty relies on you for their realization.

"The health of the King, the Queen, Madame the Duchess de Nemours and her children, and of S. A. R. Monseigneur the Duke de Montpensier, is as good as possible.

"Accept, Monsieur the Count, the assurance of my high consideration and attachment.

"The King desires me reopen my letter to beg you to give tidings of him to General Athelin, and to ask for news of him."

Louis Philippe fell asleep at Dreux in comparative tranquillity. The next day, Friday, February 25, his awakening was cruel. He was still in bed when apprised of the terrible events of the previous day: the miscarriage of the regency, the sack of the Tuileries, the proclamation of the Republic. No one knew what had become of the Duke de Nemours, the Duchess of Orleans, the Count de Paris, the Duke de Chartres, who had been carried away by the popular tumult.

This uncertainty concerning their fate plunged the unhappy King into stupor. He seemed thunderstricken. Less of an optimist than he, and long since disquieted by the direction events were taking in France, Marie Amélie was less surprised, but perhaps still more afflicted than her husband. Dreux, that lugubrious necropolis, was in harmony with the sorrowful reflections of the pious Queen. The words of great preachers on the vanity of sublunary things recurred to her mind. She prayed, she wept at this station of her Calvary. It was impossible to remain there long. They had to abandon the thought of establishing themselves at Eu, to reach the Normandy coast as soon as possible and thence embark for England. It was agreed that the Duke de Montpensier, the Duchess de Nemours, and her two sons (the Count d'Eu and the Duke d'Alençon) should be provided with passports under fictitious names and set off in a carriage, hired at Dreux, on the road to Granville, where they should embark on board the packet-boat *Jersey*. The King and Queen, under the names of M. and Madame Lebrun, accompanied by a man servant and a waiting-maid, were to start for Honfleur in one of the two berlines hired at Saint-Cloud.

Before leaving Dreux, whither she was never to return until after her death, Marie Amélie wished to pay a last visit to the subterranean abodes where several of her children were buried, and where her own tomb and that of her husband were already designated. She went down there at daybreak, while the King was discussing with General de Rumigny and General Dumas the arrangements of a journey which was to end in eternal exile.

Bowing with resignation under the hand of God which smote her, the Queen kneeled down and prayed with all her soul amid the vaults where so many hopes had been entombed. Then she said a special adieu to every grave. "Poor Marie!" she cried, before the sepulchre of the ideal princess, "poor Marie! I should have loved so to bring up her child. It is another sacrifice that must be made!" Then, kissing for the last time the tombstone of her first-born, the Duke of Orleans: "His death," said she, "has been our ruin. I felt certain, when he was taken from us, that it was for the unhappiness of France as well as ours." And, in fact, it is generally believed that if the prince-royal had lived, the Revolution of February would have been impossible. Marie Amélie would gladly have remained longer near her cherished dead. She was torn with difficulty from this dismal abode. But alas! the hour for departure had sounded. The lamentable journey must be continued.

CHAPTER XXXII

FROM DREUX TO HONFLEUR

LOUIS PHILIPPE, leaving Paris as a sovereign, did not begin to conceal his name until after quitting Dreux, February 25. From the time of his departure from this town until his embarkation for England, the King of the French was a fugitive, travelling amid real dangers, and obliged to resort to many subterfuges in order to avoid recognition.

General Dumas and Captain de Pauligue were sent away in a wretched little cabriolet to the railway between Rouen and Saint-Pierre-de-Louviers, whence they were to proceed to Havre and try to obtain a vessel on which Their Majesties might embark after quitting Honfleur.

When the berline containing the King, the Queen, and General de Rumigny left Dreux, M. Maréchal, sub-prefect of the town, mounted the coachman's box in order to protect them. People having been allowed to suppose that they were going to the château d'Eu, they set off on the high road to Verneuil, but made a sudden turn to the right by a road leading to Anet and Pacy-sur-Eure, across the forest of Dreux, which belongs to the Orleans family. The postmaster of Dreux had sent men to Anet to make ready the relays, while still ignorant that the travellers desired to maintain their incognito. When they reached this town, the former abode of Diana of Poitiers, the people received them with shouts of "Long live the King!" Dreading similar demonstrations at the next relay station, Pacy-sur-Eure, they ordered the postilions to drive to another, that of La Roche-Saint-André, on the high road to Dreux, by a cross-road which cuts through the forest of Ivry, a private estate belonging to the King, near the battle-field on which his ancestor, Henri IV., defeated the army of the League, in 1590.

The journey began to be disquieting. It was necessary to cross the Eure near a manufactory, the workmen of which, doubtless forewarned by the indiscretion of the Dreux postmaster, had assembled on the road which must be taken by the King. As the carriage had a hill to ascend after crossing the river, they pursued it, shouting: "Long live the Reform! Down with Louis Philippe!" The journey continued, however, still conducted by the sub-prefect, M. Maréchal, a man of intelligence and feeling, who had never left the driver's seat since they quitted Dreux.

They reached La Roche-Saint-André without hindrance. It was a market day. The relays were found in a very narrow street. A man looked into the carriage, and although Louis Philippe had enveloped his face in a silk handkerchief and put on spectacles, this man muttered: "It is the King!" and went to inform the gendarmes. They hastened to the place, but M. Maréchal induced them to go away again. The horses were quickly harnessed, and the postilions set off at a gallop, paying no attention to the people, who were shouting: "Stop! Stop!" behind them.

The travellers were anxiously wondering whether Évreux, which is a large city, would allow them to pass. It was still daylight; would not the inhabitants recognize them? Just then, M. Maréchal conceived a prudent idea. Seeing a small château very near the city, he asked a road-mender whose it was. The man replied that this house, which was called Mellesille, belonged to one M. Dorvilliers, who was then away from home with all his family. Now, M. Dorvilliers was the King's agent for the forest of Breteuil. M. Maréchal proposed that the travellers should stop there for a short time, until the darkness of night afforded more chances of avoiding recognition. The farmer, whose name was Renard, had a house which adjoined the château. He was told that M. and Madame Lebrun — the assumed names of the King and Queen — were friends of M. Dorvilliers, and that Madame Lebrun, being tired and suffering, desired to rest awhile, as she was unable to endure the motion of the carriage any longer. The farmer, a good and compassionate man, made haste to offer the travellers hospitality in his own dwelling. His language and manners soon made it clear that it would be safe to trust him. He was told that the so-called M. and Madame Lebrun and M. Dubreuil were no other than the King and Queen and General de Rumigny. His amazement was so great that he nearly fainted. He offered every service in his power, and immediately sent to Évreux in search of M. Dorvilliers. The latter came in haste and remitted a sum of nearly one thousand francs in partial payment of the King's income. M. Maréchal, being no longer within the limits of his sub-prefecture, now took leave of Louis Philippe, but not until he had summoned the secretary of the prefecture of the Eure, who eagerly placed himself at the King's disposal. The presence of the berline in the courtyard of the farm had attracted the attention of the neighbors, and the travellers were not free from apprehensions concerning the remainder of their journey.

No one knew the history of the French Revolution better than Louis Philippe, who had both witnessed it and been its victim. Comparisons between his own destiny and that of Louis XVI. recurred incessantly to his mind. The day before, when crossing the garden of the Tuileries to go to the Place de la Concorde, he had been reminded of the 10th of August, 1792. Now he was thinking of the flight to Varennes. He remembered that if Louis XVI.

had been arrested on the way, it was because he had travelled too slowly and been unwilling to separate from his family. If the journey had been made in two or three distinct groups, the catastrophe would doubtless have been averted. Enlightened by this example, Louis Philippe took the advice of the farmer, Renard, and consented to travel in a different carriage from the Queen. The horses obtained at the relay of La Roche-Saint-André had been sent back. The farmer procured a cabriolet and undertook to drive the King and his valet to Honfleur, eighty leagues from Évreux. As to the Queen, she entered the berline, to which two farm-horses had been attached, and went on to the Commandery, the first post-station on the road to Honfleur after leaving Évreux. Before separating, the royal pair promised to rejoin each other on the hill overlooking the latter town, in a cottage belonging to M. de Perthuis, formerly one of the King's orderlies.

General de Rumigny had entered the berline, with the Queen and her waiting-maid, Mademoiselle Muser. When the carriage stopped at the Commandery to exchange the plough-horses for post-horses, and the farm-hand who had driven them for postilions, some one approached General de Rumigny, and said in an undertone: "A berline that comes with plough-horses and takes post-horses is queer! But, as times go, sir, we ask no questions and don't look into carriages." This man was the postmaster of the Commandery. Raising his voice, he ordered the postilions to drive to the next station, Pont-Audemer, as quickly as possible. If Drouet had acted thus at Sainte-Menehould, June 21, 1791, Louis XVI. would not have been arrested at Varennes, and the face of Europe might have been changed.

The cabriolet containing Louis Philippe and his valet did not change horses, Farmer Renard, having harnessed up his own team and driven the whole eighty leagues without stopping, except at a few taverns on the road to water and feed the animals and give them a moment's rest. One of these wayside inns, situated at the limit of the department of the Eure, was called the Malbrough. The King remembered that he had received an enthusiastic welcome there fifteen years before, and that in passing under a triumphal arch he had said: "Flattery has changed sides nowadays, and the flatterers of the people are at present as dangerous to society and good government as the flatterers of kings were formerly."

They travelled all night. It was cold, and the wind blew furiously. It was the commencement of a squall which lasted for several days. Worn out with fatigue, the King reflected painfully on his fate and that of his family. It was half-past three in the morning when the cabriolet crossed Pont-Audemer. A little beyond that town, while Renard was watering his horses, the berline in which Marie Amélie was travelling with General de Rumigny and Mademoiselle Muser came in sight. The King and Queen, delighted to meet again, exchanged a few words and then continued their route, one in the cabriolet, the other in the berline, and rejoined each other on the hill overlooking Honfleur, in the pavilion of M. de Perthuis, which they reached at daybreak.

CHAPTER XXXIII

THE PAVILION DE LA GRÂCE

HONFLEUR, chief town of the canton of Calvados, is a port situated eleven kilometres southeast of Havre, at the mouth of the Seine, on the left side of the river. If you go to Honfleur by sea, you notice a wooded hill that rises above the town. At the summit of this hill is the cottage of M. de Perthuis, where Louis Philippe and Marie Amélie rejoined each other at six o'clock on Saturday morning, February 26. There is a little chapel there, dedicated to Our Lady of Grace by the piety of the sailors. It is because of the nearness of this chapel, that the cottage of M. de Perthuis is known in the vicinity as the pavilion de la Grâce. Separated from the road by a hedge and a path, it contains only two rooms, each surmounted by a sort of loft. It was a very humble refuge, but the proximity of a chapel of the Virgin seemed a good omen to the Queen, who so sorely needed protection from on high.

Renard, who had conducted the King so quickly and safely from Évreux to Honfleur, refused all remuneration. "Don't talk to me about that," he said to General de Rumigny, "matters of feeling cannot be paid for with money." At the pavilion de la Grâce, a gardener named Racine displayed equally good sentiments. At first he was not admitted to the secret, but he recognized the King from a lithograph hanging in his kitchen, and manifested absolute zeal and devotion to the august travellers.

The sea lay before them, and they would have been glad to embark on it without a moment's delay, for their anxieties were constantly increasing. They knew that the provisional government had issued strict orders for the surveillance of the littoral, that the police were on the alert, that the most revolutionary elements were unchained in Paris, that the commissioners of the Republic in the provinces were making a show of zeal, and that if the King and Queen were arrested no one could predict their fate. Marie Amélie mused on the captivity and death of her aunt, Marie Antoinette. But her courage did not falter. It was she who comforted and consoled the King.

An embarkation for England presented innumerable difficulties at that moment. The weather was detestable; the packet-boat plying between Havre and Honfleur could not undertake even that passage. Moreover, even though the sea grew smoother, an attempted embarkation in a town so important as Honfleur would still be dangerous; for the attention

of the inhabitants would be easily aroused by it.
And again, a fishing-boat would be the only one
available, because there was no steamboat plying
between Honfleur and the English coast, and at that
season of the year, and in such weather, it is no easy
task to sail on a fishing-smack.

We have said already that General Dumas and
Captain de Pauligue had left the King and Queen
at Dreux, February 25, intending to go to Havre in
search of a vessel on which Their Majesties might
embark after quitting the pavilion of M. de Perthuis.
They had not succeeded in their mission. Reaching
Rouen by train, they found such a commotion there
that they were forcibly separated from each other.
M. de Pauligue, obliged to cross the Seine at Rouen,
entered Honfleur from its own side of the river, on
February 26. General Dumas succeeded in getting
to Havre. There he met a young naval officer, M.
Edmond de Perthuis, commander of the *Rodeur*, a
small man-of-war in the roadstead of Havre. Himself the son of the proprietor of the pavilion de la
Grâce, he had a brother who was the son-in-law of
General Dumas. The General quickly confided his
errand to the naval officer, who was likewise devoted
to the royal family. Then they took a third person
into their confidence, M. Besson, formerly an officer
in the navy, and all set about finding an available
vessel at Havre. Being unsuccessful, they returned
to the King, February 27, to see whether there might
not be, either at Honfleur or in the vicinity, some

other means of getting to sea. They crossed the Seine with great difficulty, at the spot where it begins to grow narrower, between Tancarville and Quillebœuf. In the morning they arrived at the pavilion de la Grâce, where they were joined during the day by M. Besson. The latter explained to the King that, since it was impossible to procure a vessel at Havre, nothing was left but to take a fishing-smack, — a very dangerous expedient, — unless they could succeed in getting places on a Southampton steam packet, the *Express*, which lay in the roadstead of Havre and was soon to sail for England. As their embarkation at Havre might attract attention, it would be necessary for the King to go to Trouville in the first place, and they would try to induce the *Express* to manœuvre in such a way as to allow a boat containing Louis Philippe to come alongside of it at the upper end of that beach. The King charged M. Besson to sound the English steamboat captain discreetly on this point. But at the same time, wishing to have more than one string to his bow, he had recourse to the good offices of a Honfleur sailor named Hallot, a friend of Racine the gardener. Hallot had served under Prince de Joinville. He had been the coxswain of the *Belle-Poule* frigate, and his devotion to the royal family was unbounded. He thought they would certainly be discovered if they embarked at Honfleur, but that at Trouville a fishing-boat might be obtained, on which they could sail from that port to the English littoral.

Louis Philippe accepted this suggestion, and sent Hallot to Trouville in the evening of the 27th.

The great inconvenience of this arrangement, supposing it could be carried out, was that the King would be obliged to leave the Queen. He was quite willing to risk a voyage rendered so dangerous by the roughness of the sea, but utterly unwilling to expose Marie Amélie to it. He has himself written, in a manuscript from which we borrow the principal details of the present account: "My excellent queen was extremely agitated. Nevertheless, her reason, always so superior, carried the day against what her heart and her courage inclined her to brave. She comprehended, above all, that her departure with me might increase my peril, and that it was even necessary that she should remain without me at Grâce, in order that my absence might not be noticed until I should have actually embarked at Trouville. Hence she resigned herself to my departure. One absolute condition, however, she put to her consent, namely, that if I were arrested, she should instantly set out to rejoin me, no matter where. This I promised her."

Hallot came back from Trouville before M. Besson had started for Havre. He announced that he had just obtained at Honfleur, in consideration of the sum of three thousand francs, a fishing-vessel, which would be ready to set sail for England the following night, that of Monday, February 28. General Dumas, General de Rumigny, Captain de Pauligue,

M. Edmond de Perthuis, and M. Besson advised the King to embark on this vessel. On the 28th, Louis Philippe set out for Trouville. Marie Amélie remained at the pavilion de la Grâce from Monday, February 28, to Thursday, March 2, without receiving any tidings. The Queen has often said to M. Trognon, that those three mortal days had been among the most afflicting of her sorrowful existence. After chronicling this remark, M. Trognon adds: "What the Queen did not say, and what I have learned from General Dumas and Mademoiselle Muser is, that amidst all her anxieties and sorrows, amidst all the privations, annoyances, and discomforts she experienced in a narrow habitation, open on every side to the cold sea winds, not a complaint escaped her, and that not merely her patience but also the serenity of her soul, the loftiness of her sentiments and thoughts never forsook her for a single instant." And yet she no longer entertained the least political hopes. When General de Rumigny was trying to get her to look forward to a return of fortune, she said to him: "How can one lull one's self with chimeras at such a moment?" What she found hardest to endure was her uncertainty concerning the fate of her family, of whom she had received no news whatever. "If I am never to see my children again," she exclaimed, "tell them how distressed I was about them, my dear Nemours especially. . . . Perhaps we shall at least meet again in heaven." She knew that this Prince, who had displayed such chivalrous self-abnegation; that the Duchess of Orleans, who had been so courageous a mother; that the Count de Paris and the Duke de Chartres, touching and innocent victims, had disappeared, borne away by the popular flood. But what had become of them since that fatal day? Perhaps the populace had spared a woman and children. But the Duke de Nemours! And the Duke d'Aumale, the Prince de Joinville, so happy in Africa amidst the army and the fleet, how would they learn the catastrophe? What a thunderbolt for them! Then, after a long silence, the unhappy Queen resumed: "Never have I felt more vividly than now the pain caused me by the 'days' of July, 1830. I was just now recalling what I experienced in those days, and asking myself whether I am really more unhappy now than I was then. . . . And yet, when I think of the interrupted career of my poor children, of the exile which awaits them, and which they do not know as I have known it! . . ." The profound sadness which overwhelmed her soul prevented the completion of her phrase.

Ordinarily the Queen was much occupied. Her works of charity, her duties as sovereign, the long correspondence she carried on with all her children who were away from her, left her not a moment's leisure. At the pavilion de la Grâce she suffered from a lack of occupation which tormented her. To whom could she write, since she not only did not know the whereabouts of the majority of her family, but her letters could not even be posted? She had nothing to read excepting three little books of piety, among them the *Recueil de prières* of Madame de Fenoil, which she had put into her pocket as she was leaving the Tuileries. Having found some thread and needles in a bundle her maid had brought with her, she tried to sew, like Marie Antoinette in the Conciergerie, but as she was not accustomed to needlework she quickly relinquished this pastime. Her great occupation was prayer. She would go up into the chamber of her faithful servant, and place on the table a little crucifix, before which the two women knelt and prayed.

CHAPTER XXXIV

TROUVILLE

DURING these hours which Marie Amélie found so bitter, Louis Philippe was exposed to a series of dangers and tribulations at Trouville. Situated on the British Channel, at the mouth of the Toucques, the little port of Trouville is much less important than that of Honfleur, and it was hoped that the King could more easily escape the watchfulness of the authorities, and embark from there, unrecognized, on the fishing-vessel engaged by Hallot.

It had been decided at the pavilion de la Grâce that General de Rumigny, M. Edmond de Perthuis, and Captain de Pauligue should go to Trouville several hours before the King, in order to inspect the preparations made for his embarkation. One or more of these gentlemen were to await Louis Philippe at the entrance of the town and conduct him to the vessel.

M. de Pauligue set off in a stage-coach. General de Rumigny and M. Edmond de Perthuis started on foot, Monday morning, February 28, under the guidance of Hallot, who took them by cross-country roads.

After bidding the Queen a sorrowful farewell, the King, with Thuret, his valet, entered a wretched one-horse cabriolet driven by Racine the gardener. As she watched the departure of this vehicle, so different from the brilliant carriages of former days, Marie Amélie had invoked the divine protection on her spouse. The journey to Trouville was made very slowly. The horse was raw-boned and stubborn, and the King would have arrived sooner if he had walked. As it was, he reached there long after the hour appointed. The delay, however, was of small importance, since the embarkation was physically impossible. The wind was too strong and the sea too heavy. Louis Philippe was keenly disappointed when, on alighting from his cabriolet at Trouville, he found that, on account of the bad weather and the low tides, the fishing-boat he had hoped to find moored at the end of the quay, could not get afloat within twenty-four, and possibly forty-eight, hours.

Since the embarkation was impossible, it was decided that Louis Philippe should conceal himself at Trouville until it could be effected. General de Rumigny had prepared a refuge for him at the house of an old sailor, M. Victor Barbet, whose very humble dwelling was at the back of a little passage behind a lane. This sailor was the brother of the captain of the port, M. Henri Barbet, who had been decorated by the King and was very devoted to him. Accompanied by M. de Pauligue and Thuret, the King repaired to this little house, where he received the most respectful welcome. It was kept by the daughter of the proprietor, a young widow whose husband had recently been swept away by a wave during a heavy squall. This woman, who was extremely pious, had a great veneration for Marie Amélie. Her surprise at being honored by a visit from the King is easily comprehended. She herself prepared and served the sovereign's meals.

In the house of M. Victor Barbet, Louis Philippe found himself with loyal subjects, who would brave every danger for him. Nevertheless, he was in continual fear. How could a secret known to so many persons be long preserved? Would not the three thousand francs promised to the owner of the fishing-boat arouse suspicions? Would not the project of so unusual a voyage come to the ears of the authorities and custom-house officers? Was not some indiscretion to be feared, either at Honfleur or Trouville? The least indication might set the authorities on the track of the King, and then all would be lost. The King's travelling companions were still more anxious than he. He spent the night of February 28–29 in M. Victor Barbet's house, and was still there in the evening of March 1. At that moment he was apprised of news by no means reassuring. A circular from the provisional government had just been received at the custom-house, which ordered the coast-guards to use their utmost vigilance to prevent the escape of political fugitives. The posts were to be doubled, and the littoral guarded in the strictest manner. The house which had sheltered the King might be exposed at any minute to a domiciliary visit. An annoying circumstance still further increased the danger. M. Henri Barbet, without consulting the King, had had the idea of breaking the contract agreed upon between Hallot and the master of the fishing-boat, and making a new one with another mariner whose vessel seemed likely to put off sooner. He had decided to give two thousand francs to this second mariner, and one thousand to the first, in order to compensate him for the rupture of the contract. But the latter, dissatisfied with this arrangement, had gone to the authorities of the port and made a declaration that he had been engaged to transport a suspicious stranger to England.

Knowing all this, M. Henri Barbet hastened to his brother's house to inform the King. "Sire," said he, "we are betrayed; the authorities are about to make a search here. You have barely time to escape." It was eight o'clock in the evening. M. Henri Barbet at once drew Louis Philippe into a little back yard, where he passed him over to a stranger who was standing there, and then hastened back into the house to await the expected domiciliary visit.

The stranger, on finding himself alone with the

King, said to him in an undertone: "Sire, a faithful and devoted servant is about to conduct you to a place of safety." Taking a bunch of large keys, he opened several doors in succession, crossed yards and lanes, and hastily guided Louis Philippe into a house which they entered through a back door. The unknown was M. Guestier, but lately mayor of Trouville, and the house was his. There the King found several visitors, whom there had not yet been time to send away. They were all royalists. They said that out of three thousand inhabitants of the place not more than five or six held contrary views; but they added that these five or six individuals were enough to intimidate the whole town.

The King's suite, whom some one had taken pains to scatter at the first alarm, presently rejoined him at the house of M. Guestier. A longer stay at Trouville was clearly most imprudent. An embarkation there had become absolutely impossible, by reason of the alarm given to the authorities, and the probable dispute between the masters of the two fishing-smacks. They must wait until the streets were entirely empty, and then return to the pavilion de la Grâce; perhaps they might yet be able to find some way to embark, if not at Honfleur, at some other point along the coast. M. Guestier had a cabriolet, which would hold the King and Thuret, and he would take the reins himself. The proprietor of a neighboring hotel, who, like Guestier, was a royalist, had a wagonette in which he would drive

General Dumas, Captain de Pauligue, and M.
Edmond de Perthuis. Unfortunately, the harness
of the cabriolet was at the harness-maker's for repairs, and they could not procure another. While
some one went to the harness-maker's shop to find
it, Louis Philippe and his companions, sheltered by
the darkness, left the house, each by himself, and
walked as far as the village of Toucques, where the
two vehicles were to rejoin them.

To get out of Trouville, it was necessary to pass
three guard-houses. Luckily, two of them had no
sentries, and the third only one, who paid no attention either to the five men who passed singly, or,
after their passage, to the two empty carriages going
toward Toucques. When the latter came in front
of this village, the King, Thuret, General Dumas,
M. Edmond de Perthuis, and Captain de Pauligue
were there already. Louis Philippe and Thuret got
into the cabriolet, the three others into the wagonette, and set off with all speed toward Honfleur.

Between four and five o'clock on Thursday morning, March 2, just one week after the Revolution of
February, all five were set down at the foot of the
hill surmounted by the pavilion de la Grâce. They
began to ascend it, while M. Guestier drove off in
the direction of Quillebœuf, where he hoped to find
some means of embarking the King for England.

While Louis Philippe was climbing the hill, at
the top of which he was about to rejoin the Queen,
he told himself that to return thus to the point of

departure after four days and nights of perplexity
and anguish, was a dismal matter. Marie Amélie
would be greatly afflicted when she learned that all
was to begin anew, without the least appearance of
any more favorable chance occurring. But, on the
other hand, he also reflected that his faithful companion, who had witnessed him depart with so much
grief and apprehension, would be delighted to see
him again, even under such terrible circumstances.
Louis Philippe was not mistaken. As soon as she
perceived her husband, Marie Amélie began to
tremble and shed abundant tears. But they were
tears of joy. "At last," she cried, "he is here, safe
and sound. That is everything for me, God will
not abandon us!" How many times, during her
days of solitude in the pavilion de la Grâce, had
she thought of the fate of Charles I. and of Louis
XVI.! She resolved never again to separate from
her husband, under any pretext. She had prayed so
much that she hoped she had at last turned aside the
wrath of Heaven.

CHAPTER XXXV

THE EMBARKATION AT HAVRE

IT is Thursday, March 2. Day is beginning to break. Shortly after the King's return, there is an alarm at the pavilion de la Grâce. Some one is knocking at the door. Who is this early visitor? Is it an enemy? Is it an agent of the provisional government, coming to make a search? No; it is the English Vice-Consul at Havre, Mr. Jones.

We have said already, that on February 27 a former officer of the navy, M. Besson, a resident of Havre, had come to the pavilion de la Grâce and spoken to Louis Philippe about a Southampton packet-boat, the *Express*, on which it might be possible to embark. We added that the King had authorized him to find out, as secretly as possible, what Mr. Paul, the captain of the packet-boat, thought about it. M. Besson had asked the captain whether he would consent to handle the vessel in such a way as to allow a fishing-boat, containing the King, to come alongside at the upper end of Trouville. The captain of the *Express* said he could not change the usual course of his vessel without orders from his superiors. He thought, moreover, that an extraordinary manœuvre might rouse suspicions, and that they would have to run all the risks of a collision between the boats, and of a transhipment in a heavy sea. Hence he declined the proposition, and had since crossed the Channel in the *Express*. On reaching England, he made haste to inform the Admiralty, and received orders to take the *Express* immediately back to Havre, and put it at Louis Philippe's disposal. Such was the news brought to the King by Vice-Consul Jones. He announced at the same time that the Duke de Nemours, his daughter the Princess Marguerite, together with the Princess Clémentine and her husband and children, were in safety on English territory. The King and Queen, who had been especially anxious concerning the fate of the Duke de Nemours, were rejoiced to know that he was safe and sound. Unfortunately, they were still ignorant of what had befallen the other members of the royal family.

Mr. Jones was welcomed at the pavilion de la Grâce as a savior. But there were still great difficulties in the way of carrying out this scheme. How could they avoid recognition in Honfleur, and by what means get on board of the *Express?* The more they considered the matter, the more difficult it seemed. Mr. Jones had come to Havre from Honfleur on the *Courrier*, the packet plying regularly between the two ports, and returned on it during the day, bearing the thanks of the King to his chief, Mr. Featherstonhaugh, English Consul in that city, and instructions to consult with him and M. Besson as to the best manner of proceeding. The three gentlemen at once held a private conference, and decided that the *Courrier* should immediately return to Honfleur. There it was to await the King and Queen, who, after nightfall, must leave the pavilion de la Grâce, walk down the hill, and go aboard the *Courrier*, which would convey them to Havre, where they could embark for England on the *Express*. The King, provided with an English passport, was to be known as Mr. Smith, uncle to Mr. Featherstonhaugh, the English Consul, while the Queen was to keep the name of Madame Lebrun.

Such a plan was essentially hazardous, of course. Was it not to be feared that the august fugitives might be recognized, either on their way down hill, on the passage from Honfleur to Havre, or else in crossing the quay of the latter city to go on board the *Express?* But, in any case, there were no other means of getting away.

Moreover, there was not a minute to lose. Louis Philippe had barely left Trouville when the procureur of the Republic arrived with gendarmes to arrest the suspected traveller, who was none other than the King. The government magistrate learned that Louis Philippe and M. Edmond de Perthuis had been seen at Trouville, and that they had left there in the direction of Honfleur. The secret could be kept no longer. A domiciliary visit to the pavilion de la Grâce was imminent.

The *Courrier*, which had already crossed from Havre to Honfleur and back again, was not to return to Honfleur again that day. But M. Adolphe d'Houdetot, receiver of finances at Havre, brother of General Count d'Houdetot, aide-de-camp of the King, had been taken into confidence, and he called for another passage of the packet-boat under pretext of having to look up some moneys expected for the use of the receivership. The *Courrier* set out for Honfleur, therefore, with Mr. Jones and M. Besson on board. As soon as they arrived, these gentlemen repaired to the pavilion de la Grâce and announced to the King and Queen that all was ready.

They set off instantly, in several distinct groups. Louis Philippe, otherwise Mr. William Smith, uncle of the English Consul, walked with General de Rumigny and the valet. He was enveloped in a heavy overcoat and wore spectacles that partly concealed his face. Marie Amélie took a different road, leaning on the arm of M. de Perthuis. They met again on the Honfleur quay, where there were some sight-seers and gendarmes. The so-called Mr. William Smith approached Mr. Jones, and, after bidding him good evening, in English, took his arm and went aboard the *Courrier*, where he seated himself on one of the benches intended for passengers. The so-called Madame Lebrun sat down on another side with M. de Perthuis, who passed for her nephew at the pavilion de la Grâce. The boat started between five and six o'clock in the evening. Some strolling musicians were on board, who sang several pieces, among others an air by Grétry, Louis Philippe's favorite composer: *O Richard, ô mon roi! l'univers t'abandonne.* And Louis Philippe could reflect that amid all the bitter trials he was passing through, several courtiers of misfortune had already shown him the same devotion as Blondel to Richard of the Lion Heart.

Now let us leave the story to the King.

"The night was dark," he writes, "and as we were the first comers on the boat, I went to starboard and sat down between Mr. Jones and Thuret, on a bench against the bulwark netting. The Queen sat down also, but to larboard, and we were completely separated by the passengers who were promenading on both sides of the bridge. There was a man who walked up and down with a lantern, asking the passengers for their tickets and some money for the musicians; for there was a band, with men and women singers, on board, for whom, as was reasonable, they were taking up a collection. But whenever I was spoken to, I invariably replied, and always in English, that I did not understand French, and motioned them to address Mr. Jones, who would satisfy them at once."

They arrived in the port of Havre and went ashore at once. On the wharf, where there were some people, they met the English Consul. "Well, uncle," said he to the King, "how are you?" "Very well, George, I thank you," replied the King.

Louis Philippe shall go on with the story: "While continuing our conversation in English, we walked toward the not very distant point where the *Express* lay, passing a gendarme, who neither asked for a passport nor paid any attention either to me or to the Queen, who was following me rather closely. We arrived at a small, covered stairway, which we descended, and at the foot of which we found ourselves in the cabins of the *Express*, when Mr. Featherstonhaugh at once shook hands with me and said: '*Now, thank God, you are safe*'; and I replied with the same expression of gratitude toward God and those who had so efficaciously aided in extricating me from the cruel position in which I had been for the last eight days. The Queen, very much affected, arrived almost at the same moment, and threw herself into my arms. MM. Besson and Adolphe d'Houdetot knelt down at her feet, and we united in our thanksgivings to Providence." And yet all danger was not even now averted.

On the wharf there was a woman accustomed to direct travellers to different hotels and lodging-houses. Either by means of her dark lantern or the reflecting lamps, she thought she had recognized the King, and went at once to inform an officer of the port. The packet-boat had not yet started. The officer ran up, and, catching sight of Louis Philippe as he was going down into his cabin, he pressed the captain with questions. Mr. Paul replied, giving no explanation except that he was going to carry despatches. Then the officer of the port asked to visit the cabins. "Willingly," replied the captain, "but not until my next voyage, unless you want to go across with us. There is seven o'clock striking. It is the hour when I must stand out to sea."

The captain gave a signal, the cable was detached by the seamen, and the officer had barely time enough to go back to the wharf with the English Consul. Then the two men exchanged these remarks: —

"Tell me, please, who is the person you just now put on board the *Express?*"

"It is my uncle."

"Your uncle! Ah! Mr. Consul, what have you been doing?"

"What you would have done in my place, sir. . . ."

Meanwhile the packet-boat was departing, with all steam on.

The storm which had been prevailing in the Channel for several days was not yet over. The wind was blowing very hard. M. Trognon has thus described the attitude of Marie Amélie during a passage which lasted not less than ten hours. "The Queen, drenched to the bone with the chilly rain that had been pouring on her ever since she left the pavilion de la Grâce, and worn out with moral and physical fatigue, nevertheless endured courageously a long and rough voyage. She had always before been sick and frightened when at sea, but now she suffered from neither of these evils. Her soul remained mistress of her body; she had not descended from that heroic height to which circumstances had elevated her. There was in Queen Marie Amélie at once the generous exaltation which the sentiment of danger imparts to great souls, and the religious calm maintained there by the habitual sense of the presence of God." At last "this almost miraculous Odyssey," as Louis Philippe has called it, this series of tribulations, dangers, and afflictions, which had lasted more than eight days, and which his "excellent and much-loved queen," had so nobly and laboriously traversed with him, was approaching its term. On Friday, March 3, at seven o'clock in the morning, the *Express* entered the roadstead of Newhaven, and the exiles landed, respectfully greeted by a crowd of people who said to them: "Welcome to England."

CHAPTER XXXVI

THE DEPARTURE OF THE DUCHESS OF ORLEANS

NOW let us see what had become of the Duchess of Orleans and her two sons, of whose fate Louis Philippe and Marie Amélie were completely ignorant when they landed at Newhaven.

We left the Duchess and the Count de Paris with the Viscount Léon de Montesquiou-Ferenzac, at the château de Bligny, near Orsay. They had arrived there during the night of February 24-25. All the Princess thought of at first was to obtain a little nourishment for her son, who was exhausted by fatigue and emotion. Even this was not easy; for, if a fire were lighted, it was feared that it might attract the attention of the villagers.

The Duchess of Orleans had probably suffered more from disappointment and chagrin than other members of the royal family. Until that fatal session of the Chamber of Deputies was half over on the previous day, the Princess could still hope that the rights of her son would be secured. She had heard the resounding cries of "Long live the young King! Long live the Regent!" And now all seemed irrevocably lost.

Intrepid during the entire day of February 24, in the night the noble woman began to be afraid, not for herself, but for her son. She took the rustle of the wind in the fir trees for the sound of drums, and fancied every minute that the chamber where the little Prince was sleeping was about to be invaded. This night of February 24-25, and the day that followed, were one long anguish to her. And yet the energetic and persevering Princess did not even now despair. The Duke de Nemours, on taking leave of her the evening of the 24th, at the Hôtel des Invalides, had promised to examine whether anything could be done, and if there were any chance of a return. Since then, she had not heard either the Duke or the King spoken of, or any mention of a favorable demonstration on the part of the troops, the people, or the National Guards. She remained at the château de Bligny, constantly expecting some good tidings which never came.

The Duke de Nemours, for whom the police were making an active search, seeing no possibility of any further attempt on behalf of the royal cause, had left Paris the evening of February 25, with an English passport, and in company with MM. Biesta and d'Aragon, whose secretary he was supposed to be. He was so well disguised that no one recognized him between Paris and Boulogne, where he embarked on the 26th without difficulty. On their way back to Paris, MM. Biesta and d'Aragon travelled with Prince Louis Napoleon Bonaparte, who had left

England on hearing of the Revolution of February 24.

One consolation the Duchess of Orleans had, on Saturday, February 26. Her second son, the Duke de Chartres, who was not quite seven years old, was brought back to her. The poor child had been almost suffocated in the brawl at the Chamber of Deputies, where Baron de l'Espée (father of the prefect of Saint-Étienne, who was assassinated in a riot in 1871) had done much to rescue him. The unhappy mother, who for two days had been in mortal terror concerning her son's fate, poured out her heart in thanksgiving to God on finding him safe and sound. He was suffering from *la grippe*, but not seriously, and showed himself so delighted at seeing his mother and brother again, that a trace of joy reappeared on all three faces.

Bad news arrived at the same moment. The Marquis de Mornay, who brought a passport for Germany, obtained with great difficulty, declared that the police were hunting for the Princess and her sons, as they had done for the Duke de Nemours; that a longer stay at Bligny would expose them to great dangers; and that not a moment must be lost in gaining the frontier.

On March 29, 1814, when the Empress Marie Louise quitted the Tuileries, never to return, the King of Rome clung fast to the doors and banisters, crying in childish rage: "I don't want to leave my house, I don't want to go away." Neither did the

Count de Paris want to go away. This nine-year-old child incessantly repeated: "I don't want to leave my country." The Duchess was of precisely the same mind; but those about insisted so strongly that she at last decided to depart, although still hoping not to be obliged to go out of France. When M. Léon de Montesquiou came to receive her final orders, she was on her knees beside her sons, praying aloud. "My God," she was saying, "protect France; protect my poor children; protect the generous hosts who have not feared to give us hospitality in these difficult moments; may it be a source of benedictions for them and their families, and may the memory of our short stay among them never become fatal to them!" It was raining in torrents; never was there a darker night or a more dismal departure. As she was about entering the carriage, the unfortunate Princess shook hands with her hosts, and, taking off the rings she wore, she put them on their fingers. The Duchess of Orleans, the Count de Paris, and the Duke de Chartres, accompanied by the Marquis de Mornay and M. Regnier, the tutor of the young princes, left the château de Bligny at ten o'clock on Saturday evening, February 26.

Thanks to the darkness and the bad weather, which had driven the peasants out of all the streets, they were not recognized at Versailles, which they merely passed through. All the way from Pontoise to Beaumont, railway travel was cut off and the bridges were burning. They went by stage to

Amiens, where they passed the night of February 27–28, taking the train to Lille the next morning.

So long as she was still on French territory, the Princess believed that a return of good fortune was not impossible. At the same time, a secret voice told her that if she crossed the frontier, her exile would be eternal. During the passage from Amiens to Lille, the car occupied by her and her sons was next to the one containing some agents of the provisional government on their way to proclaim the Republic in the departments of the North. They recognized neither the woman nor the child who, four days before, had been saluted as the regent and the king. While travelling, the Princess was thinking that on arriving at Lille she would at once place herself in communication with General Négrier, an officer of great merit, who commanded the place, at the head of a numerous garrison.

At Lille they had to wait four hours for the train to Belgium. The Princess read the Paris journals, with the result of strengthening her resolve to have recourse to the devotion of General Négrier. The Count de Paris said to his mother: "Don't leave Lille; go into the midst of a regiment; I am sure the soldiers will receive me as a soldier's child." Those who surrounded the Princess implored her not to risk such an enterprise, nor expose the sacred deposit she had in her hands. The book the Princess had been intending to read, February 24, was the *Histoire des Girondins*. Her mind was full of the revolutionary days. These persons evoked the souvenirs connected with them; they reminded her of the flight to Varennes, the Temple, the Conciergerie. The intrepid Duchess would have braved the fate of Marie Antoinette for herself, but she shuddered when they spoke to her of Louis XVII. And yet she still resisted. "What does it matter!" she exclaimed, in response to the objections made. "God will protect us. Let us go to the citadel!" But they positively refused to follow her, if she persisted in going there. She consented then to continue her sorrowful journey. As she was crossing the frontier, she saw there were tears in the Marquis de Mornay's eyes. She wept herself. "Our tears are very different," said she; "you weep for joy because we are safe, and I for grief at quitting France, that France on which I invoke all the blessings of Heaven! In whatever place I die, may it know that the last pulsations of my heart were for its welfare!"

The Duchess passed the night at Verviers, where she took several hours of much-needed repose. She wrote from there to her stepmother, the dowager Grand-Duchess of Mecklenburg-Schwerin, who had always been tenderly devoted to her, asking her to come and console her in her exile. She signed herself the Countess de Dreux, borrowing the name from the estate where the ashes of the Orleans family reposed. Ems was the place assigned for the meeting of the two princesses. The Duchess of Orleans and her sons arrived there March 1. The courageous mother accepted the decrees of Providence with resignation. "Perhaps," said she, "this trial will be useful to my children; they will receive from exile the education it gave their grandfather. Who knows whether it will not serve them better than any other?"

CHAPTER XXXVII

THE DUCHESS DE MONTPENSIER

IT remains to relate the painful circumstances under which the departure of the Duchess de Montpensier was effected. A sister of Isabella II., Queen of Spain, the young Princess whose marriage to the youngest son of Louis Philippe and Marie Amélie had excited such wrath and jealousy in England, completed her sixteenth year on January 30. The Duke de Montpensier, when quitting the Tuileries to follow his father, on February 24, had thought it would be imprudent to take the Duchess with him, on account of her health, which demanded great attention. Hence he confided her to the care of his aide-de-camp, General Thierry, and of a deputy of the left, M. Jules de Lasteyrie, who shared the popularity of that fraction of the Chamber. The Duke charged them to conduct the Duchess to Eu, where his father intended going, and, if they did not find him, to escort her to England.

To whom was the fugitive obliged to resort for the passport needed for her melancholy voyage? To Lord Normanby, the ambassador who had been so greatly annoyed by the Spanish marriages and shown so much ill-temper to King Louis Philippe's ministry.

Lord Normanby himself wrote these lines, dated February 25, 1848, in his journal entitled: *A Year of Revolution.* A sentiment of compassion for the misfortune of the young Princess is mingled in them with a residue of bitterness against the French policy: "One could not avoid some serious private reflections on the contrast between the arrival of the Duchess de Montpensier in the land of her adoption, scarcely a year before, and the manner in which she was now leaving it, perhaps forever. All Europe had then been invited to the Tuileries in the person of its diplomatic representatives, to offer its felicitations in concert on the occasion of her happy marriage. Conformably to the attitude taken by the British government with regard to this alliance, its representative was the only one who could not be present at the ceremony, but he made haste to seize the first occasion of presenting his personal respects to Her Royal Highness as a French princess in fact. And now it was by the instrumentality of this same ambassador that she was going, under an assumed name, to reach that country in which all proscripts find an asylum! May God protect her on her way! May she find in that domestic happiness which depends neither on climate nor country, the compensation for the ill fortune which her marriage has brought her, since a cloud has suddenly obscured those ambitious expectations of which she has been rather the passive victim than the willing accomplice."

The passport, which was to serve for the Princess and the persons accompanying her, was given by the English Embassy, and remitted to General Thierry under this name: *Captain Martyn and family.*

On Friday, February 25, at eight o'clock in the morning, a train left Paris for Rouen. In the waiting-room, filled with persons who were escaping in alarm, a man wearing blue spectacles and an immense green shade was noticed. People in the throng were heard remarking: "There's a gentleman who is disguising himself to get away! He seems to be in a great hurry." Near him was a woman wearing a very simple black and white plaid woollen dress, with a large black shawl, and a hat covered with a veil of very thick lace.

Now listen to a young man who was in the waiting-room, and who, although an unexpected companion, was going to display most admirable devotion throughout the journey. This was M. Estancelin, already a married man, although only twenty-four years old, and an attaché of the legation of France at Frankfort. His account, published by M. Fernand de Montréal in *Les dernières heures d'une monarchie*, is very curious.

"Through the thick lace veil," says M. Estancelin, "I saw two fine eyes sparkling. Curious, as one is when young, I came nearer, so as to get a better notion of the woman's beauty, and saw, under the handsome eyes, a pleasant smile intended for me, and in spite of the thickness of the veil I recognized Madame the Duchess de Montpensier! I pretended not to recognize her. The man with the green shade was M. Jules de Lasteyrie. . . . I got into the first car that came along, and, as chance would have it, found myself opposite the waiting-maid of the Duchess, a Spanish woman married to a Frenchman, M. Lebeau."

At Mantes the train stopped for ten minutes. General Thierry approached M. Estancelin and said to him: "You have recognized the Princess; we are going to Eu, but the railway only goes to Rouen; you belong to this region, you ought to be able to find a postchaise at Rouen which would take us to Eu, and perhaps a little money, for we are short." M. Estancelin replied that all this was very easy.

They stopped at a house in Rouen to obtain a barouche and post-horses. A large group of workmen witnessed their departure. One of them exclaimed: "There is some one who is very anxious to get away. Perhaps it is Louis Philippe." The Princess entered the barouche with General Thierry, M. de Lasteyrie, and Madame Lebeau; M. Estancelin mounted the driver's seat.

They reached Eu about midnight. Neither prince nor princess was discoverable at the château. Princess Clémentine and her family had just departed. There were no tidings of the King. To remain at Eu under such conditions might be imprudent. Then the following remarks were exchanged: —

General Thierry. — "M. Estancelin, haven't you a habitation near here?"

M. Estancelin. — "Yes, it is ten kilometres off; it is at the disposal of the Princess."

The Duchess de Montpensier. — "Let us go home with you!"

M. Estancelin. — "Your Highness would be very badly off there! The house has not been lived in for a year."

The Duchess. — "But at least we shall be tranquil and in safety."

M. Estancelin. — "Drive on, postilions! To Baromesnil!"

They arrived at Baromesnil at one o'clock in the morning, February 26. The personnel of the household was composed of a man-servant, his wife, and a gardener.

M. Estancelin (to the servant). — "A fire and something to eat, and be quick about it!"

The servant. — "But, sir, there isn't anything."

M. Estancelin. — "Nothing! What do you mean? You surely have eggs, preserves, wine? Make an omelette, quick!"

An omelette is hastily prepared.

M. Estancelin (who is waiting on the Princess at table, near a good fire). — "I am ashamed of receiving Your Highness so badly. An omelette and farmhouse bread!"

The Duchess de Montpensier. — "But you are very lucky, I assure you. The roof that shelters you is yours, while I have nothing any more. The gown I am wearing belongs to Madame de Lasteyrie. What a singular destiny mine is! In Spain, they fought in my ante-room. In Paris, I received bullets in my chamber. How will it all end? And where can all the others be? My husband! the King! Hélène and her children! Where are they? Are they in safety, as I am?"

The eyes of the Duchess were full of tears.

They spent the 26th at Baromesnil. At seven o'clock in the evening they set off, intending to travel all night, so as to reach Boulogne by daybreak, and embark there for England. Before leaving Baromesnil, the Princess had a desire to go to the little village church and ask the protection of God and the Blessed Virgin for the royal family and herself.

To reach Boulogne it was necessary to pass through Abbeville, where the artisan class was hostile to the government of Louis Philippe. They entered at half-past nine in the evening, and saw men coming out of the wine-shops in the upper end of the Place du Pilori, shouting: "It is the King! They are the princes! Stop! Stop! You can't get away like that?" Seizing the leaders by their heads, they brought the carriage to a sudden stop. M. Estancelin, whose uncle had been a popular deputy in the country, gave his name, and said that the persons in the carriage were members of his family. He was answered by shouts of: "Long live M. Estancelin!" They drove on to a house in the town, where they hoped to obtain a few hours' repose. But some one came up suddenly and said to General Thierry: "You are not in safety. I advise you to set off at once."

M. Estancelin (to the General). — "Do you hear? There is only one thing to be done in such a situation; the Princess must go on with you and not be arrested here. I will stay, with the chambermaid, until half-past eleven; if I have not arrived by midnight with the carriage, it will be because I have been arrested. I will send the maid to warn you, if I can! Take the first street to the left; follow it straight, it is the road to Boulogne. You will see a hill at the end of the town; at midnight you will see the carriage lanterns; I will stop at the middle of the hill, if I am free! And now, if I am unfortunately arrested, God be merciful to all of us!"

The Princess, who had shown imperturbable courage throughout the journey, did not hesitate for a moment. She took General Thierry's arm and set off on foot, obeying all the instructions given her.

The weather was horrible, and the darkness complete. A storm of wind and rain was raging furiously.

At midnight M. Estancelin arrived in a carriage at the middle of the hill, as he had promised. Let him tell about it: "I stop. I call. . . . Nobody answers. . . . I run up and down the empty road, shouting and calling. . . . Silence. And besides, the wind threatens to extinguish the lanterns, which I see eclipsed for a moment every now and then. How can I tell you the anxiety of that quarter of an hour of waiting! If they are lost! If they have been arrested! All the most dismal suppositions occurred to me while I was vainly shouting and going up and down the hill, always dreading to see those blessed lanterns disappear, which were the only signal in the profound darkness. At last! I hear between the gusts of wind a clear, fresh voice calling to me: 'Here we are! Here we are!'" It was the Princess. Drenched and covered with mud, she got into the carriage. They travelled all the rest of the night, and arrived early in the morning at Boulogne, where they embarked at noon, February 27, 1848. What a difference between this date and that of November 4, 1846, the day when the young Princess, whose marriage was considered as the apogee of King Louis Philippe's success, made such a joyous entry at the château of Saint-Cloud, and found the entire royal family assembled to bid her welcome! She had arrived in France in the midst of ovations. She was leaving it a proscript.

CHAPTER XXXVIII

CONCLUSION

ON February 23, 1850, M. de Lamartine and M. Thiers each characterized the Revolution of 1848 from the tribune of the National Assembly, the one as glorious as the other, as terrible and disastrous. Whatever the judgment of posterity may be, whether it agrees with the founder of the Second Republic or with the founder of the Third, no one can shake off a sentiment of melancholy and gloom while studying that Revolution, which excited as much surprise in its authors as in its victims. The victory without a battle, which, after costing in three days the lives of 72 soldiers and 289 rioters, changed so many things in the world, is one of those events which illustrate most forcibly the inaccuracy of the calculations of human wisdom, the blindness of the most superior politicians. Assuredly, no one knew the history of the Revolution of July better than Louis Philippe did. Throughout his entire reign he might have said to himself: "I saw the mistakes of Charles X.; I shall never commit any like them; hence I am certain not to fall as he did."

And yet, neither the King of the French nor his ministers, nor the members of the dynastic opposition, profited by the lessons of a Revolution which dated back only seventeen years. As if by a mockery of fate, and in spite of all the conjectures of consummate parliamentarians, February was the imitation — I had almost said the parody — of July.

Charles X., in opening the last session of his reign, March 2, 1830, speaks of *culpable manœuvres* which raise obstacles to his government. Louis Philippe, also in opening the last session of his reign, December, 28, 1847, points out "*the agitation fomented by blind or inimical passions.*" These words, just but imprudent, *culpable manœuvres*, *blind or inimical passions*, give the signal for the contest between the Crown and the opposition.

M. de Chateaubriand, when inducing his friends to vote the Address of the 22d, M. Odilon Barrot, when organizing the banquet of the 12th arrondisement each imagines that he is merely bringing about a change of ministries, not a revolution.

The same warnings are given to Charles X. and to Louis Philippe; neither pays attention to them, — pilots who recognize the tempest only by the shipwreck.

The February days, like those of July, are three in number.

Arrested at the start, the disease would have made no progress. It is allowed to develop itself at pleasure.

There was the same insufficiency in the military preparations, the same disdain of the elements to be combatted.

The very unpopular Marshal Marmont, and Marshal Bugeaud, less unpopular than the author of the defection of Essonnes, but in bad odor with the republicans and legitimists, are not put at the head of the troops until the last moment. Apprised beforehand, they could easily have organized the resistance. Called too late, they merely organized defeat.

The plan which succeeded so badly with Marshal Marmont, namely, that of columns passing through the city and returning to their point of departure, is the one adopted by Marshal Bugeaud. This dissemination of troops, preferred to a strong concentration around the Palais-Royal, the Louvre, the Tuileries, and the Chamber of Deputies, is as fatal to Louis Philippe as to Charles X.

Bonaparte had shown how a street fight should be conducted, on the 13th Vendémiaire. Neither Marshal Bugeaud nor Marshal Marmont profits by the lesson. The latter paralyzes military action by hesitating, either through humanity or some other motive, to employ his artillery, and by forbidding his troops to fire on crowds. Marshal Bugeaud discourages and annihilates the army by permitting General Bedeau to parley with the National Guard, and by accepting the order to stop firing.

Two ways are open to them: peace or war; they

take both, but follow neither. They cover the city with guns and cannons, but make no use of them. They threaten, and do not strike. They are so bewildered by their fall that, once down, they do not even try to rise.

The inanity of Napoleon's abdication in favor of the King of Rome teaches nothing to either Charles X. or Louis Philippe. By a curious coincidence, the two children in whose favor the two sovereigns believed themselves to be abdicating were each nine years old (the Duke de Bourbon was born September 29, 1820; the Count de Paris, August 24, 1838). In July, as in February, the Revolution faced an old man, a woman, a child, and had no pity on them.

Another point of resemblance between 1830 and 1848 is that, at both epochs, the women showed more energy than the men, and that, had they been listened to, they might perhaps have saved the throne.

On the 28th of July, 1830, the Duchess de Berry prays, entreats Charles X. to let her mount a horse and go from Saint-Cloud to Paris, to show herself to the people and the army. The only reply Charles X. makes is to tell her to keep quiet, and forbid any one to give her horses. The mother of the Duke de Bourbon, shedding tears of anger, exclaims: "Oh! what a misfortune to be a woman!"

On that terrible morning of February 24, 1848, when the wind is blowing furiously, when the thunder rumbles, when the ship is deserted, who is it that adjures the pilot not to lose his head, and to renew his grasp on the helm? It is a woman, the Queen. Who advises the old King to put on a uniform and review the troops and the National Guard? It is she again. And when the unfortunate sovereign, deceived by timid counsellors, decides on an abdication, which will be not merely his own but that of his whole dynasty, who is it that cries to him: "They want to tear away your sceptre. No one but you has strength to carry it! It would be better to die with courage than to abdicate. Mount a horse! The army will follow you." It is she, always she, the worthy granddaughter of the Empress Maria Theresa.

The Duchess of Orleans is not less valiant than the Queen. A woman whose former apartments she occupies in the Tuileries, the Duchess de Berry, has shown her what can be inspired in a princess, a mother, by the horror of exile for herself and the ambition of a throne for her son. The Duchess of Orleans defends the rights of the Count de Paris with the same intrepidity shown by the Duchess de Berry for those of the Duke de Bourbon. Her noble conduct in the Chamber of Deputies, February 24, merits this eulogy from M. Dupin: "Though the day did not end in the way the friends of constitutional monarchy had a right to expect, the Princess Hélène, wife of the brave Duke of Orleans, will none the less obtain from posterity the glory of having heroically fulfilled her duty as a widow and a mother! And all my life I shall cling to the great honor granted me of accompanying and seconding her as much as I could, in the only virile action which the last day of the monarchy beheld accomplished!"

On embarking at Cherbourg with Charles X., August 16, 1830, the Duchess de Berry wears a riding-hat. There is a touch of audacity in her expression, and as she gazes at France on the horizon, she seems to be saying: "I will return."

The exiled Duchess of Orleans is not discouraged either. One day she exclaimed: "When the thought that I may never again see France occurs to me, my heart seems bursting."

We have just been pointing out numerous points of resemblance between July and February. Let us end by noting a difference between the Revolution of 1830 and that of 1848: the second had not the same character of impiety as the first.

On February 27, 1848, that is, on the first Sunday after the Revolution, Père Lacordaire, wearing the Dominican habit, which no monk had been allowed to wear in the France of 1830, ascended the pulpit of Notre Dame and said: "O God, who hast inflicted these terrible blows; God, the judge of kings and arbiter of the world, look with propitious eyes on this old French people, the eldest son of Thy law and Thy Church. Remember its past services, remember Thy first benedictions, renew with it the ancient alliance which made it Thine, appeal to its heart, which was so full of Thee, and which, even now, in the first fruits of a victory in which it spared nothing that was royal, gives to Thee the pledges of an Empire which hereafter it will accord to Thee alone. O just and holy God! by this cross of Thy Son their hands have carried from the violated palace of kings to the stainless palace of Thy Spouse, watch over us, protect us, enlighten us, prove once more to the world that a people which respects Thee is a people saved." And when Père Lacordaire spoke thus, what he had to repress were not murmurs, but cheers of approbation.

In 1830, the Archbishop of Paris, Monseigneur de Quelen, was obliged to conceal himself. In 1848, the Archbishop of Paris, Monseigneur Affre, accompanied by his two vicars-general, went to call on M. Dupont (de l'Eure), the president of the provisional government, who said to him: "Liberty and religion are two sisters equally interested in living well together."

In 1830, the clergy were treated as vanquished men, from the political point of view. In 1848, the republican Minister of Public Instruction, M. Carnot, father of the Martyr-President, addressed a circular to the archbishops and bishops of France, which ended thus: "Do not allow the priests of your diocese to forget that, being citizens by participation in all political rights, they are children of the great French family, and that in the electoral assemblies or on the benches of the National Assembly, to which the confidence of their fellow-citizens may call them, they have but one interest to defend, — that of the country, intimately allied to that of religion."

In 1830, the priests did not dare to wear their cassocks in the streets. In 1848, they solemnly blessed the liberty trees.

In short, the Revolution of July remained as Christian as that of 1830 was Voltairian. It is certain that between the two dates a change had been produced in the tendencies of the Parisian people. From the depths of her exile, Marie Amélie could do herself the justice of having been no stranger to this alteration. It is in this sense that she had not ceased to exert an influence, discreet and reserved, but very real, throughout her husband's entire reign. Accustomed to place the interests of religion above all others, the pious Queen, who had been so afflicted by the sack of Saint-Germain-l'Auxerrois and the destruction of the archbishop's palace, returned thanks to God on learning that the revolutionists of 1848 meditated nothing of the sort. They had sacked the Palais-Royal and the Tuileries. They destroyed and burned the château of Neuilly from top to bottom. But they had not profaned the churches. They had burned the throne, but had respected the altar. France has not ceased to be the great Catholic nation. The crowns are broken. The Cross remains.

INDEX

Abbatucci, M., on the new Cabinet, 182, 185.
Abd-el-Kader, surrender of, 2–4.
Address, the, debated in the Chamber of Peers, 14, 15, 21, 27, 28; paragraph in, by Baron de Barante, 27; discussed in the Chamber of Deputies, 65 et seq.; Amendments to, 72 et seq.
Adelaide, Madame, see Eugénie
Adelaide, Louise, Princess of Orleans.
Affre, Monseigneur, Archbishop of Paris, 334.
Alençon, Duke d', 209.
Algeria, conquest of, 2–5.
Alton-Shée, Count d', 21, 22, 101, 146.
Amendments to the Address, 72 et seq.
Andryane, 252, 253.
Arago, 248, 249, 250.
Aubernon, M., Prefect of Versailles, 277.
Augustus, Duke of Saxe-Coburg-Gotha, 7, 209; rejoins the royal family in flight, 277.
Aumale, Duke d', in Algeria, 2–5, 54, 63.
Aupick, General, 36.

Banquet, the scheme, 80, 82; conditions and arrangements of, 89–96; measures to preserve peace at, 97–99; the programme of the manifestation, 99–103; order of the procession, 102; change in the character of, 105; the arrangement of February 19 not universally approved, 106, 107; not approved by the ministry and King, 107; the government's measures to prevent, 107, 108; placard of the government against the manifestation, 107; given up by the deputies, 111–113, 116; Louis Philippe's words to de Salvandy concerning the abandonment of, 117.
Barante, Baron de, paragraph in the Address by, 27.
Barbet, Henri, 301.
Barbet, Victor, Louis Philippe at the house of, 299, 300.
Barrot, Odilon, 66, 70; his idea of the banquet scheme, 83, 89; at the reunion in the Durand café, 84; his part in the plan of the banquet, 91; his words on the arrangements for the banquet, 93; his desire for peace, 97; his words on the programme of the manifestation, 103, 104, 105, 109, 110; his words on the government's resistance to the banquet, 109; tries to heal the breach between the government and the opposition, 108; meeting of the deputies at the house of, 110, 111; his proposition to the Chamber of Deputies, 125, 133, 155; demonstration at the house of, after the retirement of the ministry, 159, 160, 171; and the new ministry,

z 337

174, 182; not mentioned in news reports of the military command, 181; his excursion on the boulevards, 185-188; attended to his house by the mob, 187, 188, 189; wanted by the people in place of Thiers, 201; recommends the Duchess of Orleans not to go to the Chamber of Deputies, 215; arrives at the Chamber of Deputies, 232-234; declares for the Duchess of Orleans and the Count de Paris, 234-236; his illusions concerning Lamartine, 239; urges the Duchess of Orleans to leave Paris, 268, 269; his bitter words concerning the Revolution, 270, 271, 329.

Basire, Captain, 211.

Beaufort, Colonel de, brings tidings of Abd-el-Kader's surrender, 2.

Beaumont, M. de, his words concerning the Chamber of Deputies, 233.

Bedeau, General, 176, 177; his note to Marshal Bugeaud, 178, 179; Marshal Bugeaud's reponse to, and instructions to, 179, 181, 182; recommended to Thiers by Marshal Bugeaud, 180; harangues the crowd, 191; his retreat, 188-190, 194.

Belgian Embassy, ball at the, on February 21st, 118, 119.

Berger, 90.

Berry, Duchess de, and Charles X., 331, 333.

Berryer, M., his conduct toward Louis Philippe, 39; in the reunion at the Durand café, 84.

Besson, M., assists Louis Philippe in flight, 292-294, 305, 307, 308.

Biesta, M., 215, 270.

Bilfeldt, Colonel, 127.

Billault, M., 169.

Blanc, Louis, at the reunion in the *Réforme* office, 114.

Bled, Victor du, his *Histoire de la Monarchie de Juillet* quoted, 221.

Bocage, 226, 247.

Boissy, Marquis de, 21; his proposition to the Chamber of Peers on February 22d, 124; his motion in the Chamber of Peers on February 23d, 146.

Boulevard des Capucines, the firing on the, 161-166.

Broglie, Duke de, quoted, 5, 6, 14; his words concerning Louis Philippe's Cabinet, 34.

Bugeaud, Marshal, his character, 167, 168, 175; is placed in command, 167-173; his birth, 173; his words of confidence to Thiers, 173, 174; his plan of action, 175, 176; and the National Guards, 173, 174, 176; his billet to General Bedeau, 179; accepts General Lamoricière for command of National Guard, 184; his vain attempts at pacification, 191, 192; M. Fauvelle-Delabarre's advice to, 179, 180, 181; offers to form a new Cabinet with Thiers, 180; recommends General Bedeau and Magne to Thiers, 180; condemns Fauvelle-Delabarre for his advice, 181, 195; harangues the people and National Guards, 198; the people want him displaced, 201; his portrait slashed, 256; mistakes of, 330.

Camp, Maxime du, his *Souvenirs de l'année 1848*, quoted, 98; his account of the firing on the Boulevard des Capucines, 163-165; his account of scenes of vandalism in the Tuileries and Palais Royal, 255, 257, 262, 263.

Capucines, Boulevard des, the firing on the, 161-166.

Carnot, M., his circular to the archbishops and bishops of France, 334, 335.

Caussidière, M., 114; quoted, 133.

Cavaignac, General, 5.
Chamber of Deputies, the, its duty, 38; blindness and weakness of, 38; Louis Philippe's attitude toward, 38, 39; character and personnel of, 40; the discussion of the Address, 45, 65 et seq.; de Tocqueville's speech of alarm in, 49-51; excitement and confusion in, 70, 71; discussion and vote on the Amendments to the Address, 72-77; the session of February 22d, 124, 125; Barrot's proposition to, 125; its session of February 23d, 147; interpellations to the ministry proposed by M. Vavin, 151, 152; Guizot announces the retirement of the ministry to, 151-153; effect of the announcement on, 153-155; the Duchess of Orleans in, 221 et seq.; de Tocqueville's words concerning the importance of, 233, 234; the invasion of, 238 et seq.; the mob meeting in, 247 et seq.
Chamber of Peers, the, Address debated in, 14, 15, 21, 27, 28; Montalembert's speech before, 15-20; character and attitude of, 21-28; proposition to, by the Marquis de Boissy, on February 22d, 124; motion in, by the Marquis de Boissy, on February 23d, 146.
Charles Albert, King of Piedmont, his words concerning Pope Pius IX., 22, 23, 25.
Charles X., Louis Philippe compared with, 328, 329, 331, and the Duchess of Berry, 331, 333.
Chartres, Duke de, 214, 222; separated from his mother in the escape from the Chamber of Deputies, 244, 245; restored to his mother, 315.
Chateaubriand, M. de, 329.
Clémentine, Princess, 7, 209; rejoins the royal family in flight, 277; safe on English territory, 306.

Countermand, the, of the military preparations, 120, 132.
Couraud, Lieutenant-Colonel, at the firing on the Boulevard des Capucines, 162-165.
Court of Cassation, the, question of the banquet to be submitted to, 91, 93.
Cousin, M., his words on Italian affairs, 25.
Crémieux, M., expresses the wishes of the people to the King, 201, 209; urges a provisional government, 231, 248, 250.

Deputies, Chamber of, see Chamber of Deputies.
Dorvilliers, M., 285, 286.
Dreux, chapel of, 8, 10; Louis Philippe and Marie Amélie at, during their flight, 277-282.
Duchâtel, Count, 6; his position in the government, and character, 43, 44; in the discussion of the Address, 68, 69; his words on the banquet manifestation, 109, 110; favors countermanding the military preparations, 120; his conversation with Louis Philippe and Marie Amélie at the Tuileries concerning the public situation, 147-149, and the nomination of Marshal Bugeaud, 170, 172.
Dufaure, M., 51, 169.
Dumas, Alexandre, 247.
Dumas, General, with the King in flight, 209, 275, 277; his letter from Dreux, to Count de Montalivet, 279, 280, 282; at Havre, 292, 293, 303.
Dumoulin, M., in the Chamber of Deputies, 238.
Dupin, his words on the banquet arrangement, 94; his words to Louis Philippe on the imminent danger, 143, 144, 155; his words on the abdication of Louis Philippe, 205; accompanies the Duchess of Orleans to the Cham-

ber of Deputies, 214-219, 244; speaks in the Chamber of Deputies in behalf of the Duchess of Orleans, 223, 224.
Dupont, M. (de l'Eure), takes the President's chair in the Chamber of Deputies, 247, 250, and the Archbishop of Paris, 334.
Durand café, reunion of the opposition in, 80, 84-87.

Estancelin, M., assists the Duchess of Montpensier in flight, 322-327.
Estissac, Duchess d', 118
Estourmel, Count d', quoted, 131, 271, 272.
Eugénie, Adelaide Louise, Princess of Orleans, called Madame Adelaide, death of, 1, 2; obsequies of, 7-10.

Falloux, Count de, quoted, 84, 86, 87, 253, 254.
Fauvelle-Delabarre, M., his advice to Marshal Bugeaud, 179-181.
Featherstonhaugh, M., 306, 307.
Flaubert, Gustave, 255.
Flocon, M., editor of the *Réforme*, 113, 114; his article, 115; proposes the use of National Guard uniforms for rioters, 140, 141.
Friant, Count, 275.

Garnier-Pagès, M., his words concerning the banquet arrangement, 95, 105, 106, 114; his words on the excessive prudence of the military authorities, 130, and Marshal Bugeaud's billet, 182; his words concerning Duke de Nemours, 218, 232, 250; his sentiments on the Revolution, 265, 274.
Genoude, M. de, 232.
Gérard, Marshal, 108; wanted by the people in place of Bugeaud, 201; announces the abdication of Louis Philippe to the people, 206.

Giacomo, fires the first shot of the Revolution, 163-165.
Gioré, Desmousseaux de, proposes amendment to the Address, 72, 73.

Girardin, Emile de, demands Louis Philippe's abdication, 202, 203.
Grammont, Marquis de, 214.
Guestier, M., Louis Philippe at the house of, 302.
Guivard, M., 98.
Guizot, M., 6, 21; his attitude in Italian affairs, 25, 26; and the Court, 29 *et seq.*; his words on the Court, 30; offers to withdraw, 30; his conversation with Court affairs with Louis Philippe, 31; his words on Italian events, 36; Duchâtel compared with, 43, 44; opposition of the Prince de Joinville to, 56, 57; his efforts to win over the Prince de Joinville, 56, 57, 58; his words of reply to Lamartine, 66; his words of 1830 quoted, 68; and the amendments to the Address, 73, 77; his words on the banquet arrangement, 95; his words on the change in the character of the banquet plan, 105; he reads the accusation of the ministry by the deputies, 125; his astonishment, 126; his confidence in the military, 131; his words concerning the countermand of the military preparations, 132; his words concerning Marie Amélie, 148; his conversation with Louis Philippe concerning the retirement of the ministry, 150; announces to the Chamber of Deputies the retirement of the ministry, 151-153; his position in regard to the change of ministry, 157, 159; the mob in front of the residence of, 162; urges the King to put Marshal Bugeaud in command, 167; his words con-

cerning the King's confident attitude, 172, 173; at the Tuileries on the occasion of the visit of the new ministry to Louis Philippe, 184.

Hallot, a Honfleur sailor, assists in flight of Louis Philippe, 293, 294.
Hauranne, M. Duvergier de, his words in the discussion of the Address, 67, 68; one of the five negotiators, 90; his conversation with de Tocqueville, 93; tries to heal the breach between the government and the opposition, 108, 174; on the new Cabinet, 182, 183, 185; at the last breakfast of the King at the Tuileries, 194.
Hébert, M., speech of, in the discussion of the Address, 69, 70; de Tocqueville's words concerning, 69; his words concerning the banquet, 107; disapproves of the King's change of ministry, 157.
Honfleur, Louis Philippe and Marie Amélie at, 290, 291.
"Hospital for Invalid Citizens," an inscription on the Tuileries, 272.
Hôtel-de-Ville, Lamartine leads the people to, 249, 254; the appearance of, occupied by the crowd, 273, 274.
Houdetot, Adolphe d', 308.
Hugo, Victor, his words concerning Pope Pius IX., 23, 24.

Italy, discussion over affairs in, 22 et seq.; Guizot's words concerning affairs in, 36.

Jacqueminot, General, 108, 111; favored countermanding the military preparations, 120, 137.
Janvier, M., his speech in the Chamber of Deputies, 52.
Jayr, M., warns Louis Philippe of the public disturbance, 121, 122; disapproves of the King's change of ministry, 157.
Joinville, Prince de, his *Vieux Souvenirs* quoted, 3, 7, 27; his attitude at Court, 29; joins the Duke d'Aumale in Algeria, 54, 59, 63; his apprehensions, 54, 55; in command of the Mediterranean squadron, 55; his ideas opposed to those of Guizot, 56, 58; his words on the Spanish marriages, 56; resigns his commandership and returns home, 58, 59.
Jollivet, M., death of, 190.
Jones, M., Vice-Consul at Havre, assists in the flight of Louis Philippe, 305–309.
Journal des Débats, quoted on the state of public uneasiness, 45–47; its words on the banquet scheme, 81, 82; on the public disturbances, 133, 134.

Lacordaire, Père, 333.
Lagrange, M., 114, 163.
Lamoricière, General de, in Algeria, 4, 5; on the new Cabinet, 182; appointed to command the National Guard, 183, 184, 195; accompanies Louis Philippe on his last review, 195, 202; a prisoner of the insurgents, 208.
Lamartine, M. de, 47; his words in the discussion of the Address, 65; his words at the reunion in the Durand café, 84–86; the hero of the day, 87; his words concerning his speech at the reunion, 87, 88; his characterization of the *National*, 99, 100; opposes giving up the banquet, 111; his words concerning the *Réforme*, 113; his words concerning Molé, 168, 169; his words concerning Louis Philippe, 172; his words concerning Marshal Bugeaud, 175; his words concerning the Queen, 196, 197; in the Chamber of Deputies

on the occasion of the presence of the Duchess of Orleans, 225 et seq.; becomes a republican, 226; his description of the arrival of the Duchess of Orleans, 226, 227; his pity for the Duchess, 226-228; his speech from the tribune of the Chamber of Deputies, 239-242; illusions of Barrot and Sauzet concerning, 239; declares for a provisional government, 241, 242, 247, 248; the speech he might have addressed to the Duchess of Orleans, 239, 240; the tool of the crowd, 240; before the crowd in the Chamber, 247 et seq.; leads the people to the Hôtel-de-Ville, 249, 254; drinks a glass of wine to symbolize the banquet, 254; his words on the Revolution, 266; his description of the crowd at the Hôtel-de-Ville, 274; his characterization of the Revolution, 328.

Lasteyrie, Jules de, his words concerning the change of ministry, 160, 269, 270; accompanies the Duchess de Montpensier in flight, 320 et seq.

Laubespin, Capt. de, brings tidings of Bedeau's retreat to the King, 194.

Ledru-Rollin, M., his republican opinions, 40, 41; denied admission to the banquet, 83, 113; at the reunion in the *Réforme* office, 114, 115, 133; in the Chamber of Deputies, 238, 239; a rival of Lamartine, 249; addresses the crowd in the Chamber, 250, 251.

Louise Marie Adelaide, of Bourbon, 1.

Louis Philippe Joseph, Prince of Orleans, 1.

Louis XVI., his purchase of Rambouillet, 8.

Louis Philippe, King, mourns for his sister Eugénie Adelaide Louise, 1, 2; at the funeral of his sister, 7-10; his grief, 10, 11; his strength and confidence in his public office, 11; the Address presented to, 27, 28; his conversation with Guizot on the condition of affairs at Court, 31; his resolution not to change his ministry, 31-33, 35; his attitude toward Thiers, 33-35; his position in the affairs of Europe, 35, 36; his attitude toward the Chamber of Deputies, 38, 39; his words to M. Sallandrouze, 39; his fear of the deputies of the dynastic opposition, 42; his optimism, 45; gloried in preserving the pacific character of his reign, 65; receives the Address from the Chamber of Deputies, 78, 79; hears of the giving up of the banquet, 111; his pleasure and increased confidence, 117, 121, 122, 134, 135; his conversation with M. de Salvandy, 117; countermands the military preparations, 120; is warned of public disturbance by M. Jayr, 122; his attitude toward the National Guard, 137; his surprise at the sentiments of the National Guard, 143; allowed no thought of change of ministry, 144, 147; his conversation with Duchâtel concerning the public situation, 147-149; his conversation with Guizot, 149; decides to part with his ministry and form a new Cabinet, 150-153; places Marshal Bugeaud in command, 167-172; his conversation with Thiers concerning a new Cabinet, 171; his confidence unshaken, 172, 173; his meeting with the new ministry, 183, 184; refuses to dissolve the Chamber, 183, 184; his last day at the Tuileries and last review of his troops, 193-198; abdicates and

INDEX

leaves the Tuileries, 202-211; his horror of bloodshed, 205; his portrait in the Chamber of Deputies fired upon, 251, 252; drives to Saint-Cloud, 275, 276; at Dreux, 277-281; his letter to Count de Montalivet, 278, 279; from Dreux to Honfleur, 283-289; travels under the name of Lebrun, 281, 283, 285, 286; at Honfleur, 290 *et seq.*; at Trouville, 298-304; rejoins Marie Amélie at Honfleur, 303, 304; the embarkation at Havre, 305 *et seq.*; travels under the name of William Smith, 308; his own story of the embarkation, 309, 310; reaches England, 312; compared with Charles X., 328, 329; 331, 332.

Lucerne, surrenders, 14.

Magne, M. 180.
Maleville, Léon de, his words in the discussion of the address, 68; one of the five negotiators, 90; on the new cabinet, 182.
Marie Antoinette, 195.
Marie, M., his words to the radicals concerning the banquet scheme, 80; in the Chamber of Deputies, 225, 228; proposes a provisional government, 230, 231, 249.
Marie, Princess, the models of sculptured statues by, 259.
Marie Amélie, Queen, 1, 7; at the burial of Madame Adelaide, 10; similarity of her ideas to those of Montalembert, 13; her apprehensions, 45; entreats the Prince de Joinville to remain at home, 59; reopens her salon for a small party, 60, 61; her receptions, 61, 62; as a hostess, 62; her parting with her son, the Prince de Joinville, 62, 63; her uneasiness concerning public affairs, 117, 118, 134; her reassurance, 118; Guizot's words concerning, 148; her conversation with the King and Duchâtel concerning the public situation, 148, 149; knew that the hour of the last crisis had come, 193; and the last review of Louis Philippe, 196; Lamartine's words concerning, 196, 197; her self-possession, 200; urges the King not to abdicate, 203; her flight with the King to Saint-Cloud, Dreux, and to Honfleur, 275 *et seq.*; her visit to the tombs of her children, 282; rejoins the King at Honfleur, 290; at the Pavilion de la Grâce, 290-297; her words concerning her fate, 295, 296; her occupations, 296, 297; rejoined by the King, 303, 304; embarks with the King for England, 308, 309; her fortitude, 311, 312, 332.

Maréchal, M., assists Louis Philippe in flight, 283-286.
Marmont, Marshal, 330.
Marrast, Armand, and the programme of the manifestation, 99-105; his birth, career, and character, 100, 101; his opinion on the giving up of the banquet, 111, 226.
Mazzini, his words to Pope Pius IX., 22.
Military preparations, the, countermanded, 120, 132.
Ministry of Foreign Affairs, the affair in front of, 162-166.
Ministry, the new, 168, 169, 171; and Louis Philippe at the Tuileries, 182-184.
Molé, Count de, 33; selected by Louis Philippe to form a new Cabinet, 151, 153; his efforts to form a new ministry, 168, 169; his character, 168, 169.
Molitor, Marshal, 267.
Montalembert, Count de, his birth, parentage, and early life, 12, 13; chief of the Catholics, 13; simi-

larity of his ideas to those of Marie Amélie, 13; his condition of mind in 1848, 13; his speech on the Address before the Chamber of Peers, 15-20.

Montalivet, Count de, his words on the change of ministry, 161, 196, 210; Louis Philippe's letter to, 278, 279; General Dumas' letter to, 279, 280.

Montesquiou, Viscount Léon de, 270.

Montpensier, Duchess de, the flight of, 320-327.

Montpensier, Duke de, 7, 27, 78, 148, 151, 195; urges the King to abdicate, 203; leaves the Tuileries with the King, 209, 320.

Mornay, Marquis de, 267, 269, 315.

Morny, Count de, in the Chamber of Deputies, 76, 77, 89; his career and character, 90; one of the five negotiators, 89, 90, 107.

Muser, Mademoiselle, 287, 289.

Musset, Alfred de, his verses on the château of Neuilly, 264.

National, the, Lamartine's characterization of, 99, 100, 133; its words on the Revolution, 265.

National Guard, the, its part in the programme of the manifestation, 102, 103; called out by the government, 136 *et seq.*; attitude of Louis Philippe toward, 137; Count de Pont-Martin's words on, 138; the feelings of, 138-144; rioters in the ranks of, 140; the legions move, 141; Marshal Bugeaud and, 173, 174; and the new ministers, 182; General Lamoricière appointed to command of, 183, 184; powerless to repress the crowd, 187; Louis Philippe's last review of, 195-197.

Nemours, Duke de, 7, 20, 27; his attitude at Court, 29, 78; goes into the ranks of soldiery to quell the disturbances, 128, 150, 195; obtains carriages for the royal family to leave the Tuileries, 209, 210; in command at the Tuileries, 213; his plan to carry the Duchess of Orleans to Mont Valérien, 215, 217; follows the Duchess of Orleans to the Chamber of Deputies, 218, 219; Garnier-Pagès' words concerning, 218; in the Chamber of Deputies, 223, 229, 230; his escape from the Chamber, 245, 246; goes to the house of M. Biesta, 270; safe on English territory, 306; his flight from Paris, 314.

Neuilly, the château of, destroyed, 264.

Normanby, Lord, his experience at the dinner of the Minister of Finance, 130, 131; his words concerning the Duchess of Montpensier, 321, 322.

Ochsenbein, M., 23.

Orleans, Duchess of, 29, 94; her words on the change of ministry, 158; with the Queen the last night at the Tuileries, 194, 196; her fidelity to the King, 200; the people demand the regency of, 203, 204, 207; urges the King not to abdicate, 203; left behind at the Tuileries, 209; leaves the Tuileries soon after the King and goes to the Chamber of Deputies, 213-220; in the Chamber of Deputies, 221 *et seq.*; Lamartine's description of the entrance of, to the Chamber of Deputies, 226, 227; refuses to withdraw, 228; did not share the illusions concerning Lamartine, 241; her exit from the Chamber, 243-245; her flight from Paris, 267-270; at the Château de Bligny, 313-315; her son the Duke of Chartres restored to her, 315; her flight to Germany, 315-319; her courage, 318, 332; arrives at Ems, 319.

Orleans, Duke of, his apartments

in the Tuileries respected by the mob, 259, 260.
Oudinot, General, his words concerning the Duchess of Orleans in the Chamber of Deputies, 229, 252.

Palais-Royal, the gathering at the, 133; sacked by the mob, 262-264.
Palmerston, Lord, M. Thiers an ally of, 34, 36.
Paris, Count de, Louis Philippe abdicates in favor of, 207, 212, 214; in the Chamber of Deputies, 222 et seq.; separated from his mother in the exit from the Chamber, 244; restored to his mother, 245; leaves Paris with his mother, 269; his reluctance to leave France, 316.
Passy, M., 169.
Pasquier, Duke de, his words to Count d'Alton-Shée, 22.
Paul, M., 305, 310.
Pauligue, M. de, with Louis Philippe in flight, 276, 283, 292, 298, 300, 303.
Pavilion de la Grâce, Louis Philippe and Marie Amélie at, 290, 291.
Peers, Chamber of, see Chamber of Peers.
Perthuis, Edmond de, 292, 298, 303.
Perthuis, M. de, Louis Philippe and Marie Amélie rejoin each other at the cottage of, 290.
Piscatory, M., urges the King not to abdicate, 203, 204.
Pius IX., Pope, his attitude in Italian affairs, 22, 23; admirers of, in the Chamber of Peers, 23, 24; Mazzini's words to, 22; King Charles Albert's words concerning, 22; Victor Hugo's words concerning, 23, 24; Cousin's words concerning, 25.
Pontécoulant, Count de, his words concerning the banquet arrangement, 106; criticises the lack of vigor on the part of the authorities, 129; his words on the abdication of Louis Philippe, 204, 205.
Pontmartin, Count de, his words on the National Guard, 138.
Programme of the Manifestation, the, 99-103, 104 et seq.; de Tocqueville's words concerning, 104; Barrot's words concerning, 104, 105.
Provisional Government, a, proposed in the Chamber of Deputies, 230-232; Lamartine declares for, 241, 242; acclaimed, 247 et seq.

Quelen, Monseigneur de, Archbishop of Paris, 334.

Racine, a gardener at Honfleur, 291, 293.
Rainneville, M. de, 86, 87.
Raucourt, 247.
Réforme, the, Lamartine's characterization of, 113; the reunion at the office of, 113-115, 133.
Regnault, General de Saint-Jean-d'Angély, 275.
Rémusat, M. de, 77, 174; on the new Cabinet, 182, 185; at the last breakfast of the King at the Tuileries, 194.
Renard, farmer, 286-288, 290.
Renault, General, 176, 177.
Revolution, of 1848, note of alarm sounded by de Tocqueville, 47 et seq.; the discussion of the Address the prologue of the, 65; the banquet scheme, 80 et seq.; the reunion in the Durand café, 84-88; the reunion in the Réforme, 113-115; the gathering of people on February 22d, 121-123; the first attempts at disorder, 126-128, 135, 136; lack of vigor on the part of the authorities, 129, 130; the countermand of the military preparations, 120, 132; the National Guard called out, 136 et

seq.; the firing on the Boulevard des Capucines, 162-166; how the first shot was fired, 163-165; Marshal Bugeaud in command, 167-173; plan of action, 175, 176; Marshal Bugeaud's billet, 181, 182; the retreat of General Bedeau, 188-190; Louis Philippe's last review, 194-198; Louis Philippe abdicates and leaves the Tuileries, 202-211; the affair at the guard-house on the Place du Palais-Royal, 202, 208; the Chamber of Deputies is invaded, 238 *et seq.;* accomplished, 254; effect of, 265; *et seq.;* comments on by the *National*, 265; by Garnier-Pagès, 265; by Lamartine, 266; by Odilon Barrot, 270, 271; by Count d'Estournel, 271, 272; characterized by Thiers and Lamartine, 328; lessons of, 328 *et seq.;* difference between Revolution of 1830 and, 333-335.
Revue des Deux-Mondes, quoted, on the government and condition of public affairs, 47, 59, 60.
Rewbell, Colonel, 211, 275.
Rochejaquelein, M. de la, in the Chamber of Deputies, 236, 237.
Rumigny, General de, with Louis Philippe in flight, 286, 287, 298, 299.

Sainte-Aulaire, Count de, his words to the Chamber of Peers, 26.
Sallandrouze, M., 39; proposes amendments to the Address, 72, 75.
Salvandy, M. de, his words concerning the banquet, 107; Louis Philippe's conversation with, concerning the abandonment of the banquet, 117; disapproves of the King's change of ministry, 157.
Sauzet, M., President of the Chamber of Deputies, 75; his words on the arrangement for the banquet, 94; in the Chamber on the occasion of the presence of the Duchess of Orleans, 221, 224, 228, 229; his illusions concerning Lamartine, 239; adjourns the Chamber, 243.
Sébastiani, General Tiburce, 120; clears the approaches to the Chamber of Deputies, 123; at the Hôtel-de-Ville, 176, 177.
Scheffer, Ary, 209.
Six, Theodore, 252.
Sonderbund, the, 13, 14, 34, 35.
Soult, Marshal, 204, 269.
Switzerland, civil discord in, 14, 15.

Talabot, Colonel, 162, 163.
Thierry, General, accompanies the Duchess de Montpensier in flight, 320 *et seq.*
Thiers, M., 32, 33; his attitude toward Louis Philippe, 34; an ally of Lord Palmerston's, 34; his words on the Swiss question, 66; belongs to the party of the Revolution, 66; favors wholesale resignation of the opposition, 80; at the reunion in the Durand café, 86, 87; his opinion on the banquet manifestation, 110, 111, 159; and the new Cabinet, 169-172, 174; his conversation with Louis Philippe, 171, 172; his ministry, 182; urges the King to dissolve the Chamber, 183, 184, 185, his characterization of the Revolution, 328; not mentioned in news reports of the military command, 181; at the last breakfast of the King at the Tuileries, 194; proposes a retreat to Saint-Cloud, 194; his presence in the Cabinet an anomaly, 201; his sole idea to escape, 222.
Thureau-Dangin, M., his words concerning the departure of the Duchess of Orleans, 217.
Tocqeville, M. de, his words on the

government, 42, 43; his birth and parentage, 47; his *Democracy in America*, 48; his position in public affairs, 48; his speech of alarm in the Chamber of Deputies, 49-51; his lack of complete faith in his sinister predictions, 51; his conversation with Duvergier de Hauranne, 93; his words on the programme of the manifestation, 104; his words on the disturbance of February 22d, 123; his description of the effect on the Chamber of Deputies of the retirement of the ministry, 153, 154; his words on the change of ministry, 160, 161; his words to Lamartine in the Chamber of Deputies, 227; on the importance of the Chamber, 233, 234; incident attending his exit from the Chamber of Deputies, 252, 253.

Trézel, General, 170.

Trognon, M., his words concerning Marie Amélie at Honfleur, 295.

Tuileries, the, Louis Philippe's last day at, 193 *et seq.*; disorder at, 199-201; Louis Philippe leaves, 208-211; the sack of the, 255-264; "Hospital for Invalid Citizens," inscription on, 272; the people occupying, 272, 273,

Vavin, M., addresses interpellations to the ministry in the Chamber of Deputies, 151, 152.

Vernet, Horace, Colonel of National Guards, 185.

Vitet, M. de, one of the five negotiators, 89, 90.

FAMOUS WOMEN OF THE FRENCH COURT

CHARLES SCRIBNER'S SONS, PUBLISHERS.

" In these translations of this interesting series of sketches, we have found an unexpected amount of pleasure and profit. The author cites for us passages from forgotten diaries, hitherto unearthed letters, extracts from public proceedings, and the like, and contrives to combine and arrange his material so as to make a great many very vivid and pleasing pictures. Nor is this all. The material he lays before us is of real value, and much, if not most of it, must be unknown save to the special students of the period. We can, therefore, cordially commend these books to the attention of our readers. They will find them attractive in their arrangement, never dull, with much variety of scene and incident, and admirably translated." — THE NATION, *of December 19, 1890.*

NEW VOLUME

THE REVOLUTION OF 1848.

With four portraits. Price $1.25.

M. Imbert de Saint-Amand's volume on "The Duchess of Berry and the Revolution of 1830," which described the turbulent accession of Louis Philippe to the throne of France, is now followed by the account of the Citizen King's equally agitated abdication and exile during the Revolution of 1848, — the title of a new volume just issued in the author's popular and admirable series, "Famous Women of the French Court." As heretofore, the historian writes from the inside, and his description of the exciting events of the February days that led to the overthrow of the Orleanist dynasty, the flight of the last king France has had, and the dramatically sudden establishment of the Second Republic is familiar and intimate rather than formal, and the reader gets a view of what passed behind the scenes as well as on the stage at that interesting and fateful moment.

VOLUMES PREVIOUSLY ISSUED.

THREE VOLUMES ON MARIE ANTOINETTE.

Each with Portrait, $1.25. Price per set, in box, cloth, $3.75; half calf, $7.50.

MARIE ANTOINETTE AND THE END OF THE OLD RÉGIME.
MARIE ANTOINETTE AT THE TUILERIES.
MARIE ANTOINETTE AND THE DOWNFALL OF ROYALTY.

In this series is unfolded the tremendous panorama of political events in which the unfortunate Queen had so influential a share, beginning with the days immediately preceding the Revolution, when court life at Versailles was so gay and unsuspecting, continuing with the enforced journey of the royal family to Paris, and the agitating months passed in the Tuileries, and concluding with the abolition of royalty, the proclamation of the Republic, and the imprisonment of the royal family, — the initial stage of their progress to the guillotine.

THREE VOLUMES ON THE EMPRESS JOSEPHINE.

Each with Portrait, $1.25. Price per set, in box, cloth, $3.75; half calf, $7.50.

CITIZENESS BONAPARTE.
THE WIFE OF THE FIRST CONSUL.
THE COURT OF THE EMPRESS JOSEPHINE.

The romantic and eventful period beginning with Josephine's marriage, comprises the astonishing Italian campaign, the Egyptian expedition, the *coup d'état* of Brumaire, and is described in the first of the above volumes; while the second treats of the brilliant society which issued from the chaos of the Revolution, and over which Madame Bonaparte presided so charmingly; and the third, of the events between the assumption of the imperial title by Napoleon and the end of 1807, including, of course, the Austerlitz campaign.

FOUR VOLUMES ON THE EMPRESS MARIE LOUISE.

Each with Portrait, $1.25. Price per set, in box, cloth, $5.00; half calf, $10.00.

THE HAPPY DAYS OF MARIE LOUISE.
MARIE LOUISE AND THE DECADENCE OF THE EMPIRE.
MARIE LOUISE AND THE INVASION OF 1814.
MARIE LOUISE, THE RETURN FROM ELBA, AND THE HUNDRED DAYS.

The auspicious marriage of the Archduchess Marie Louise to the master of Europe; the Russian invasion, with its disastrous conclusion a few years later; the Dresden and Leipsic campaign; the invasion of France by the Allies, and the marvellous military strategy of Napoleon in 1814, ending only with his defeat and exile to Elba; his life in his little principality; his romantic escape and dramatic return to France; the preparations of the Hundred Days; Waterloo and the definitive restoration of Louis XVIII. closing the era begun in 1789, with "The End of the Old Régime,"— are the subjects of the four volumes grouped around the personality of Marie Louise.

FAMOUS WOMEN OF THE FRENCH COURT

TWO VOLUMES ON THE DUCHESS OF ANGOULÊME.

Each with Portrait, $1.25.   *Price per set, in box, cloth*, $2.50; *half calf*, $5.00.

THE YOUTH OF THE DUCHESS OF ANGOULÊME.
THE DUCHESS OF ANGOULÊME AND THE TWO RESTORATIONS.

The period covered in this first of these volumes begins with the life of the daughter of Louis XVI. and Marie Antoinette imprisoned in the Temple after the execution of her parents, and ends with the accession of Louis XVIII. after the abdication of Napoleon at Fontainebleau. The first Restoration, its illusions, the characters of Louis XVIII., of his brother, afterwards Charles X., of the Dukes of Angoulême and Berry, sons of the latter, the life of the Court, the feeling of the city, Napoleon's sudden return from Elba, the Hundred Days from the Royalist side, the second Restoration, and the vengeance taken by the new government on the Imperialists, form the subject-matter of the second volume.

THREE VOLUMES ON THE DUCHESS OF BERRY.

Each with Portrait, $1.25.   *Price per set, in box, cloth*, $3.75; *half calf*, $7.50.

THE DUCHESS OF BERRY AND THE COURT OF LOUIS XVIII.
THE DUCHESS OF BERRY AND THE COURT OF CHARLES X.
THE DUCHESS OF BERRY AND THE REVOLUTION OF JULY, 1830.

The Princess Marie Caroline, of Naples, became, upon her marriage with the Duke of Berry, the central figure of the French Court during the reigns of both Louis XVIII. and Charles X. The former of these was rendered eventful by the assassination of her husband and the birth of her son, the Count of Chambord, and the latter was from the first marked by those reactionary tendencies which resulted in the dethronement and exile of the Bourbons. The dramatic Revolution which brought about the July monarchy of Louis Philippe, has never been more vividly and intelligently described than in the last volume devoted to the Duchess of Berry.

FOUR VOLUMES ON WOMEN OF THE VALOIS AND VERSAILLES COURTS.

Each with Portraits, $1.25.   *Price per set, in box, cloth*, $5.00; *half calf*, $10.00.

WOMEN OF THE VALOIS COURT.
THE COURT OF LOUIS XIV.
THE COURT OF LOUIS XV.
THE LAST YEARS OF LOUIS XV.

The splendid pageantry of the court over which Catherine de Medici presided and in which she intrigued, and the contrasting glories and shames of the long reigns of the "Sun King" and of Louis XV. are the subjects of these four volumes which depict the most brilliant days of the Valois and Bourbon dynasties.

CRITICAL NOTICES.

"Indeed, a certain sanity of vision is one of M. de Saint Amand's characteristics. . . . He evidently finds it no difficult task to do justice to Legitimist and Imperialist, to the old world that came to an end with the Revolution and to the new world that sprang from the old world's ashes. Nor do his qualifications as a popular historian end here. He has the gift of so marshalling his facts as to leave a definite impression. These are but short books on great subjects; for M. de Saint Amand is not at all content to chronicle the court life of his three heroines, and writes almost more fully about their times than he does about themselves; but yet comparatively short as the books may be, they tell their story, in many respects, better than some histories of greater pretensions."—*The Academy, London.*

"The volumes are even more pictures of the times than of the unhappy occupants of the French throne. The style is clear and familiar, and the smaller courts of the period, the gossip of the court and the course of history, give interest other than biographical to the work."—*Baltimore Sun.*

"M. de Saint-Amand makes the great personages of whom he writes very human. In this last volume he has brought to light much new material regarding the diplomatic relations between Napoleon and the Austrian court, and throughout the series he presents, with a wealth of detail, the ceremonious and private life of the courts."—*San Francisco Argonaut.*

"The sketches, like the times to which they relate, are immensely dramatic. M. Saint-Amand writes with a vivid pen. He has filled himself with the history and the life of the times, and possesses the art of making them live in his pages. His books are capital reading, and remain as vivacious as idiomatic, and as pointed in the translation as in the original French."—*The Independent.*

"The last volume of the highly interesting series is characterized by all that remarkable attractiveness of description, historical and personal, that has made the former vo'umes of the series so popular. M. de Saint-Amand's pictures of court life and of the brilliant men and women that composed it, make the whole read with a freshness that is as fascinating as it is instructive."—*Boston Home Journal.*

www.ingramcontent.com/pod-product-compliance
Lightning Source LLC
Chambersburg PA
CBHW020229240426
43672CB00006B/461